Applied Mathematics to Mechanisms and Machines II

Applied Mathematics to Mechanisms and Machines II

Guest Editors

Higinio Rubio Alonso
Alejandro Bustos Caballero
Jesus Meneses Alonso
Enrique Soriano-Heras

MDPI

Basel • Beijing • Wuhan • Barcelona • Belgrade • Novi Sad • Cluj • Manchester

Guest Editors
Higinio Rubio Alonso
Department of Mechanical Engineering
Universidad Carlos III de Madrid
Madrid
Spain

Alejandro Bustos Caballero
Department of Mechanics
National University of Distance Education
Madrid
Spain

Jesus Meneses Alonso
Department of Mechanical Engineering
Universidad Carlos III de Madrid
Madrid
Spain

Enrique Soriano-Heras
Department of Mechanical Engineering
Universidad Carlos III de Madrid
Madrid
Spain

Editorial Office
MDPI AG
Grosspeteranlage 5
4052 Basel, Switzerland

This is a reprint of the Special Issue, published open access by the journal *Mathematics* (ISSN 2227-7390), freely accessible at: https://www.mdpi.com/journal/mathematics/special_issues/T2B4OLUO0T.

For citation purposes, cite each article independently as indicated on the article page online and as indicated below:

Lastname, A.A.; Lastname, B.B. Article Title. *Journal Name* **Year**, *Volume Number*, Page Range.

ISBN 978-3-7258-6504-8 (Hbk)
ISBN 978-3-7258-6505-5 (PDF)
https://doi.org/10.3390/books978-3-7258-6505-5

Contents

mathematics

Article

Development of an Algorithm for Computing the Force and Stress Parameters of a Cycloid Reducer

Egor A. Efremenkov [1], Sergey A. Shanin [1] and Nikita V. Martyushev [2,*]

[1] Department of Mechanical Engineering, Tomsk Polytechnic University, 30, Lenin Ave., 634050 Tomsk, Russia
[2] Department of Advanced Technologies, Tomsk Polytechnic University, 30, Lenin Ave., 634050 Tomsk, Russia
* Correspondence: martjushev@tpu.ru

Abstract: The paper is devoted to the development of an algorithm for the automated calculation of force characteristics of cycloid toothing when the initial parameters vary widely. The algorithm forms a structured data array that accelerates finding and outputting the necessary parameters and reduces the probability of error in determining these parameters. The algorithm serves the basis for a program that allows for the examination of the change in force and geometrical parameters in various combinations. The study includes the analysis of the dependence of forces and contact stresses in transmission toothing with intermediate rolling elements and a free cage on the initial parameters of this transmission. The obtained results will make it possible to select optimal combinations of initial parameters in order to minimize the force impact on the mechanism parts when designing modern compact mechanisms based on the cycloid with intermediate rolling elements and a free cage.

Keywords: automated calculation; modeling; algorithm; cycloid toothing; transmission toothing; cycloid with intermediate rolling elements

MSC: 65Z05

1. Introduction

Currently, it is impossible to develop modern mechanical transmissions in general and transmissions with intermediate rolling elements (IRE) in particular without the automated design of structures and design calculations.

The automation of calculations of cycloids increases the quality of selection of the functional parameters and reduces the time for determining the technical parameters provided by the designed mechanism. In addition, it reduces the probability of design errors in the finished product. Modern mathematical methods allow us to determine stresses and strains in the toothing of various transmissions with high accuracy, and the capabilities of processing a large amount of data allow us to study the cycloid profile in detail.

The transmission with intermediate rolling elements and a free cage (IREFC) is the most promising for use in modern mechatronic and automated systems, since it most fully provides a set of the required technical characteristics. This transmission provides compactness and, at the same time, a high load capacity owing to the toothing multipairing, has a high efficiency due to the replacement of sliding friction in the toothing with rolling friction, and a high toothing accuracy and small angular gaps. The entire set of these characteristics is the most in-demand when designing modern mechanisms.

Currently, the calculation of cycloids with IRE and, especially, transmissions with IREFC, is quite time consuming. The calculation and design of the transmission with IRE often require several iterations of the recalculation of the force characteristics of the mechanism with different combinations of the cycloid initial parameters. This process takes a lot of time, which delays the design stage. Therefore, it is quite relevant to create an algorithm for the automated determination of forces and contact stresses of cycloid toothing of the transmission with IREFC.

Many authors [1–16] are engaged in the study of cycloids using mathematical methods, including the force characteristics of pin gears and transmissions with IRE [17–29]. The determination of forces through deformations in the toothing of the transmission with IRE and a loaded separator is considered in [1]. In [2], the author analyzes the kinematic error and tolerance allocation of cycloidal gear reducers. In another work [3], the author analyzes a cycloidal reducer output mechanism while taking into account machining deviations. In [4], the authors propose a technology for reducing the accuracy of performing cycloid profiles while maintaining the toothing accuracy. The authors in [5,6] investigate the changes in the torque of the drive gearing system. In [7], the dynamic behavior of a two-stage pin cycloid reducer of a new design is analyzed, and the effect of vibrations on the cycloid toothing is considered. In [8,9], the authors analyze the operation of the cycloid. The author [10] describes the design features of the transmission when contacting fixed intermediate links with grooves cut in the torus. He also presents the equations of the spirals used for cutting these grooves. Studies [11,12] analyze contact stresses in a spherical transmission with intermediate rolling elements and propose an algorithm for calculating the number of rolling elements simultaneously transmitting the load. In [13], the authors investigate the forces and torque in a two-stage sine wave gearbox with IRE and analyze the changes in the output torque together with the main parameters. In [14], the authors present methods for generating profiles of plane cycloids with improved geometry; numerical examples are given to illustrate the proposed methods. In [15], the authors propose a generalized dynamic model for the pin gear transmission, which allows for the estimation of the intensity in the contact of the pin with the cycloid profile. Study [16] proposes an approach to optimizing the cycloid drive profile, stress, and efficiency. The authors in [17,18] develop an algorithm for determining contact stresses in the toothing of a pin gear transmission, and the maximum force in the toothing is determined by the method of successive iterations. Works [19–22] consider the contact characteristics of the pins with the cycloid profile. The forces in the pin gear engagement are determined using a single contact stiffness. The forces obtained using the finite element method, including experimental data, are compared. An algorithm for determining the torque, taking into account the friction forces in the engagement of the pin gear toothing, is developed. In [23], the authors analyze the loadings of the cycloid disk using the finite element method. The authors in [24] use an analytical method for determining forces in cycloid toothing and present a program interface for their calculation. The authors of [25] propose a method for calculating the deformation of the cycloid tooth and the gap between the cycloid profile and the rolling element. Study [26] proposes an expression to determine the geometric parameter of a transmission with intermediate rolling elements based on the contact strength condition. Another study, [27], performs the analysis of forces and contact stresses in cycloid toothing of the end transmission with intermediate rolling elements using the numerical modeling of the finite-element model. The author of [28] proposes a new design of a two-stage cycloid with IRE and studies the forces and stresses in toothing. The clearances in the pin toothing are analyzed in [29]. The authors in [30] determine defects in the cycloid toothing of the pin gear based on vibration signals. The authors consider and improve not only the geometry of the cycloid engagement, but also the design of the transmission in [31]. In [32], the authors present a method for diagnosing cycloidal gear damage on a laboratory stand.

The presented analysis of sources confirms various studies of transmissions with cycloid toothing and works on the algorithms to determine stresses and forces in cycloid toothing; however, there was no algorithm for automated calculation and analysis of the connection of force and geometrical parameters of transmissions with IREFC.

Thus, the algorithm for the automated calculation of force parameters of the IRE transmission is relevant. It will expand the field of knowledge on cycloids with intermediate rolling elements and a free cage.

The purpose of this work is to develop an algorithm for the automated determination of the maximum contact stress in a transmission with rolling elements and a free cage, which makes it possible to determine the parameters of the transmission IREFC corresponding to the maximum stress. This will require the solution of the following tasks:

1. To identify the dependence of geometric parameters from initial parameters of the transmission with IREFC.
2. To identify the dependence of force characteristics from initial parameters of the transmission with IREFC.
3. To develop an algorithm for calculating the force parameters (contact stresses and forces) in toothing with the specified initial parameters of the transmission with IREFC.
4. To create the software according to the developed algorithm that allows studying the dependence of force parameters on the initial ones in the transmission with IREFC.
5. To analyze the obtained results.

2. Materials and Methods

To solve the set tasks, the authors developed a methodological model of the sequence of determining the force characteristics of the transmission with IREFC and the procedure for their analysis with the initial parameters of this transmission.

When finding the curvature radii of cycloid profiles to determine contact stresses, an analytical expression of the Bobillier geometric construction was used based on the Euler-Savary theorem. The forces in toothing and stresses in the contact of the rolling elements with cycloid profiles of wheels were determined on the basis of the Hertz elasticity theory.

A unique data structure was created for the software implementation of the algorithm for the complex calculation of the force parameters of the transmission with IREFC according to a set of parameters, each of which is varied in its range. The calculation implies that a structure sample is created as a dynamic array element for each combination of input parameters. To determine the range of valid values, the calculation algorithm iteratively selects among all the parameters, each of which has its own step and range of changes.

3. Cycloid with Intermediate Rolling Elements and a Free Cage

The transmission with IREFC [26] having a single-pole engagement (Figure 1) consists of an input link–a planet carrier (1), an internal cycloid wheel–a cam (2) installed on a rolling bearing on the planet carrier (1), rolling elements (3) in a cage (4) and an external cycloid wheel–a crown (5). The cam (2) or the crown (5) may serve as the output link. If the output link is the cam (2), then the crown (5) is rigidly fixed in the mechanism body and is stationary. If the output link is the crown (5), then the cam (2) should be fixed. However, due to the specifics of the transmission with IREFC, the cam (2) has tow motions as a rotation and linear motion; its complete fixation is impossible. In this case, the rotation is locked, and the linear motion remains.

Since two toothings are connected in one transmission with IREFC, there are situations when the pitch points P (Figure 2) of the first and the second toothings do not coincide; then the transmission has two pitch points, and it is named as a double-pole transmission. When the pitch point of both toothings in the transmission coincide, such transmission is called single-pole.

The transmission ratio of the rolling elements and a cam is defined as follows:

$$i_{21} = 1 - \frac{1}{Z_2}. \tag{1}$$

The transmission ratio of the rolling elements and a crown is defined as follows:

$$i_{23} = 1 + \frac{1}{Z_2}. \tag{2}$$

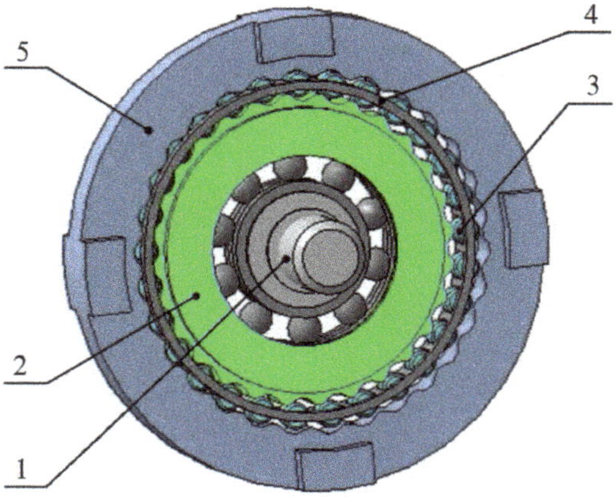

Figure 1. Diagram of the transmission with intermediate rolling elements and a free cage.

The transmission with IREFC has two toothings: rolling elements and a cam (Figure 2a); rolling elements and a crown (Figure 2b) [26].

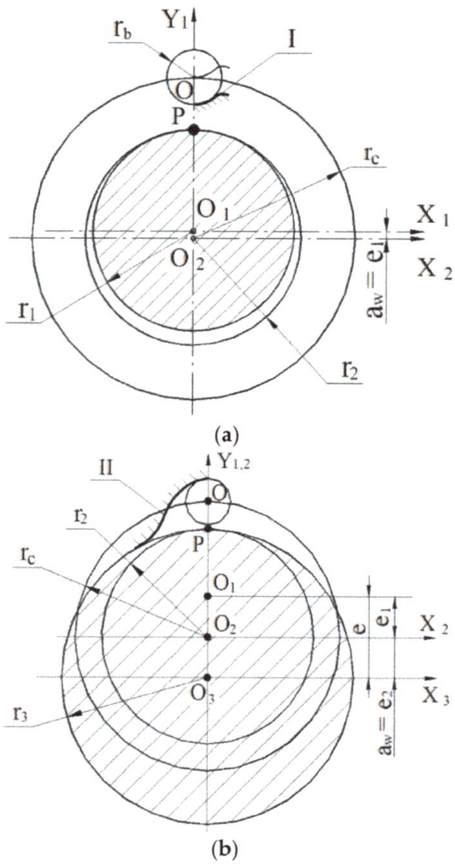

Figure 2. Toothing of the transmission with intermediate rolling elements and a free cage: (**a**)—rolling elements with a cam; (**b**)—rolling elements with a crown.

In expressions (1) and (2), Z_2 is the number of rolling elements, which is one of the initial transmission parameters. In addition, before the beginning of the design, the following initial parameters are set: the generating circle radius r_2 and the displacement factor χ [26]. After choosing the specified three parameters, the range of possible values of the rolling elements radius r_b is determined based on the dependence [26]:

$$2\frac{r_2}{Z_2} < r_b < r_2 \cdot \chi \cdot \sin\left(\frac{180^\circ}{Z_2}\right). \tag{3}$$

The radius (Figure 2) r_c of the centers of the rolling elements is determined using the following expression:

$$r_c = r_2 \cdot \chi. \tag{4}$$

The displacement coefficient χ in the transmission with IREFC is an important parameter, because it influences the cycloid profile geometry and the transmission assemblability; it cannot be less than 1.25. This parameter shows (4) to what degree the radius of the centers of the rolling elements r_c is greater than the radius of the generating circle r_2, and therefore it has a direct impact on the force values in the cycloid toothing.

One should note that in case of the single-pole transmission with IREFC, the initial parameter r_2 is the same for both toothings (rolling elements with the cam and the crown). In the case of the double-pole transmission, different values of this parameter are used. At the same time, the parameter χ is the same for both single-pole and double-pole transmissions. Further, let us consider the calculations intended for designing a single-pole transmission.

Since the initial parameters are preset arbitrarily at the beginning of designing, the geometry of the cycloid toothing, the power characteristics of the transmission with the IREFC, and the designed mechanism depend on them. The equations presented below to represent the transmission geometry and to determine the mesh forces will be written mainly using the initial parameters of the transmission with IREFC.

The axial distance (eccentricity) is determined according to the following expression:

$$a_w = e_i = \frac{r_2}{Z_2}. \tag{5}$$

The total eccentricity of the transmission with IREFC is calculated using the following formula:

$$e = e_1 + e_2,$$

where e_1 and e_2 are the eccentricities of the engagement of the rolling elements with the cam and the crown, respectively (Figure 2b).

The angle φ_2 is present in all the expressions for calculating and designing the transmission with IREFC, which will be observed further. The cycloid profiles are formed when the rolling elements begin to migrate together with a circle of the radius r_2. The angle of this migration is calculated in the same way as φ_2 is.

The rotation angle φ_2 of the separator with rolling elements is used to determine all geometrical parameters of the transmission with IREFC. It is a basic variable in the calculation of geometry and transmission force parameters. To determine the force parameters of the transmission with IREFC, φ_2 should be taken in the range from 0 to 180°. The rotation angle φ_1 of the cam and the rotation angle φ_3 of the crown also depends on φ_2 [26]:

$$\varphi_1 = \frac{\varphi_2}{i_{21}} = \frac{\varphi_2}{\left(1 - \frac{1}{Z_2}\right)}; \tag{6}$$

$$\varphi_3 = \frac{\varphi_2}{i_{23}} = \frac{\varphi_2}{\left(1 + \frac{1}{Z_2}\right)}. \tag{7}$$

These angles determine the position of the cycloid teeth of the cam and crown, depending on the position of the rolling elements.

The radius of the initial circle of the cam (Figure 2) is determined depending on r_2:

$$r_1 = r_2\left(1 - \frac{1}{Z_2}\right).$$

The geometrical parameters of cycloid wheels are determined according to the following expressions:

- cam tip radius

$$r_{tip}^{cm} = r_2\left(\chi + \frac{1}{Z_2}\right) - r_b; \quad (8)$$

- cam root radius

$$r_{root}^{cm} = r_2\left(\chi - \frac{1}{Z_2}\right) - r_b; \quad (9)$$

- crown tip radius

$$r_{tip}^{cn} = r_2\left(\chi - \frac{1}{Z_2}\right) + r_b; \quad (10)$$

- crown root radius

$$r_{root}^{cn} = r_2\left(\chi + \frac{1}{Z_2}\right) + r_b. \quad (11)$$

The expressions (8)–(11) make it possible to define the range of coordinates of the distribution of contact points of cycloid profiles with rolling elements.

4. Loading Characteristic of the Cycloid

To determine the forces in the transmission toothing with IREFC, let us consider the design model (Figure 3). The torque on the cam through toothing forces is expressed through the formula:

$$T_{cam} = \sum F_i \cdot h_i. \quad (12)$$

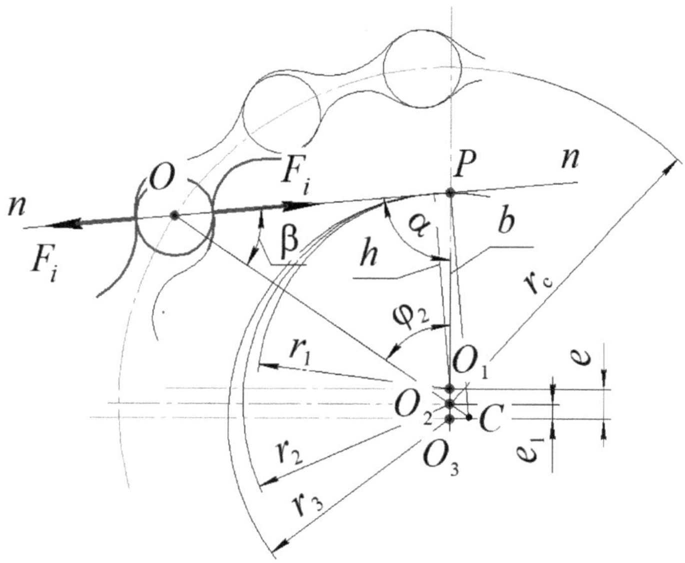

Figure 3. Calculation of forces in the toothing of the transmission with intermediate rolling elements and a free cage.

The arm h is calculated according to the geometry (Figure 3) as follows:

$$h_i = b \cdot sin\alpha_i. \tag{13}$$

where b is the distance from the center of the profile wheel (cam or crown) to the pitch P, which is equal to r_1 for the cam or r_3 for the crown.

The rotation angle α of the normal profile relative to the vertical transmission axis is found via the sine theorem based on the triangle OPO_2 (Figure 3):

$$sin\alpha_i = \frac{sin\varphi_{2i} \cdot r_c}{L_i} \rightarrow \alpha_i = \arcsin\left(\frac{sin\varphi_{2i} \cdot r_c}{L_i}\right) \tag{14}$$

where the distance L_i is determined through the rotation angle φ_2 of the cage with rolling elements and through the initial parameters:

$$PO = L_i = r_2\sqrt{1 + \chi^2 - 2\chi cos\varphi_{2i}} \tag{15}$$

Assuming the fact that the forces in toothing are connected by the linear dependence with the deformations [33], the correspondence of the maximum force and the maximum deformation can be considered. Then the ratio of the force to the corresponding arm in the toothing of one transmission is equal. We know the position of the line of action of the maximum force, because we know the inclination angle of the normal profile at this point of contact and the arm of this force [26]. Thus, let us determine the force on each rolling element using the proportion:

$$\frac{F_i}{h_i} = \frac{F_{max}}{b},$$

Then the force on the i rolling element equals:

$$F_i = \frac{F_{max} \cdot h_i}{b}. \tag{16}$$

Let us substitute the obtained expression into (13), and after conversion we get an expression to determine the maximum force to engage the transmission with IRE and a free cage through the input torque:

$$F_{max} = \frac{T_{cam} \cdot b}{\sum h_i^2}. \tag{17}$$

Then, according to (17), let us determine the force on each rolling element transmitting the load.

By determining all forces in the transmission toothing with IREFC, i.e., at the points of contact of the rolling elements with the profiles of the cam and the crown, it is possible to determine the stresses in these points. The literature [26] provides the formula for determining the contact strength in the toothing of planetary cycloids:

$$(\sigma_H)_i = \sqrt{\frac{T_{cam} h_i E(\rho_{2i} + \rho_{1i})}{2\pi \cdot l_b \cdot \rho_{1i}\rho_{2i}(1 - \mu^2)\sum h_i^2}}. \tag{18}$$

where T_{cam} is the torque on the cam;

ρ_{1i}, ρ_{2i} are radii of the profile curvature of the first and second contacting bodies at the contact point (cycloid profile of the wheel and the rolling element, respectively);

μ is the Poisson's ratio for the first and second contacting bodies, respectively;

E is the elongation modulus of the first and second bodies, respectively;

h_i is the shortest distance from the axis of the cam center to the normal profile and to the cycloid profiles;

l_b is the large side of the contact spot rectangle, in our case equal to the length of the roller.

To determine the radii of the profile curvature of the cam ρ_{1i} and the crown ρ_{3i}, we use the Euler–Savary theorem [34], which can be expressed through the Bobillier construction [33].

The curvature radius of the cycloid profile of the cam and the crown is then determined using the following relationship:

$$\rho_i = \pm L - r_b \mp l_{MP}, \tag{19}$$

where it should be noted that the upper sign is used to calculate the curvature radius of the cycloid profile of the cam, and the lower sign is used to calculate that of the crown profile. The distance l_{MP} from the pitch to the center of the curvature radius of the cycloid profile is defined based on the expression:

$$l_{MP} = \frac{r_2\left(1 - \frac{1}{Z_2}\right)}{\frac{sin\alpha}{tg\beta} + cos\alpha}. \tag{20}$$

In this case, the tangent of the angle of location of the curvature radius center of the cycloid profile is determined based on the following expression:

$$tg\beta = \frac{l_{O_2C} sin\varphi}{l_{O_2C} cos\varphi + \frac{r_2}{Z_2}}.$$

$$l_{O_2C} = \frac{r_2}{sin\varphi \cdot tg\alpha - cos\varphi}.$$

When determining the curvature radius of the corresponding profile from the expression (20), we get a negative radius for the concave section of the profile and a positive radius for the convex section of the profile.

5. Automatization Calculation Algorithm of Loading Characteristic

Specifying the initial radius of the generating circle (r_2) and the radius of the rolling element (r_b), as well as the number of rolling elements (Z_2) and the displacement coefficient (χ), let us determine the geometrical parameters of the transmission with IREFC. By setting the output torque T_{out} and the length of the rolling body l_b, let us determine the forces in the cycloid toothing and the contact stresses. These calculations are performed using expressions (1)–(20) according to the sequence in the algorithm (Figure 4).

Let us note that we should set the range of changes Z_2 and χ before starting the calculations to analyze the change in the maximum contact stress and the corresponding forces in the toothing of the cycloid with IREFC, as well as other parameters. In this case, the number of rolling elements Z_2 can vary arbitrarily, but only in increments of one, and the displacement coefficient χ is always considered in the range of 1.25–1.67, but in arbitrary increments.

When developing the algorithm, specifying the length of the rolling body is provided: it is equal to the diameter of the rolling body by default and, if required, it is arbitrary. Next, the maximum toothing force is determined by creating a temporary data array.

After determining the maximum force in the cycloid toothing, we generate an array of data for the angle φ_2 of the position of the rolling elements in increments of 0.02°. The study of the cycloid profile is performed in the range of angle φ_2 from 0° to 180°.

Further, using the received ranges Z_2 and χ, as well as the maximum force determined earlier (18), the geometrical parameters of cycloid toothing, forces, and contact stresses at each point of the cycloid profile are calculated. All calculated parameters are entered into the structured array base. After filling the data array, the maximum and corresponding initial data, forces in toothing, and geometrical parameters of the cycloid with IREFC are determined using a sequential comparison according to contact stresses.

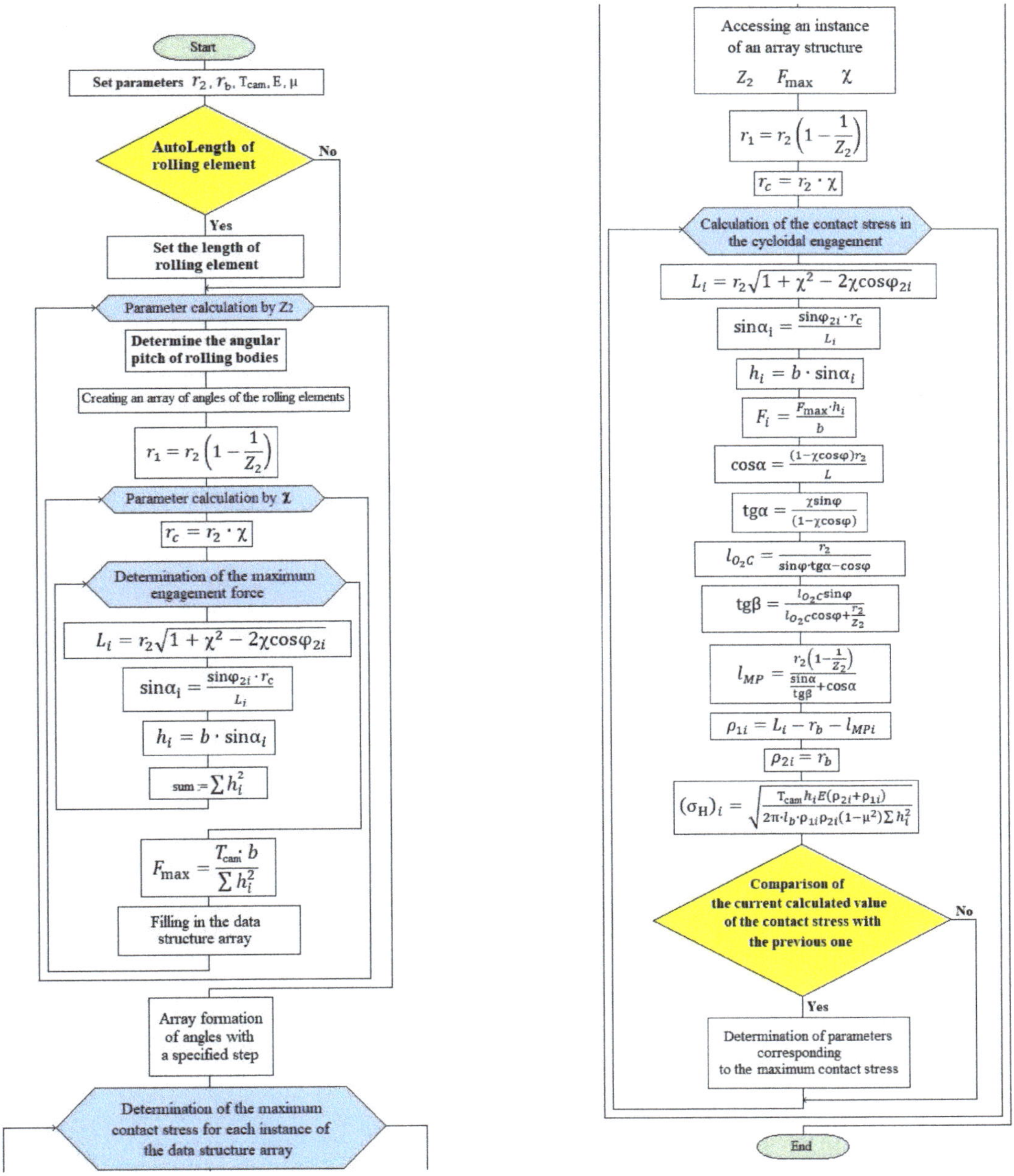

Figure 4. Algorithm for determining the maximum contact stresses in a cycloid.

Having determined the maximum contact stress in the cycloid toothing, let us determine the dependencies between the force and geometrical parameters in the form of graphs.

Thus, a data structure was created for the software implementation of a complex transmission calculation with intermediate rolling elements based on a set of parameters, each of which varies in its range. The calculation implies that a structure sample is created as a dynamic array element for each combination of the input parameters. To determine the range of valid values, the calculation algorithm iteratively selects among all the parameters, each of which has its own step and range of changes. The calculation results are recorded in the corresponding copy of the dynamic array. After calculating all the combinations of the parameters, the results are displayed on the screen as a text and a graph.

6. Results and Discussions

A calculation program was written in the Lazarus cross-platform development environment according to the developed algorithm. The average calculation and plotting time is 0.2 s for the parameters taken as examples. However, the calculation time directly depends on the specified ranges and the steps of the calculated parameters, such as the number of rolling elements Z_2 and the displacement coefficient χ. That is, the wider the ranges and the smaller the calculation step, the longer the calculation time. However, in the case of our calculations, having different ranges and calculation steps up to 0.002, the calculation time was not more than 0.3 s. A personal computer with an Intel(R) Core(TM) i5-9400F 2.9 GHz processor and random-access memory of 8 GB was used for the calculations.

According to the algorithm of the automated calculation of the force parameters of the cycloid with IREFC, the major result is the multiple of force characteristic values of the transmission with IRE and the geometrical parameters corresponding to them. In contrast to [35], where a computational program with a user-friendly interface is proposed, this algorithm allows us to comprehensively study the changes in the power characteristics in a wide range of several initial parameters of the transmission with IREFC.

The algorithm makes it possible to obtain a large amount of data on the values of forces and contact stresses in the toothing of the cycloid with IREFC by determining these data at high resolution (small step). This allows for a more accurate analysis of the cycloid profile loading. The use of a structured data array allows us to reduce the time taken to find the necessary information and the time taken for designing the entire mechanism.

Figure 5 shows the interface of the program developed according to the above algorithm, which allows us to quickly change the initial parameters of the transmission with IRE and their limits of testing (on the left). The calculated values of the force parameters and geometrical parameters corresponding to them (on the right) are immediately displayed with high accuracy. The use of the algorithm makes it possible to obtain an exact value of the contact stress, since the cycloid profile is analyzed in increments of 0.02° over the angle.

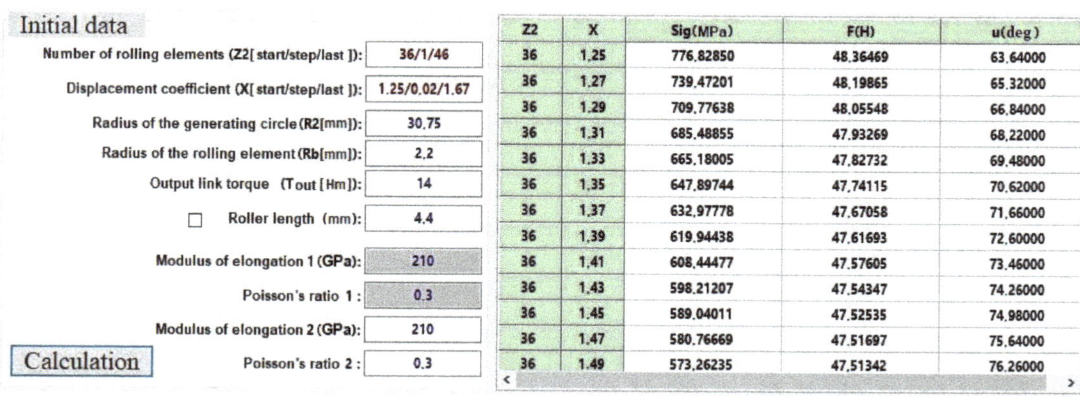

Figure 5. Interface of the program for automated calculation of the transmission force parameters with intermediate rolling elements and a free cage according to the developed algorithm.

According to the obtained data, the structured array element allows us to build and study the dependencies of various parameters of the transmission with IREFC. For example, the maximum contact stress for different values of χ and Z_2 corresponds to the graph of studying the change in the position angle of rolling elements (Figure 6). The graph (Figure 6) shows that for different values Z_2, the angle of occurrence of the maximum contact stress varies within different limits in the specified range of the variation of the displacement coefficient χ. In this way, in the presence of definite parameters Z_2 and χ, one angle φ_2 corresponds to the maximum contact stress. Thus, the use of a structured array allows us to quickly obtain a change in the force parameters depending on the initial ones for the transmission with IREFC, which is also illustrated below.

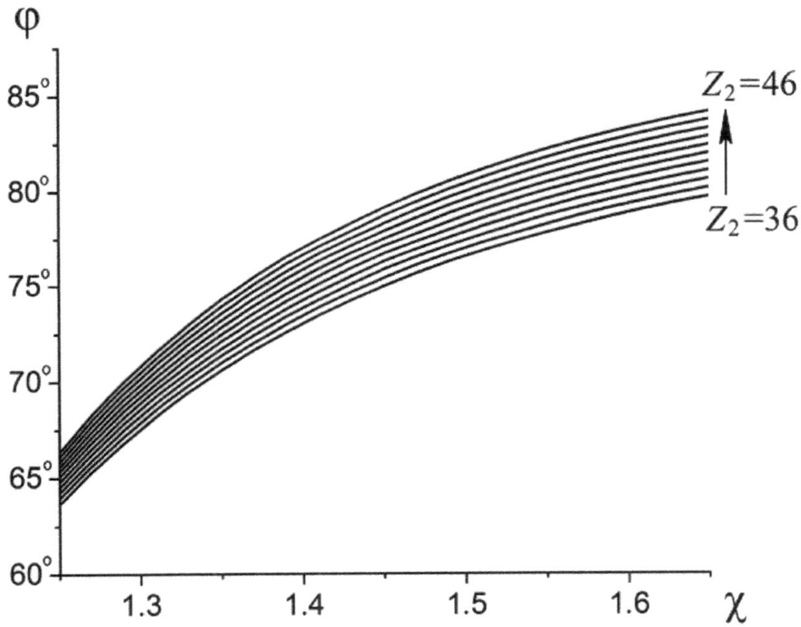

Figure 6. Dependence of the maximum contact stress angle on the displacement coefficient χ at different values of the rolling elements number Z_2.

Figure 7 shows the multiple of the graphs of the change in the maximum contact stress in the cycloid toothing with IREFC for the same range χ and a different number of transmission rolling elements. The algorithm makes it possible to clearly see what displacement factor should be selected for a particular number of rolling elements in order to obtain the minimum value of the contact stress in the designed mechanism. Or otherwise, it allows us to select the number of rolling elements for a particular displacement factor in order to minimize loads in the designed product.

It is also possible to study the change in the maximum force in the toothing of the cycloid with IREFC (Figure 8). The use of the algorithm makes it possible to see that the maximum force in the cycloid toothing for a certain number of rolling elements almost does not depend on the displacement coefficient χ.

The results of the algorithm operation determine the dependence of the force characteristics on the initial geometric parameters of the cycloid with IREFC; the composite parameters, such as eccentricity, circle radius of centers, etc., are not analyzed at this stage.

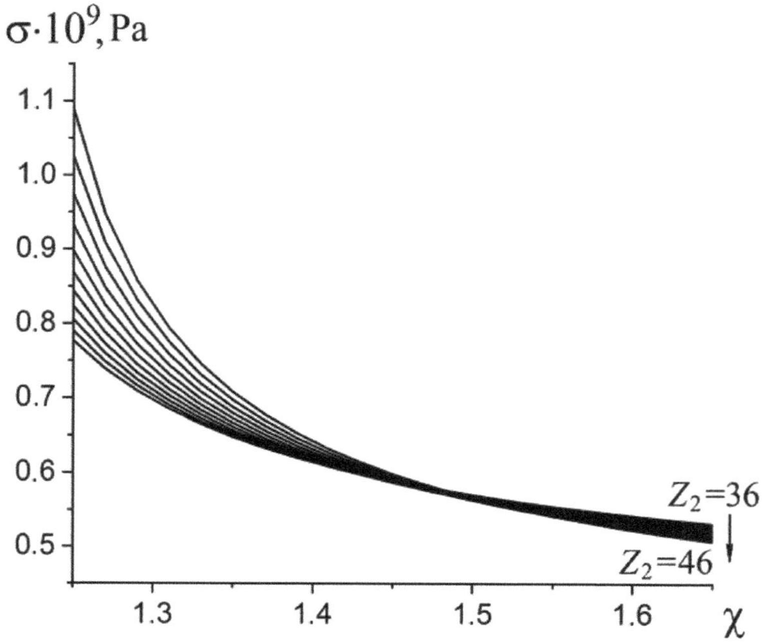

Figure 7. Dependence of the maximum contact stress on the displacement coefficient χ at different values of the rolling elements number Z_2.

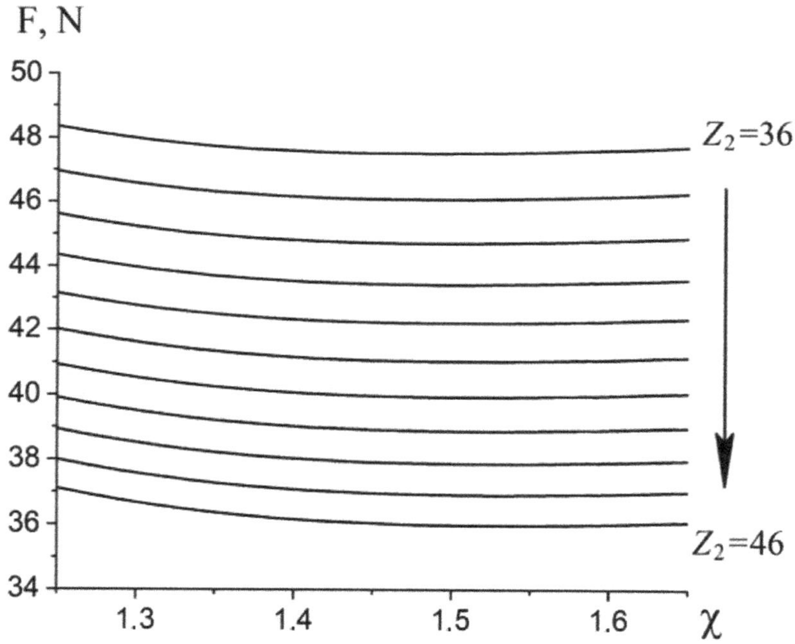

Figure 8. Dependence of the maximum force in the toothing on the displacement coefficient χ at different values of the rolling elements number Z_2.

7. Conclusions

Thus, the developed algorithm of the automated determination of force characteristics depending on the initial and geometrical parameters of the cycloid with intermediate rolling elements and a free cage allows us to reduce the time required to provide data for the design of the information mechanism. The proposed algorithm made it possible to build a program into the Lazarus cross-platform development environment. The program allows us to study various combinations of the force and geometrical parameters, such as:

- the maximum contact stress in toothing;
- angles of rolling element positions corresponding to the maximum contact stress;
- toothing forces corresponding to the maximum contact stress;
- number of rolling elements varying over a wide range; and
- the displacement factor varying over a wide range.

These studies can also be carried out for various materials of contacting links: both cycloid wheels and rolling elements.

The algorithm made it possible to create a structured array of force and geometric parameters of the transmission with IREFC, which facilitates the access to the necessary parameters and eliminates errors in providing the incorrect combination of the requested parameters.

The work of the algorithm and the developed program, as compared to the design time without using the algorithm, allowed us to reduce the time allotted for selecting the correct parameters by 30% and the time for designing the mechanism based on the transmission with IREFC by 15%. Without the proposed algorithm, the selection of operable transmission parameters and the process of designing the mechanism on its base took more time.

The algorithm allows us, with a new degree of accuracy, to analyze the cycloid profile, which, in turn, makes it possible to determine most accurately both the values of the maximum force and contact stress in the cycloid toothing, and the accuracy of the values themselves.

The algorithm allows us to analyze both the dependence of the mesh force on the displacement coefficient and the forces arising due to the change in the radius of the generating circle or the center circle of the rolling elements. It is also possible to analyze changes in contact stresses arising due to the eccentricity of the transmission with IREFC and the number of rolling elements, the change in the number of rolling elements owing to the displacement coefficient, and the number of rolling elements due to the mesh force. Obviously, not all of these graphs have been presented in this work. The radius of the centers of the rolling elements and the eccentricity of the transmission are complex composite parameters, and the analysis of changing the forces owing to these parameters is the next stage of the work. The analysis of the influence of clearances in the toothing on the distribution of forces, when rolling elements contact with the cycloid profile, is also planned to be included in the next stage of the work.

The developed algorithm can be used when designing one-, two-stage, etc., reducers, but it is necessary to design each stage separately. In the long term, the end-to-end design of multi-stage cycloids is planned to be studied thoroughly. The algorithm may also be extended to determine the gap in the toothing of the designed cycloid.

Author Contributions: Conceptualization, E.A.E.; methodology, S.A.S.; software, S.A.S.; validation, E.A.E.; formal analysis, N.V.M.; investigation, E.A.E.; resources, N.V.M.; data curation, S.A.S.; writing—original draft preparation, E.A.E.; writing—review and editing, N.V.M.; visualization, S.A.S. All authors have read and agreed to the published version of the manuscript.

Funding: This research received no external funding.

Institutional Review Board Statement: Not applicable.

Informed Consent Statement: Not applicable.

Data Availability Statement: The data presented in this study are available from the corresponding authors upon reasonable request.

Conflicts of Interest: The authors declare no conflict of interest.

References

1. Kan, A.; Il'In, A.S.; Lazurkevich, A. Load analysis of the planetary gear train with intermediate rollers. Part 2. *IOP Conf. Ser. Mater. Sci. Eng.* **2016**, *124*, 012004. [CrossRef]
2. Lin, K.-S.; Chan, K.-Y.; Lee, J.-J. Kinematic error analysis and tolerance allocation of cycloidal gear reducers. *Mech. Mach. Theory* **2018**, *124*, 73–91. [CrossRef]
3. Bednarczyk, S. Analysis of the cycloidal reducer output mechanism while taking into account machining deviations. *Proc. Inst. Mech. Eng. Part C J. Mech. Eng. Sci.* **2021**, *235*, 7299–7313. [CrossRef]
4. Efremenkov, E.A.; Martyushev, N.V.; Skeeba, V.Y.; Grechneva, M.V.; Olisov, A.V.; Ens, A.D. Research on the Possibility of Lowering the Manufacturing Accuracy of Cycloid Transmission Wheels with Intermediate Rolling Elements and a Free Cage. *Appl. Sci.* **2021**, *12*, 5. [CrossRef]
5. Ren, Y.; Bian, W.; Yan, R. Optimization analysis of air gap magnetic field in electromagnetic harmonic movable tooth drive system. *Int. J. Comput. Eng.* **2019**, *4*, 132–135.
6. Ren, Y.; Ma, Y.; Wan, R. Parametric design of inner teeth of center wheel in electromagnetic harmonic movable teeth transmission. *J. Phys. Conf. Ser.* **2021**, *1965*, 012009.
7. Blagojević, M.; Matejic, M.; Kostić, N. Dynamic Behaviour of a Two-Stage Cycloidal Speed Reducer of a New Design Concept. *Teh. Vjesn.—Technol. Gaz.* **2018**, *25*, 291–298. [CrossRef]
8. Bechhoefer, E. Automated Condition Monitoring of a Cycloid Gearbox. In *Maintenance Management-Current Challenges, New Developments, and Future Directions*; IntechOpen: London, UK, 2022. [CrossRef]
9. Grosso, P.; Massaccesi, G.; Cavalaglio Camargo Molano, J.; Mottola, G.; Borghi, D. Signal model of a cycloidal drive for diagnostic purposes. In Proceedings of the ISMA-USD Conference, Leuven, Belgium, 12–14 September 2022; pp. 750–764.
10. Prudnikov, A.P. Planetary Torus Helical Transmission. *IOP Conf. Ser. Mater. Sci. Eng.* **2020**, *795*, 012022. [CrossRef]
11. Lustenkov, M.E.; Lustenkova, E.S. Load Capacity of Spherical Roller Transmission with Double-Row Pinion. *IOP Conf. Ser. Mater. Sci. Eng.* **2020**, *795*, 012020. [CrossRef]
12. E Lustenkov, M.; Moiseenko, A.N. Analysis of contact strength of spherical roller transmission with double-row pinion. *IOP Conf. Ser. Mater. Sci. Eng.* **2021**, *1118*, 012006. [CrossRef]
13. Xu, L.; Song, W. Two-step sine movable tooth drive. *Adv. Mech. Eng.* **2017**, *9*, 1–9.
14. Litvin, F.L.; Feng, P.-H. Computerized Design and Generation of Cycloidal Gearing. *Mech. Mach. Theory* **1996**, *31*, 891–911. [CrossRef]
15. Xu, L.X.; Chen, B.K.; Li, C.Y. Dynamic modelling and contact analysis of bearing-cycloid-pinwheel transmission mecha-nisms used in joint rotate vector reducers. *Mech. Mach. Theory* **2019**, *137*, 432–458.
16. Sensinger, J.W. Unified Approach to Cycloid Drive Profile, Stress, and Efficiency Optimization. *J. Mech. Des.* **2010**, *132*, 024503. [CrossRef]
17. Hu, Y.H.; Li, G.; Zhu, W.D.; Cui, J.K. An Elastic Transmission Error Compensation Method for Rotary Vector Speed Re-ducers Based on Error Sensitivity Analysis. *Appl. Sci.* **2020**, *10*, 481.
18. Li, X.; Tang, L.; He, H.; Sun, L. Design and Load Distribution Analysis of the Mismatched Cycloid-Pin Gear Pair in RV Speed Reducers. *Machines* **2022**, *10*, 672. [CrossRef]
19. Malhotra, S.; Parameswaran, M. Analysis of a cycloid speed reducer. *Mech. Mach. Theory* **1983**, *18*, 491–499. [CrossRef]
20. Blanche, J.G.; Yang, D.C.H. Cycloid Drives with Machining Tolerances. *J. Mech. Des.* **1989**, *111*, 337–344. [CrossRef]
21. Gorla, C.; Davoli, P.; Rosa, F.; Longoni, C.; Chiozzi, F.; Samarani, A. Theoretical and Experimental Analysis of a Cycloidal Speed Reducer. *J. Mech. Des.* **2008**, *130*, 112604. [CrossRef]
22. Wang, H.; Shi, Z.-Y.; Yu, B.; Xu, H. Transmission Performance Analysis of RV Reducers Influenced by Profile Modification and Load. *Appl. Sci.* **2019**, *9*, 4099. [CrossRef]
23. Thube, S.V.; Bobak, T.R. *Dynamic Analysis of a Cycloidal Gearbox Using Finite Element Method*; American Gear Manufacturers Association: Alexandria, Virginia, 2012; 13p.
24. Bao, J.; He, W. Parametric Design and Efficiency Analysis of the Output-Pin-Wheel Cycloid Transmission. *Int. J. Control Autom.* **2015**, *8*, 349–362. [CrossRef]
25. Blagojevic, M. Analysis of clearances and deformations at cycloid disc. *Mach. Des.* **2014**, *6*, 79–84.
26. Efremenkov, E.A.; Efremenkova, S.K. Design of a heavily loaded cycloidal transmission with a free cage based on the contact strength condition. Bulletin of Tomsk Polytechnic University. *Eng. Georesour.* **2021**, *332*, 182–188.
27. Nam, W.K.; Shin, J.W.; Oh, S.H. Design of thin plate-type speed reducers using balls for robots. *J. Mech. Sci. Technol.* **2013**, *27*, 519–524. [CrossRef]
28. Wu, S.; Yan, H.-Z.; Bi, R.; Wang, Z.; Zhu, P. Nonlinear Optimization Method for Transmission Error of Hypoid Gear Machined by the Duplex Helical Method. *Math. Probl. Eng.* **2020**, *2020*, 626089. [CrossRef]
29. Król, R. Analysis of the backlash in the single stage cycloidal gearbox. *Arch. Mech. Eng.* **2022**, *69*, 693–711.

30. Al Hajj, M.A.; Quaglia, G.; Schulz, I. Condition-Based Monitoring on High-Precision Gearbox for Robotic Applications. *Shock. Vib.* **2022**, *2022*, 6653723. [CrossRef]
31. Maccioni, L.; Concli, F.; Blagojevic, M. A new three-stage gearbox concept for high reduction ratios: Use of a nested-cycloidal architecture to increase the power density. *Mech. Mach. Theory* **2023**, *181*, 105203. [CrossRef]
32. Komorska, I.; Olejarczyk, K.; Puchalski, A.; Wikło, M.; Wołczyński, Z. Fault Diagnosing of Cycloidal Gear Reducer Using Statistical Features of Vibration Signal and Multifractal Spectra. *Sensors* **2023**, *23*, 1645. [CrossRef]
33. Kudryavtsev, V.N. *Planetary Gears*; M/S: Moscow, Russia, 1966.
34. Litvin, F.L.; Fuentes, A.; Curti, G. *Gear Geometry and Applied Theory*; Cambridge University Press: Cambridge, UK, 2004; pp. 267–286.
35. A Efremenkov, E.; Bonnard, E. Power Parameters Automated Calculation for Transmission with Intermediate Rolling Bodies and Free Cage. *IOP Conf. Ser. Mater. Sci. Eng.* **2020**, *795*, 012025. [CrossRef]

mathematics

MDPI

Article

Analytical Modelling of an Active Vibration Absorber for a Beam

Carlos Rincon *, Jorge Alencastre and Richard Rivera

Engineering Department, Pontificia Universidad Catolica del Peru, San Miguel 15088, Peru; jalenca@pucp.edu.pe (J.A.); rrivera@pucp.edu.pe (R.R.)
* Correspondence: rinconr.carlos@pucp.pe

Abstract: Attenuation of mechanical vibrations is an ongoing field of research in engineering aiming at reducing damage and improving performance in the presence of dynamical forces. Different alternatives have been proposed over time; the active vibration absorber can be highlighted as an alternative which can absorb the vibration from system in real time. In this study, an active vibration absorber was modelled as an electromechanical device. It was applied to a cantilever beam, mathematically modelled as a continuous beam. A set of differential equations representing the dynamical behaviour of the cantilever beam and active vibration absorber was obtained and it was simulated in Matlab Simulink®. Results indicated that the active vibration absorber is able to significantly reduce the vibration amplitudes of a system, especially in resonance conditions. The analytical model and procedure developed here can easily spread to any more complex system.

Keywords: vibration absorber; tuned mass damper; active vibration absorber model; active control; electromagnetic vibration absorber

MSC: 37M05

1. Introduction

Mechanical vibrations are manifested in almost any human activity. In the engineering field, they appear in structures, machinery, piping systems and other areas as a consequence of dynamic forces over time. High vibration amplitudes affect negatively the performance of a system and damage its structure, components and other systems which are connected in some way. Vibrations are usually monitored in specific locations which provide useful information in order to prevent catastrophic failures and correct them in an initial stage [1,2]. In this sense, attenuation of vibration amplitudes has been a continuous field of research for engineering. The dynamic vibration absorber invented by Frahm in 1909 [3] can be highlighted as a mechanical device capable of changing the dynamical characteristics of an existing system. It consists of a secondary system tuned to a specific excitation frequency in order to produce an opposite equal force to the perturbation in a primary system over time [4].

The main disadvantage of the passive vibration absorber is it is not effective if the perturbation changes its frequency since the vibration absorber parameters are not able to change. On the other hand, the active vibration absorber compensates for this characteristic since it is able to tune its parameters for different requirements. In active absorption, an actuator component is added to the vibration absorber in order to tune it to any excitation frequency in real time. Control strategies of this active component have been developed, especially in active control for structural engineering [5,6]. One of the first active vibration absorbers was designed in order to reduce the vibration amplitudes of a tall building, modelled as discrete masses [7,8]. Chang and Yang proposed an active mass damper for a structure modelled as discrete masses, but actuator dynamics was not considered [9]. Kwak,

Yang and Shin proposed a semi active absorber, where the active component was controlled by a correlation with the current magnitude through a solenoid [10]. Yu, Thenozhi and Li studied the active vibration absorber implemented in a discrete structure model with PD/PID control of the active force using position over time as feedback [11]. Yang, Shin, Lee, Kim and Kwak used an acceleration feedback, since it was the simplest variable which can be measured directly by accelerometers [12]. Chang developed an LQR control of an AMD with an acceleration feedback for a scaled bridge modelled as a rigid body [13]. Ramesh and Narayanan presented a better accurate structure model of a beam based on the finite element method (FEM) [14]. Cao and Li proposed a new control algorithm, with a better response than LQR under same conditions, based on the calculation of the optimal gains in order to obtain the minimum variance of the displacement response over time [15]. Zhou and Li applied an active tuned mass damper (AMTD) with an LQR control algorithm to a tall building represented as an FEM model calibrated by its dynamical response measurement [16]. In these studies, primary systems were modelled as discrete systems. However, real systems are more complex than a discrete model as well as their dynamical behaviours. Different control strategies and feedback variables have been implemented, where PD/PID control algorithms can be highlighted as the standard industrial controllers due to its simplicity and the theory being well known [11]. Other current strategies consist of adding devices for damping. Some authors proposed structural damping for controlling the vibration amplitude [17]. Active damping was also proposed based on magnetorheological damper [18]. Linear motion is not the only consequence of vibration, torsional vibration is also a field of research. An electromagnetic torsion active vibration absorber has been proposed [19]. Applications of an active vibration absorber are not limited to structural and mechanical engineering, The concept has been extended to the medical field in order to reduce the vibration amplitude of tremor in human arms [20]. Passive vibration absorber has been effective for this application [21–23]. The main advantage for patients is that it is a non-invasive device. However, it is not able to tune its parameters for different requirements as an active absorber.

In this paper, an active vibration absorber (AVA) is modelled as an electromechanical device. A cantilever beam is chosen as a primary system since it can be used to represent different structures. This was represented as a continuous model which is the most accurate model of a real body since it is based on a strong formulation of the differential equations. The main advantage of a continuous model is that it allows to quantify the influence of the AVA when it is placed in different positions along the structure. The PD control algorithm is used for controlling the active force. The developed procedure is not limited to structures, it can be applied to different systems by coupling the AVA equations.

2. Materials and Methods

2.1. Active Vibration Absorber Model

The active vibration absorber can be modelled as a 1-DOF system, Figure 1. It consists of a mass m_a, a damper that is represented by a damping coefficient b_a, stiffness k_a and an external active force produced by an actuator u. The magnitude and direction of the active force is calculated in order to tune this system to any excitation frequency.

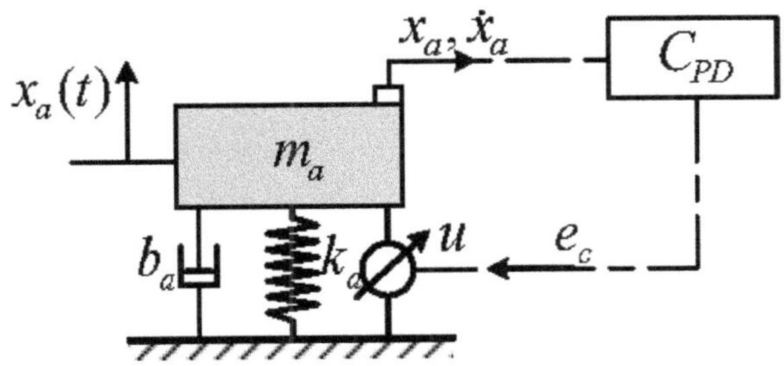

Figure 1. Active vibration absorber.

By using Newton's 2nd Law, the equation of motion for this vibration absorber is given by (1).

$$m_a\ddot{x}_a + b_a\dot{x}_a + k_a x_a = u \tag{1}$$

The actuator is modelled as an electromagnetic actuator. Thus, the dynamic behaviour is obtained from its geometric and electromagnetic characteristics according to the modelling presented in [24,25]. It can be simplified as an equivalent electrical LR circuit given by (2), where L is inductance, R is resistance, I is current and e_c is excitation voltage.$K_b\dot{x}_a$ is a voltage induced by the relative movement in the presence of current through a solenoid [26], where K_b is the actuator constant.

$$L\dot{i} + Ri + K_b\dot{x}_a = e_c \tag{2}$$

The interaction between an electromagnetic field and the current through a circuit of the electromagnetic actuator produces the active force over time according to Lorentz's Law, (3), where u is the active force and K_c is an actuator constant.

$$u = K_c i \tag{3}$$

According to the vibration absorption theory, the natural frequency of the decoupled system must be equal to the excitation frequency of the primary system. The same working concept is used to tune the active vibration absorber. In this sense, a PD control is able to modify the real part as well as the imaginary part of the poles of its characteristic equation in order to locate these poles in the imaginary axis with a frequency equal to the excitation frequency. The PD control of the electromagnetic actuator voltage was proposed in [26] and it has the following form (4), where K_p and K_d are the PD gains for the position and velocity feedback.

$$e_c = K_p x_a + K_d\dot{x}_a \tag{4}$$

Using Laplace transform in Equations (1)–(3) and ordering, Equations (5) and (6) in the Laplace domain are obtained.

$$X_a(s) = \frac{K_c}{(m_a s^2 + b_a s + k_a)(sL + R) + K_b K_c s} E(s) \tag{5}$$

$$E_c(s) = K_p X_a(s) + sK_d X_a(s) \tag{6}$$

Solving the characteristic equation of the system, the PD gains which tune the natural frequency of the active vibration absorber to the excitation frequency ω_c are given by (7) and (8) according to [26].

$$K_p = \mathrm{Re}\left(\frac{-(Ls+R)(m_a s^2 + c_a s + k_a) - K_b K_c s}{K_c} \right)_{s=\omega_c i} \tag{7}$$

$$K_d = \frac{1}{\omega_c}\mathrm{Im}\left(\frac{-(Ls+R)(m_a s^2 + c_a s + k_a) - K_b K_c s}{K_c} \right)_{s=\omega_c i} \tag{8}$$

The equations above in the Laplace domain of the active vibration absorber response are represented as a control diagram with the position and velocity of the absorber feedback, Figure 2.

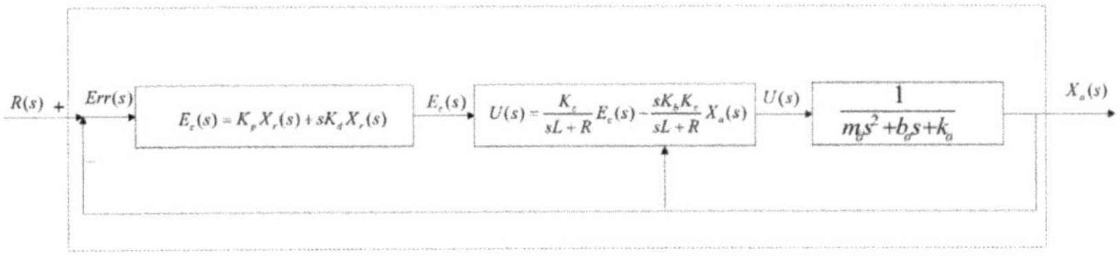

Figure 2. Scheme of active vibration absorber control diagram.

2.2. *Active Control for a Cantilever Beam*

The active vibration absorber is implemented to a cantilever beam, Figure 3. The force produced by the absorber to the beam is considered as a punctual force. A continuous model of a cantilever beam is used for the analysis. Kinetic and potential energy expressions of the cantilever beam have the following form (16) and (10), where $\rho(x)$ is the density, $A(x)$ is the section transversal area, $w(x,t)$ is the deflection over time, $E(x)$ is the Young modulus and $I(x)$ is the inertia of the transversal area along the x axis. The perturbance is considered an external force over time $p(t)$ placed at a position l_p.

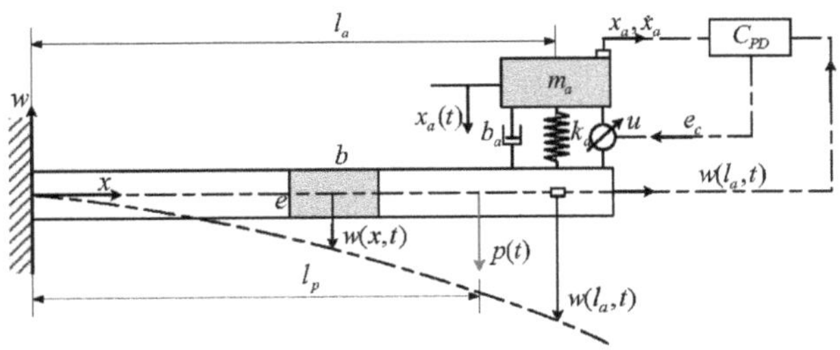

Figure 3. Cantilever beam implemented with an active vibration absorber at its free end.

$$T = \frac{1}{2}\int_0^l \rho(x)A(x)\left(\frac{\partial w}{\partial t}\right)^2 dx \tag{9}$$

$$V = \frac{1}{2}\int_0^l E(x)I(x)\left(\frac{\partial^2 w}{\partial^2 x}\right)^2 dx \tag{10}$$

The deflection of any position along the beam can be represented as the superposition of the modal coordinates [27], which is given by (11), where $q_i(t)$ is the generalized coordinate related to i-mode of vibration and $\varphi_i(x)$ is the normal mode function defined by (12)

$$w(x,t) = \sum_{i=1}^{n} q_i(t)\varphi_i(x) \tag{11}$$

$$\varphi_i(x) = C_i[sen\beta_i x - senh\beta_i x - \alpha_i(\cos\beta_i x - \cosh\beta_i x)],\ \ i = 1\ 2\ 3\ \ldots n \tag{12}$$

$$\alpha_i = \frac{sen\beta_i l - senh\beta_i l}{\cos\beta_i l - \cosh\beta_i l} \tag{13}$$

According to the procedure developed in [28], using the Lagrange equations for (16) and (10), the dynamics of the cantilever beam are represented by the differential equations system in (14), where m_{ij} is the generalized mass, k_{ij} is the generalized stiffness, $h^1{}_j$ is the generalized force of disturbance and $h^2{}_j$ is the generalized force of the force produced by the active vibration absorber at its position along the beam.

$$\sum_{i=1}^{n} m_{ij}\ddot{q}_i(t) + \sum_{i=1}^{n} k_{ij}q_i(t) = h^1{}_j + h^2{}_j, \quad j = 1\ 2 \ldots n \tag{14}$$

$$\begin{cases} m_{ij} = \int_0^l \rho(x)A(x)\varphi_i(x)\varphi_j(x)dx = 0 \\ k_{ij} = \int_0^l E(x)I(x)\frac{d^2\varphi_i}{dx^2}\frac{d^2\varphi_j}{dx^2}dx = 0 \end{cases} \quad Si\ \ i \neq j \tag{15}$$

$$\begin{cases} h^1{}_j = p(t)\varphi(l)_j \\ h^2{}_j = f(t)\varphi(l)_j \end{cases} \quad j = 1\ 2 \tag{16}$$

Solving the differential equations system in (14) in the Laplace domain and substituting it in (11), the deflection, in the Laplace domain, along the beam as a function of the disturbance $P(s)$ and active force $U(s)$ is obtained:

$$W(l,s) = \sum_{i=1}^{2} G^i{}_p P(s) + \sum_{i=1}^{2} G^i{}_u U(s) \tag{17}$$

where

$$\begin{cases} G^i{}_p(s) = G_i{}^{-1}\ \varphi_i{}^2(l) \\ G^i{}_u(s) = G_i{}^{-1}\left(-\frac{m_a s^2}{m_a s^2 + b_a s + k_a}\right)\varphi^2{}_i(l) \end{cases} \tag{18}$$

$$G_i = m_{ii}s^2 + k_{ii} + \frac{m_a s^2(k_a + b_a s)}{m_a s^2 + b_a s + k_a}\varphi_i(l)^2 \tag{19}$$

Hence the active control is obtained coupling the equations of the PD control, the electromagnetic actuator and the cantilever beam. Figure 4 shows a scheme of the developed active control of the cantilever beam using the relative position and velocity feedback.

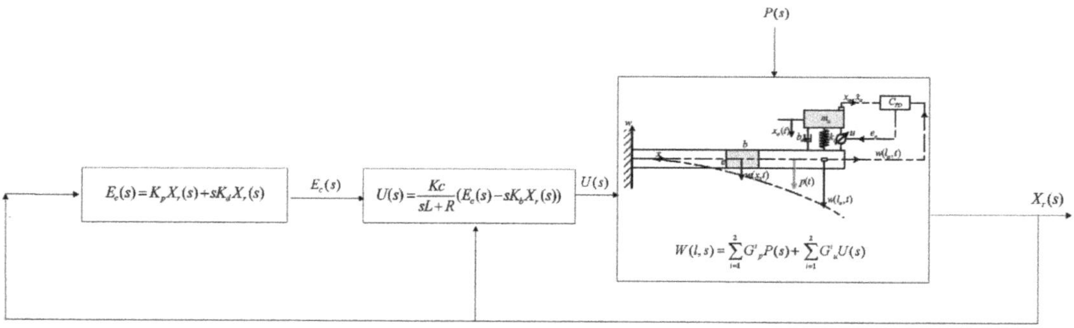

Figure 4. Active control diagram of a cantilever beam implemented with the active vibration absorber.

2.3. Simulation

The developed model was simulated using Matlab Simulink® R2022a. Parameters used for the simulation are listed in Table 1. Parameters of the electromagnetic actuator presented in [26] were used. PD control gains must change the dynamic characteristics of the active vibration absorber. Thus, its natural frequency has to be equal to the excitation frequency of the primary system since the inertial force must be equal and opposite to the excitation force. By using Equations (7) and (8), the PD gains were calculated for the second resonant frequency; K_p is 606.87 V/m and K_d is −3.22 V-s/m.

Table 1. Parameters of the cantilever beam and active absorber.

Description	Parameter	Value
Cantilever beam	b	50 mm
	e	5 mm
	ρ	7850 kg/m^3
	A	250 mm^2
	E	210 GPa
	I	5000 mm^4
	l	1 m
Active vibration absorber	m_a	0.05 kg
	k_a	141.8 N/m
	b_a	0.1 N.s/m
	R	1.6 Ohm
	L	0.75 mH
	K_c	3.5 N/A
	K_b	3.5 V.s/m

2.3.1. Dynamic Characteristics of the AVA

The dynamic behaviour of only the AVA was evaluated with the parameters established. The step response was calculated with and without control represented as Xa(s)/Ec(s) and Xa(s)/Err(s). The first condition simulates the dynamic behaviour considering just dynamic characteristics of the actuator and the mechanical absorber as an open loop. In this case, the step signal was a voltage unit for the actuator. The second condition simulates the PD control, the actuator and the absorber as an open loop. In this case, the step signal was the error signal calculated as the difference between reference and absorber position.

2.3.2. Natural Frequencies of the Cantilever Beam

The addition of a mass and spring after absorber implementation to the cantilever beam changes the original natural frequencies without them. When AVA is off, its dynamical behaviour depends on mass and stiffness mainly while the actuator acts as damping. In this case, natural frequencies of the cantilever beam were calculated numerically with Equation (14) by solving an eigenvalue problem with and without absorber mass and stiffness, simulating a passive absorber case. Three modes of vibration were considered in order to model the dynamical behaviour in Equation (11), since excitation frequency for evaluation was within the first and second modes of vibration.

When AVA is activated, free vibration was simulated by the dynamical response in the time domain after a unitary impulse application in Matlab Simulink.

2.3.3. Dynamic Response of the Cantilever Beam

Attenuation of vibration amplitude was evaluated under different conditions with an excitation force located at the free end of the cantilever beam model since it is the most critical location for an external force. The cantilever beam model was excited in its first and second resonant frequency with and without an absorber. Likewise, the dynamic influence of the absorber position at the cantilever beam was evaluated since the maximum vibration attenuation is one of the objectives for designing a solution. The absorber was placed in three different positions at 1/3, 2/3 of its length relative to the fixed end. For each absorber position, the displacement of the free end was obtained over time when the primary system was excited in the second resonant frequency,

3. Results

3.1. AVA Dynamic Characteristics

Natural frequencies of the cantilever beam with and without mass and stiffness of the absorber are shown in Table 2. The response of only the active vibration absorber to a step signal is shown in Figure 5a without a control algorithm. Figure 5b shows the response with PD control in an open loop tuned to the second resonant frequency. In Figure 5a, the input signal was a unit voltage step, there are no overshoots over time and the settling time was 0.87 s. In Figure 5b, the input signal was a unit error step which is the difference between reference and absorber position; the settling time was 0.875 s.

Figure 6 shows the dynamic response in the frequency domain when it is tuned to first and second resonant frequencies. Peaks show the natural frequencies of only the AVA. It can be noticed that they match the desired absorption frequency of the primary system.

Table 2. Natural frequencies of the cantilever beam.

Natural Frequency	Without Absorber	With Absorber
First	4.14 Hz	3.50 Hz
Second	26.26 Hz	4.93 Hz
Third	73.53 Hz	26.26 Hz

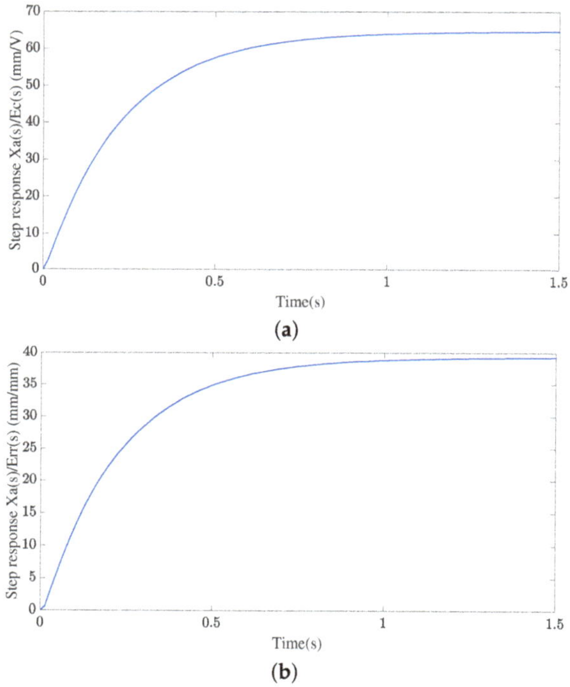

Figure 5. Step response of the active vibration absorber: (**a**) without PD control in open loop; (**b**) with PD control from an error signal in open loop.

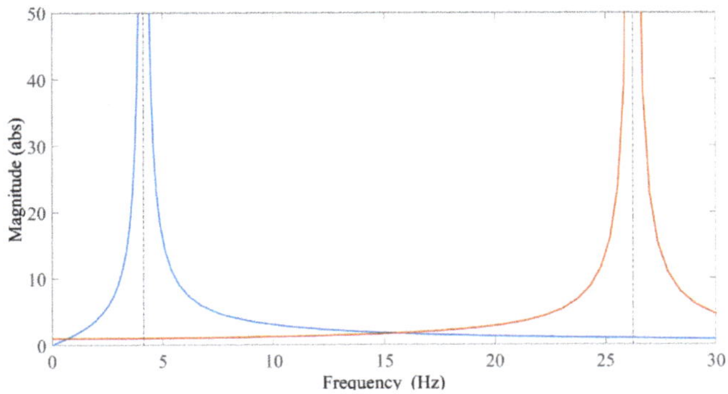

Figure 6. Frequency response of the active vibration absorber.

3.2. Dynamic Response

Figure 7 shows the impulse response of the cantilever beam over time with a passive, an active and without an absorber when a unitary impulse was applied at the free end. The AVA was tuned to the second natural frequency of the cantilever beam. It can be seen that response periods of the cantilever beam were different in each case. Likewise, each signal was composed of different frequencies corresponding to the multiples modes of vibration. When a passive absorber was added, the contribution of other modes of vibration increased. The best controlled response was obtained with the AVA. Furthermore, the response period increased with AVA with respect to the cantilever beam without absorber.

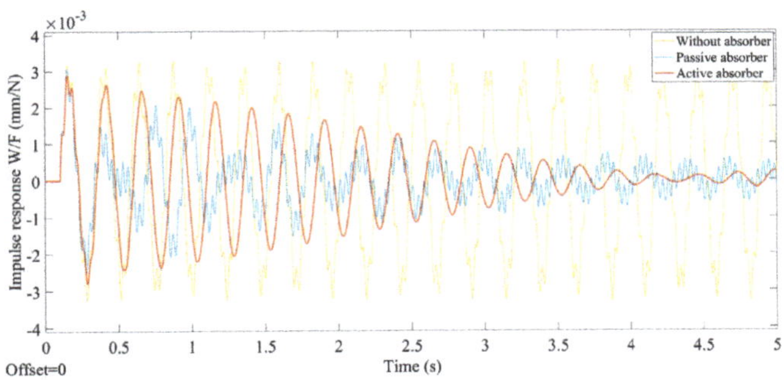

Figure 7. Impulse response of the cantilever beam at free end.

Figure 8 shows the dynamic response of the cantilever beam over time with a passive, an active and without an absorber when it is excited in its first resonant frequency. Without an absorber, the vibration amplitude increased over time due to the resonance condition. However, with a passive or an active absorber, the amplitude value was controlled within a range. Figure 9 shows the dynamic response when it is excited in its second resonant frequency. Without an absorber, the vibration amplitude greatly increased over time. A passive absorber was not more effective in this case. The active vibration absorber was effective and controlled a low vibration amplitude over time. Figure 10 shows the active force and relative displacement over time when the cantilever beam was excited in its second resonant frequency. It can be seen that the active force was always opposite and proportional to the relative displacement as an artificial stiffness tuned to that frequency.

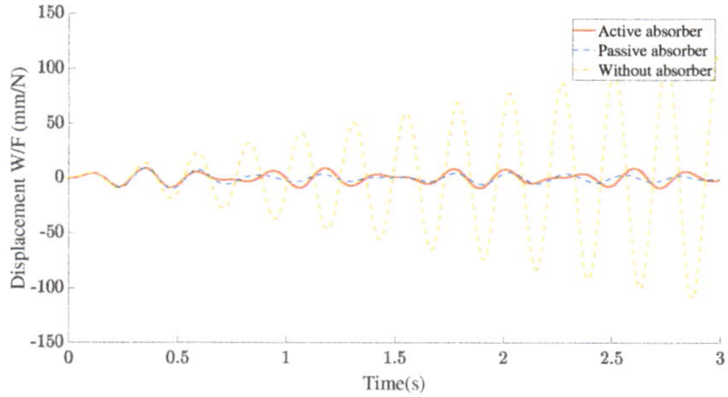

Figure 8. Dynamic response under the first resonant frequency.

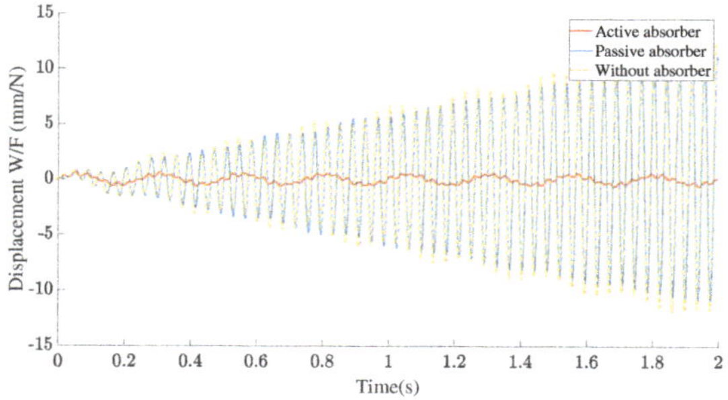

Figure 9. Dynamic response under the second resonant frequency.

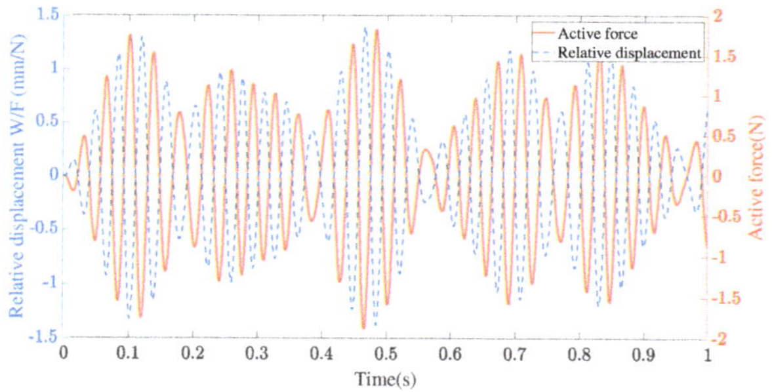

Figure 10. Active force and relative displacement under the second resonant frequency.

3.3. Position Influence

Figure 11 shows the displacement of the cantilever beam free end when the AVA was placed in three different positions. For all positions, it was effective and reduced the vibration amplitude. Nevertheless, the maximum absorption was obtained when the AVA was placed at the free end, where the external dynamical force acts. Figure 12 shows the dynamic response when the AVA was placed in a node of the primary system and the response was without AVA. The second mode of vibration contains a node at 0.783 of its length where the amplitude is zero. In this case, the AVA was not effective and the vibration amplitude increased over time. It is shown that there was not a significant difference between the case with AVA and without it when it is placed in a node.

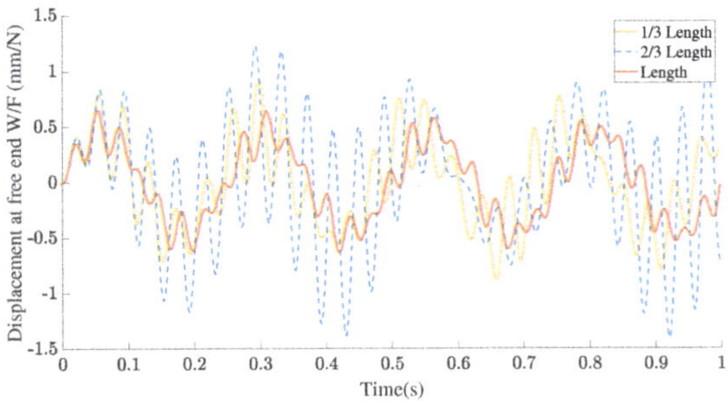

Figure 11. Displacement at free end under the second resonant frequency for the active vibration absorber placed in 1/3, 2/3 of the length and at free end.

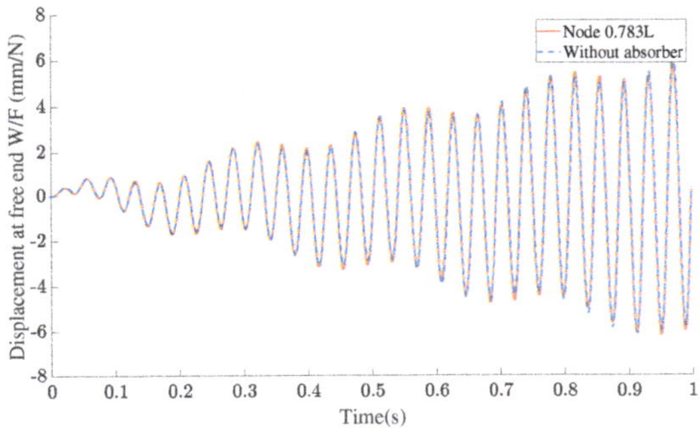

Figure 12. Displacement at free end under the second resonant frequency for the active vibration absorber placed in a node of the second vibration mode at 0.783 of its length.

4. Discussion

The dynamic behaviour of the cantilever beam is a superposition of modes of vibration with a pounded contribution since a continuous model was used. The addition of an AVA produced a modification of the original dynamic characteristics of the structure. With a passive absorber, mass and stiffness determined how intense the change was in the natural frequencies. With an AVA, the change also depended on control and actuator dynamic characteristics. Impulse responses in time domain have shown that the contribution of different modes of vibration increased with a passive absorber. Nevertheless, with an AVA, the response was more uniform and better controlled with a period higher than the cantilever beam without absorber.

Natural frequencies 3.5 and 4.93 Hz after a passive absorber addition were introduced around the tuning frequency 4.14 Hz. The difference was 15% and 19% when the absorber mass was 2.54 % of the cantilever mass. Since the absorber mass is a few percentage of cantilever mass, the second mode of vibration was not altered and the natural frequency kept its value. Step response of the AVA has shown how intense the PD control gains were in an open loop when this receives the error signal. Since PD gains were calculated in order to tune the AVA to the excitation frequency exactly, the values are unique. However, tuning frequency can be slightly different and continue being effective as passive absorbers within a narrow range around the desired tuning frequency. The frequency range where AVA is effective depends on the components' capacity. Absorption frequency must be equal to the natural frequency of only the AVA. This relation required an artificial stiffness proportional to the squared absorption frequency. In this sense, a higher absorption frequency increased the active force. Thus actuator capacity must be able to provide a sufficient force with a dynamic behaviour fast enough to keep the AVA tuned.

The vibration amplitude of the cantilever beam increased over time without an absorber in a resonance condition. There were no differences between passive and active absorbers when both were tuned to the same frequency. This is due to the working concept of the AVA. Actuator force is designed to produce a proportional opposite force to the relative displacement between the absorber and the cantilever beam as an artificial stiffness. In this sense, since mass and stiffness of the absorber are tuned to the first resonant frequency, the AVA is already tuned without the active force. The position of the absorber was a significant parameter for the dynamic response. Although the AVA was effective in all positions, the exceptions were nodes of vibration where the amplitudes are zeros. The AVA needed to be placed in positions able to transmit movement in order to produce an inertial force opposite to the excitation external force over time.

5. Conclusions

A model of an active vibration absorber implemented to a continuous cantilever beam was developed, this continuous model represents the most accurate dynamic response of the real structure. Results indicate that the active vibration absorber is able to be tuned to a desired frequency within an excitation frequency range from a primary system and reduce the vibration amplitude, especially in critical conditions corresponding to the resonant frequencies.

The vibration amplitude is absorbed in the whole continuous cantilever beam model, not only at the position of the active vibration absorber. The position of the active absorber at the cantilever beam has a significant influence at the reduction of vibration, especially if it is placed near a vibration node from the primary system, where the active absorber is not effective. It was found that the optimum position for the active vibration absorber corresponds to the position of the maximum vibration amplitude at the primary system. In this sense, a proper formulation of the primary system model and experimental validation are required, especially for complex systems in order to establish the absorption frequency range, optimum position and active absorber physical characteristics.

The analysis of the developed active vibration absorber model is not limited to structures, but is also effective in application to any system.

Author Contributions: Conceptualization, C.R. and J.A.; methodology, C.R. and J.A.; software, C.R.; validation, C.R., J.A. and R.R.; formal analysis, C.R.; investigation, C.R.; data curation, C.R.; writing—original draft preparation, C.R.; writing—review and editing, C.R.; visualization, C.R.; supervision, J.A.; project administration, C.R. All authors have read and agreed to the published version of the manuscript.

Funding: This research received no external funding.

Data Availability Statement: The data presented in this study are available on request from the corresponding author. The data are not publicly available due to the modelling is a part of a research in progress.

Conflicts of Interest: The authors declare no conflict of interest.

References

1. Orhan, S.; Aktürk, N.; Çelik, V. Vibration monitoring for defect diagnosis of rolling element bearings as a predictive maintenance tool: Comprehensive case studies. *NDT E Int.* **2006**, *39*, 293–298. [CrossRef]
2. Sofronas, A. *Case Histories in Vibration Analysis and Metal Fatigue for the Practicing Engineer*; John Wiley & Sons: Hoboken, NJ, USA, 2012; pp. 245–268.
3. Frahm, H. A Device for Damping Vibrations of Bodies. US Patent 989958A, 18 April 1911
4. Hartog, J.D. *Mechanical Vibrations*, 4th ed.; McGraw-Hill: New York, NY, USA, 1956; Volume 1.
5. Soong, T.T. Active structural control in civil engineering. *Eng. Struct.* **1988**, *10*, 74–84. [CrossRef]
6. Housner, G.W.; Bergman, L.A.; Caughey, T.K.; Chassiakos, A.G.; Claus, R.O.; Masri, S.F.; Skelton, R.E.; Soong, T.T.; Spencer, B.F.; Yao, J.T. Structural control: Past, present and future. *J. Eng. Mech.* **1997**, *123*, 897–971. .:9(897). [CrossRef]
7. Kobori, T.; Koshika, N.; Yamada, K.; Ikeda, Y. Seismic-response-controlled structure with active mass driver system. Part 1: Design. *Earthq. Eng. Struct. Dyn.* **1991**, *20*, 133–149. [CrossRef]

8. Kobori, T.; Koshika, N.; Yamada, K.; Ikeda, Y. Seismic-response-controlled structure with active mass driver system. Part 2: Verification. *Earthq. Eng. Struct. Dyn.* **1991**, *20*, 151–166. . [CrossRef]
9. Chang, C.; Yang, H.T. Control of Buildings Using Active Tuned Mass Dampers. *J. Eng. Mech.* **1995**, *121*, 355–366. [CrossRef]
10. Kwak, M.K.; Yang, D.H.; Shin, J.H. Active vibration control of structures using a semi-active dynamic absorber. *Noise Control Eng. J.* **2015**, *63*, 287–299. [CrossRef]
11. Yu, W.; Thenozhi, S.; Li, X. Stable active vibration control system for building structures using PD/PID control. *IFAC Proc. Vol.* **2014**, *47*, 4760–4765. [CrossRef]
12. Yang, D.H.; Shin, J.H.; Lee, H.W.; Kim, S.K.; Kwak, M.K. Active vibration control of structure by Active Mass Damper and Multi-Modal Negative Acceleration Feedback control algorithm. *J. Sound Vib.* **2017**, *392*, 18–30. [CrossRef]
13. Chang, S. Active mass damper for reducing wind and earthquake vibrations of a long-period bridge. *Actuators* **2020**, *9*, 66. [CrossRef]
14. Kumar, K.R.; Narayanan, S. Active vibration control of beams with optimal placement of piezoelectric sensor/actuator pairs. *Smart Mater. Struct.* **2008**, *17*, 055008. [CrossRef]
15. Cao, H.; Li, Q.S. New control strategies for active tuned mass damper systems. *Comput. Struct.* **2004**, *82*, 2341–2350. [CrossRef]
16. Zhou, K.; Li, Q.S.; Li, X. Dynamic Behavior of Supertall Building with Active Control System during Super Typhoon Mangkhut. *J. Struct. Eng.* **2020**, *146*, 04020077. [CrossRef]
17. Babaei, M.; Asemi, K.; Safarpour, P. Natural Frequency and Dynamic Analyses of Functionally Graded Saturated Porous Beam Resting on Viscoelastic Foundation Based on Higher Order Beam Theory. *J. Solid Mech.* **2019**, *11*, 615–634. [CrossRef]
18. Wang, J.; Liu, Y.; Qin, Z.; Ma, L.; Chu, F. Dynamic performance of a novel integral magnetorheological damper-rotor system. *Mech. Syst. Signal Process.* **2022**, *172*, 109004. [CrossRef]
19. Xu, J.; Zhou, W.; Jing, J. An electromagnetic torsion active vibration absorber based on the FxLMS algorithm. *J. Sound Vib.* **2022**, *524*, 116734. [CrossRef]
20. Mo, J.; Priefer, R. Medical Devices for Tremor Suppression: Current Status and Future Directions. *Biosensors* **2021**, *11*, 99. [CrossRef]
21. Fromme, N.P.; Camenzind, M.; Riener, R.; Rossi, R.M. Design of a lightweight passive orthosis for tremor suppression. *J. Neuroeng. Rehabil.* **2020**, *17*, 47. [CrossRef]
22. Tremelo for Essential Tremor | Effective Hand Tremor Device. Available online: https://fivemicrons.com/tremelo/ (accessed on 25 February 2023)
23. Rudraraju, S. Wearable tremor reduction device (trd) for human hands and arms. In *Frontiers in Biomedical Devices*; American Society of Mechanical Engineers: New York, NY, USA, 2018.
24. Palomera-Arias, R.; Connor, J.J.; Ochsendorf, J.A. Feasibility Study of Passive Electromagnetic Damping Systems. *J. Struct. Eng.* **2008**, *134*, 109–158. .:1(164). [CrossRef]
25. Diez-Jimenez, E.; Rizzo, R.; Gómez-García, M.J.; Corral-Abad, E. Review of Passive Electromagnetic Devices for Vibration Damping and Isolation. *Shock Vib.* **2019**, *2019*, 1250707. [CrossRef]
26. Elmali, H.; Renzulli, M.; Olgac, N. Experimental comparison of delayed resonator and PD controlled vibration absorbers using electromagnetic actuators. *J. Dyn. Syst. Meas. Control. Trans. ASME* **2000**, *122*, 514–520. [CrossRef]
27. Rao, S.S. *Mechanical Vibrations*, 5th ed.; Pearson: London, UK, 2010; Volume 169, p. 641. [CrossRef]
28. Łatas, W. Application of the continuous dynamic absorbers in local and global vibration reduction problems in beams. *Vib. Phys. Syst.* **2016**, *27*, 245–254.

mathematics

MDPI

Article

A New RP1PR Type Coupling for Shafts with Crossed Axes

Stelian Alaci [1,*], Ioan Doroftei [2], Florina-Carmen Ciornei [1], Ionut-Cristian Romanu [1], Ioan-Alexandru Doroftei [2] and Mariana-Catalina Ciornei [3,4,*]

[1] Mechanics and Technologies Department, "Stefan cel Mare" University of Suceava, 720229 Suceava, Romania
[2] Mechanical Engineering, Mechatronics and Robotics Department, "Gheorghe Asachi" Technical University, 700050 Iasi, Romania
[3] Physiology Department, "Carol Davila" University of Medicine and Pharmacy, 020021 Bucharest, Romania
[4] Medical Engineering Faculty, "Politehnica" University of Bucharest, 060042 Bucharest, Romania
* Correspondence: stelian.alaci@usm.ro (S.A.); catalina.ciornei@umfcd.ro (M.-C.C.)

Abstract: There are few examples of mechanical coupling solutions for the transmission of high torques between two rotating shafts that have non-coplanar, non-parallel axes. Based on the structural analysis, the paper proposes a solution for an RP1PR-type symmetrical coupling. The Hartenberg–Denavit methodology is not applicable for performing the kinematical analysis, hence the solution starts from the geometrical condition of the creation of planar pairs of the mechanism, expressed in vector form. The absolute motion of all elements of the mechanism's structure can be expressed after developing the kinematical analysis. The theoretical results are validated via numerical analysis. By comparing the analytical results with the CATIA-modeled results, excellent compatibility is obtained. We also propose a constructive solution for the newly designed coupling mechanism.

Keywords: spatial coupling; crossed axes; kinematic analysis; constructive solutions; numerical validation

MSC: 70B15; 70B10; 00A06; 65D17

1. Introduction

One of the main tasks of the Theory of Machines and Mechanisms is the transmission of rotational motion between two fixed axes. The problem arose even from the first machines, which had complex requirements while the driving possibilities were limited, as is still the case [1,2]. A mobile assembly is actuated for most cases by rotational engines—cc, dc, or internal combustion engine—when the driving element has a rotational motion, and by free piston linear engine when a translational motion is needed. Obviously, the motion of the final element depends on the construction of the kinematical chain interposed between the driving and driven elements. The designer is responsible for choosing amongst possible solutions the one that best runs the transmission [3]. From these criteria, one can mention a kinematical criterion [4,5], which imposes a certain law of motion for the driven element, constructive simplicity [6–8], high efficiency, low production costs, high accuracy [9,10], etc. However, the higher the number of imposed criteria, the fewer possibilities of completely fulfilling them. Therefore, a prioritization of criteria is necessary for choosing the final solution [11]. The solution can either be adapted to the actual necessities, or a completely new one must be found. The latter case requires comprehensive study and research work since a new solution should be original and comparable or superior to the existing ones from the point of view of fulfilling the imposed criteria.

The present paper proposes a new coupling mechanism with high reliability and an original method for the kinematical analysis, based on a geometrical condition concerning the creation of planar pairs.

The kinematics analysis of a spatial mechanism can be completed by the general methodology proposed by Hartenberg and Denavit [12], known as the "the method of homogenous operators", which is appropriate for spatial bar mechanisms having in their structure only cylindrical pairs, or particular cases of cylindrical pairs: revolute pair, prismatic pair, or helical pair [13]. The method is based on the relations of transformation of a point's coordinates when the reference system is changed and expresses the condition of closure of the mechanism's kinematic chain in matrix form—using square type 4×4 matrices. For the situations when other than cylindrical pairs occur in the structure of the mechanisms, the method proposed by Hartenberg and Denavit can be applied after each of the non-cylindrical joints is replaced by a kinematical chain that has in its structure only cylindrical pairs [14,15].

Fisher presents solutions for substituting the spherical joints by an assembly of three revolute pairs with concurrent and reciprocally perpendicular axes [16]. Fisher also proposes the replacement of a planar joint by an assembly of two prismatic joints with perpendicular axes and a revolute joint with the axis normal to the plane defined by the revolute pairs. In [17] there is presented a methodology of replacing a class 1 pair with a mechanism consisting of two shafts with direct contact and crossed directions. Generally, when applying the Hartenberg and Denavit method, this produces complicated systems of trigonometrical equations that can rarely be solved analytically. One of the difficulties met in the positional solutioning of a spatial mechanism is the fact that the system of trigonometrical equations obtained presents multiple solutions—solutions corresponding to all assembling possibilities of the mechanism when the values of the driving element's position parameters are stipulated.

Another aspect that complicates solving the positional analysis of a spatial mechanism is the structure of a homogenous operator's matrix. This matrix has a structure that contains the rotational matrix, which describes the position of the new system of coordinates with respect to the initial one, and the displacement vector corresponding to the translation of the old origin into the new position. Two displacements are identical when the matrices corresponding to the homogenous operators correlated to the two displacements are identical [12]. The identification of the elements of displacement vectors produces three scalar equations and the identification of the rotation matrices gives nine scalar equations from which only three are independent. These three independent equations are recognized by deconstructing the rotation matrix into symmetric and antisymmetric matrices [18], followed by finding the versor of the rotation axis and the rotation angle. At this stage the conditions of equality of rotations can be imposed, specifically the axis parallelism, resulting in two scalar equations, and the equality of the rotation angles, which results in the third scalar equation.

Lastly, six scalar trigonometrical equations result from the condition that two displacements are identical. From here, the conclusion is that the simplest spatial mechanism with mobility $M = 1$, which has the kinematic completely determined by the conditions developed from the contour closure condition, has the position described by six scalar parameters. Uicker et al. [19] developed a numerical methodology that considers a constrained system of 12 scalar equations obtained by equalling all components of the displacement vectors and rotation matrices. The procedure is iterative, rapidly converging, and finally offering the position parameters of the mechanism of single-contour mechanism. The fact that the numerical methodology is appropriate to an over-constrained system of equations leads to the idea of applying it to over-constrained mechanisms. In the literature, there are presented the kinematical solutions for the Bricard mechanism $M = 0$ [12,20], and Benett mechanism $M = -2$ [12]. In the case where the mechanism contains numerous contours whose positions cannot be described by six scalar parameters, the equations resulting from the closing matrix equations of some loops will be considered until the number of obtained scalar equations will equal the number of scalar parameters of position of all the considered kinematical chains.

There are numerous types of couplings in technical applications [1,14,21–25], but the couplings with crossed axes of high reliability and that transmit important torques are rather infrequent. The present paper proposes a new coupling mechanism of an RP1PR type, an original method for the kinematics analysis, and the design of the corresponding constructive solution.

2. Structural Considerations

Figure 1 shows two shafts with crossed axes and the coupling intermediate kinematic chain consisting of m elements and $c_k, k = 1 \div 5$ kinematic pairs of class k. The two shafts are joined to the ground by revolute pairs c_5. The transmission has a unique driving element, 1 and that means that the mobility of the transmission should be $M = 1$. The formula for the calculus of the mobility degree of spatial mechanisms [21] is:

$$M = 6(n-1) - \sum_{k=1}^{5} k \cdot c_k \quad (1)$$

Applying the relation (1) for the particular case from Figure 1 gives:

$$1 = 6(3+m-1) - \sum_{k=1}^{5} k \cdot c_k - 2 \cdot 5 \quad (2)$$

where $\sum_{k=1}^{5} k \cdot c_k$ represents the number of degrees of freedom nulled by the coupling kinematic chain composed of m elements.

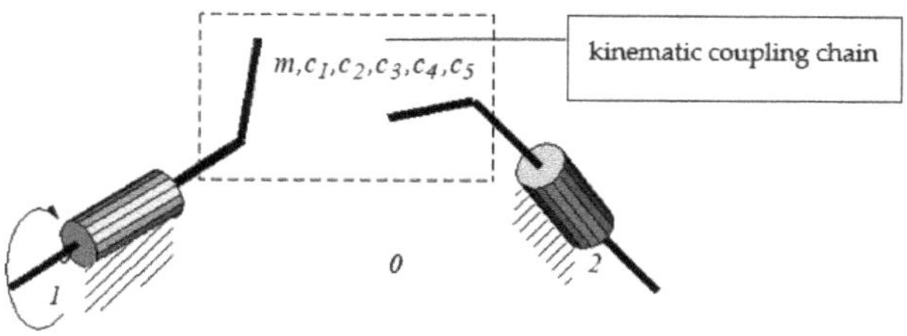

Figure 1. Transmission of rotation motion between two shafts with crossed axes through an intermediate chain.

The final relation is:

$$\sum_{k=1}^{5} k \cdot c_k = 6m + 1 \quad (3)$$

Equation (3) allows for finding the number of elements and kinematic joints from the structure of the coupling chain. The simplest coupling solution corresponds to $m = 0$, that is direct coupling of the two shafts. For $m = 0$ Equation (3) has one solution:

$$c_1 = 1, \; c_k = 0, \quad k \geq 2 \quad (4)$$

which shows that between the two shafts a pair of c_1 class (direct point contact) must exist. The concrete form can be the contact between two surfaces (gear mechanisms with crossed axes [26,27] or spatial cam mechanisms [28]), two curves [29], the contact between a surface and a point, point-curve contact, or curve-surface contact [30]. The above enumeration demonstrates that even for the simplest case of direct transmission, the constructive solutions are numerous. The advantage of this structural solution is its constructive simplicity. While the main drawback can be considered to be the high contact stresses from the contact pair between the two elements [31–34]. The next structural solution, $m = 1$, with a single intermediate element, gives the relation:

$$\sum_{k=1}^{5} k \cdot c_k = 7 \quad (5)$$

There are multiple structural solutions since the kinematic coupling chain can contain any type of kinematic pair. In [35] it is presented the constructive solution:

$$c_1 = 0,\ c_2 = 2,\ c_3 = 1 \tag{6}$$

Next, a new solution is presented, where the coupling consists of revolute–planar–contact–c_1–planar–revolute (acronym RP1PR) joints. Possible pairs that can be used in the structure of the mechanism are:

- the sphere–plane joint, (class 1 pair), with a unique representation, a ball on a plate (Figure 2a);
- the planar class 3 pair, represented in Figure 2b;

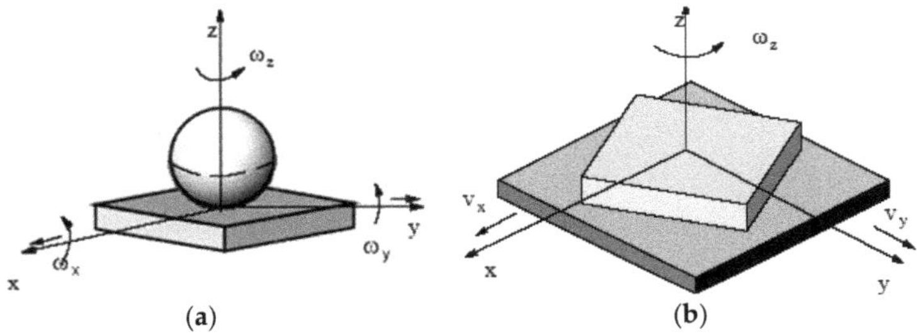

Figure 2. Types of pairs involving the middle element: (**a**) sphere–plane pair; (**b**) planar pair.

- another class 3 pair could be the spherical joint, Figure 3a.

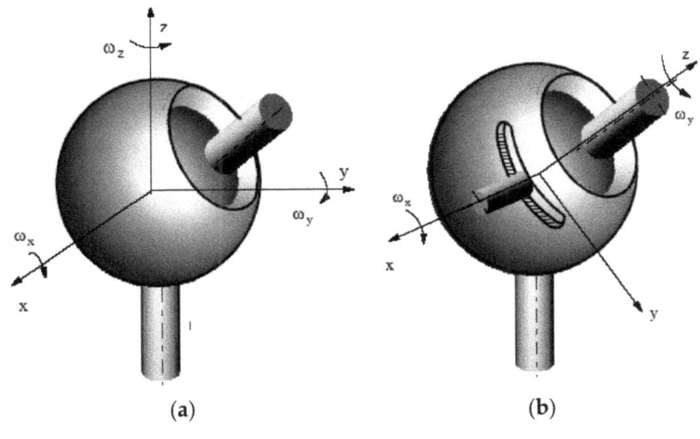

Figure 3. Constructive solution for spherical pairs: (**a**) spherical pair; (**b**) spherical pair with pin.

Therefore, an alternate mechanism (to our proposed RP1PR) is RS1SR, that is, to use spherical joints (Figure 3a). In this case, the first significant problem that arises concerns a passive motion of the intermediate element about the axis passing through the centers of spheres. To eliminate this passive motion, one of the spherical joints must be replaced by a joint of finger-sphere type of class 4 (Figure 3b). From the figures representing the planar and spherical joints, it is obvious that the class 3, planar joint is preferable. In the case of a spherical pair, the constructive solution is more complex from a manufacturing point of view [36,37] because the planar pair consists of plane surfaces obtained by high machining conditions, compared to the spherical surfaces, (especially inner spherical surfaces) which are difficult to obtain technologically.

From a functional perspective, the planar pair is also desirable because it presents the advantage that the three allowed motions (two translations and one rotation) are not limited, while, for the spherical joint, (three rotations allowed) there are imposed some constructive restrictions and locking of the mechanism may occur.

2.1. Proposed Solution

One of the possible solutions that verify the relation (5) corresponds to the case when the intermediate element makes with the rest of the elements two planar pairs of class 3 and a pair of class 1 (RP1PR). The principle scheme for designing the mechanism is presented in Figure 4a, and the kinematic diagram of the mechanism is shown in Figure 4b. The middle element consists of the planes P' and P'' fixed together, having a dihedral angle of π and B the point from the intersection line. Driving shaft 1 and driven shaft 2 have the planes P_1 and P_2 attached respectively and P_0 is the plane fixed to the ground. The mechanism is created when the coincidence between the planes $P_1 - P'$, and $P_2 - P''$ respectively is ensured and the point B is obliged to lay in the plane P_0.

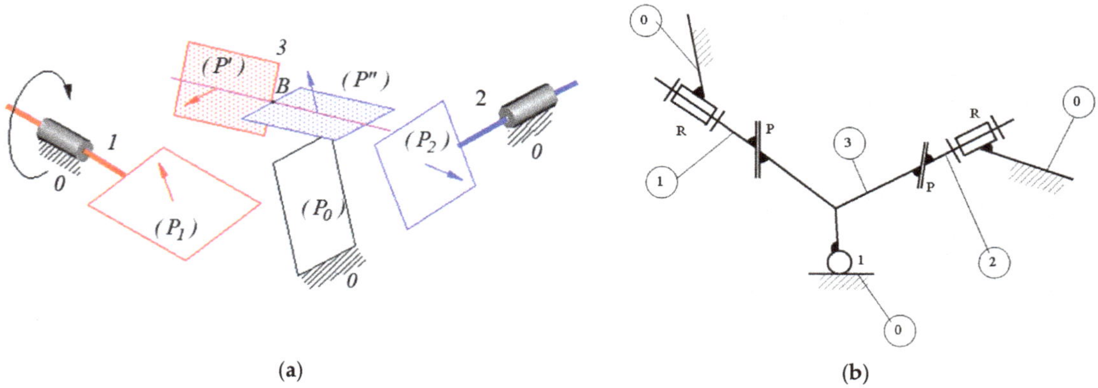

Figure 4. Proposed mechanism (0—the ground; 1—the driving element; 2—the driven element; 3—the middle element): (**a**) principle schematics for designing the mechanism; (**b**) kinematic diagram.

The elements of the mechanism are shown in Figure 4b, represented according to international standards [38]: the ground 0, the driving element 1, the driven (exit) element 2, and the intermediate element 3. The joints of the mechanism are: two revolute pairs R (first, between the ground and the driving element and the second, between the driven element and the ground), two planar pairs P (between the driving element and the intermediate element and, between the intermediate element and the driven element, respectively), and 1, a class 1 pair (point contact between the middle element and the ground). The succession of the pairs is the origin of the abbreviation of the name of the mechanism: RP1PR. We must mention that in the literature [1,39], only nine possible structural solutions for spatial mechanisms with intermediate elements are presented. The proposed RP1PR coupling is an entirely new solution.

The kinematic analysis of the mechanism requires finding the motion from the pairs of the mechanism. A convenient method consists in equivalating the planar joints with an assembly of two prismatic pairs with perpendicular axes and a revolute pair with the axis normal to the prismatic pairs and then replacing the class 1 pair with a series Oldham coupling–Cardan coupling [21]. The Hartenberg–Denavit method could be applied to the obtained mechanism. The disadvantage of the kinematic solution resides in a great number of elements and kinematic pairs of the substituting mechanism.

The graph of the mechanism is presented in Figure 5 and it contains two independent contours: $0 - 1 - 3 - 0$ and $0 - 2 - 3 - 0$. The position of the first contour is defined by $3 + 5 = 8$ scalar parameters and the position of the second is described by $3 + 5 + 1 = 9$ scalar parameters.

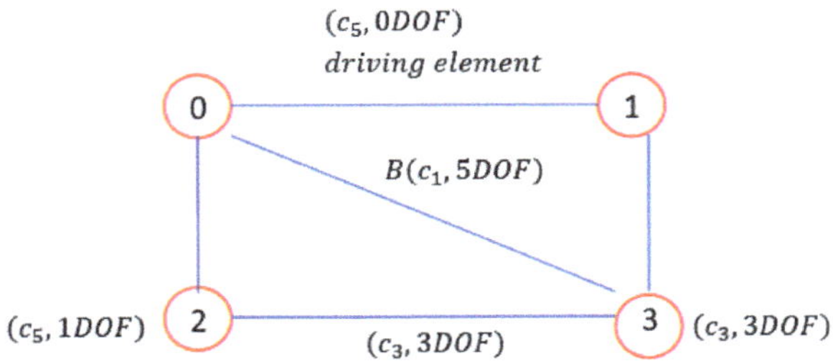

Figure 5. The graph of the mechanism.

Thus, we conclude that neither of the two contours can be analyzed independently, through the six scalar equations obtained from the condition of the closed kinematic chain. Instead, considering the two contours simultaneously, for obtaining the complete stipulation of the positions, there are required $3 + 5 + 3 + 1 = 12$ scalar parameters that can be unequivocally found from the 12 scalar equations of closure of the two loops. As mentioned above, solving the system of 12 trigonometrical equations will encounter difficulties. Therefore, a method where the conditions of forming the joints of the mechanism are directly used is preferred to the classical Hartenberg–Denavit method.

Several coordinate systems are used for solving the problem, as shown in Figure 6. The coordinate system of the ground, with the Ox axis as common normal for the axes of the two shafts. The origin O of the fixed system is in the middle of the common normal A_1A_2. The axes of the two shafts make two planes with the common normal, and their bisecting plane is Oxz. The distance between the axes of the shafts is $2a$ and the angle between them is $\pi - 2\alpha$. The axis Oy is in completion for the tri-orthogonal right reference system.

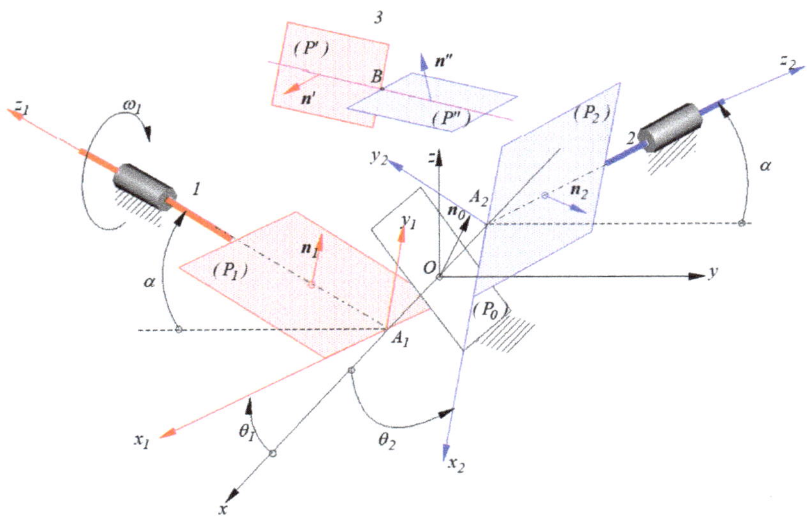

Figure 6. The coordinate systems and the kinematic and constructive parameters of the mechanism.

To each of the two shafts, a mobile coordinate system is attached, with the Oz axis in coincidence with the axis of the shaft, with the origin in the foot of the common normal. The plane $A_1x_1y_1$ is the plane with the normal $\boldsymbol{n}_1$ that contains the point A_1 and the plane $A_2x_2y_2$ is the plane with the normal $\boldsymbol{n}_2$ that contains the point A_2. The plane P_0, of normal $\boldsymbol{n}_0$ in which the point B is obliged to move, is considered to be a plane containing the common normal of the axes z_1 and z_2 of the two shafts, and making the angle β with the axis Oy. This position was chosen in order to obtain simpler relations. Obviously, a generic position can be chosen for the plane (P_0) and the methodology for finding the solution is the same, but only with increased amounts of calculus. The positions of the two shafts will be stipulated by the angles θ_1 and θ_2 made by the axes A_1x_1 and A_2x_2 respectively, with the Ox axis.

The creation of planar joints imposes the next geometrical conditions:

- the planes (P_1) and (P_2) should be perpendicular:

$$\boldsymbol{n}_1 \cdot \boldsymbol{n}_2 = 0 \tag{7}$$

- the point B belongs to the plane (P_1):

$$\boldsymbol{n}_1 \cdot \left(\boldsymbol{r}_B - \boldsymbol{r}_{A_1}\right) = 0 \tag{8}$$

- the point B belongs to the plane (P_2):

$$\boldsymbol{n}_2 \cdot \left(\boldsymbol{r}_B - \boldsymbol{r}_{A_2}\right) = 0 \tag{9}$$

The creation of the contact between the sphere and the plane requires:

- the point B belongs to the plane (P_0):

$$\boldsymbol{n}_0 \cdot \left(\boldsymbol{r}_B - \boldsymbol{r}_O\right) = 0 \tag{10}$$

where $\boldsymbol{r}_B, \boldsymbol{r}_{A_1}, \boldsymbol{r}_{A_2}, \ \boldsymbol{r}_O$ are the position vectors of the points B, A_1, A_2, and O respectively.

For the proposed RP1PR mechanism, the relations (7)–(10) are needed and all vectors must be expressed in the same frame. The coordinate system of the ground is chosen for this purpose. The notation $\boldsymbol{v}^{(k)}$ will be subsequently used to specify the coordinate system, other than the fixed one, where the Cartesian components of the vector $\boldsymbol{v}$ are stipulated. For a simplified notation, the lack of exponent indicates that the $\boldsymbol{v}$ vector is outlined by the Cartesian projections on the axes of the fixed system (of the ground) $Oxyz$.

The transformation relations [12] are used for expressing the coordinate transformations for a point when changing the coordinate system. Thus, the matrix describing the transformation from the frame "k" to the frame "$k+1$" is:

$$\boldsymbol{T}_{k,k+1} = \boldsymbol{Z}(\theta_k, s_k)\boldsymbol{X}(\alpha_{k,k+1}, a_{k,k+1}) \tag{11}$$

where $\boldsymbol{Z}(\theta, s)$ is the matrix describing the roto-translation with respect to the axis of motion Oz by a rotation of θ angle and a translation of s distance:

$$\boldsymbol{Z}(\theta, s) = \begin{bmatrix} cos\theta & -sin\theta & 0 & 0 \\ sin\theta & cos\theta & 0 & 0 \\ 0 & 0 & 1 & s \\ 0 & 0 & 0 & 1 \end{bmatrix} \tag{12}$$

The roto-translation with respect to Ox, the common normal of two axes of motion from the same element is $\boldsymbol{X}(\alpha, a)$:

$$\boldsymbol{X}(\alpha, a) = \begin{bmatrix} 1 & 0 & 0 & a \\ 0 & cos\alpha & -sin\alpha & 0 \\ 0 & sin\alpha & cos\alpha & 0 \\ 0 & 0 & 0 & 1 \end{bmatrix} \tag{13}$$

By choosing the position of the frames attached to the elements of the kinematic chain where only cylindrical pairs exist, the relative position between two frames could be described by only four scalar parameters, θ, s, α and α (named D-H parameters) instead of six scalar parameters required by the general case.

To bring a system "k" over the system "$k+1$", the matrix $\boldsymbol{T}_{k,k+1}$ is required:

$$\boldsymbol{T}_{k,k+1} = \begin{bmatrix} \underset{(3\times3)}{\boldsymbol{R}_{k,k+1}} & \underset{(3\times1)}{\boldsymbol{d}_{k,k+1}} \\ \begin{bmatrix} 0 & 0 & 0 \end{bmatrix} & 1 \end{bmatrix} \tag{14}$$

$\boldsymbol{R}_{k,k+1}$ is an orthogonal matrix with columns elements as the projections of the versors of the frame "$k+1$" on the axes of the frame "k", and the matrix $\boldsymbol{d}_{k,k+1}$ contains the components of the displacement vector of the origin of frame "k" for the superposition with the origin of the "$k+1$" system of coordinates.

Applying the above relations:

$$\boldsymbol{T}_{01} = \boldsymbol{X}\left(\frac{\pi}{2} - \alpha, a\right)\boldsymbol{Z}(\theta_1, 0) = \begin{bmatrix} cos\theta_1 & -sin\theta_1 & 0 & a \\ sin\alpha\ sin\theta_1 & sin\alpha\ cos\theta_1 & -cos\alpha & 0 \\ cos\alpha\ sin\theta_1 & cos\alpha\ cos\theta_1 & sin\alpha & 0 \\ 0 & 0 & 0 & 1 \end{bmatrix} \tag{15}$$

But $\boldsymbol{n}_1^1 \equiv \boldsymbol{j}_1^1 = \begin{bmatrix} 0 & 1 & 0 \end{bmatrix}$ and this gives:

$$\boldsymbol{n}_1^0 = \boldsymbol{T}_{01}\boldsymbol{n}_1^1 = \begin{bmatrix} -sin\theta_1 & \sin\alpha cos\theta_1 & cos\alpha cos\theta_1 \end{bmatrix}^T \tag{16}$$

Similarly:

$$\boldsymbol{n}_2^0 = \boldsymbol{T}_{02}\boldsymbol{n}_2^2 = \begin{bmatrix} -sin\theta_2 & \sin\alpha cos\theta_2 & -cos\alpha cos\theta_2 \end{bmatrix}^T \tag{17}$$

where:

$$\boldsymbol{T}_{02} = \boldsymbol{X}(-\pi/2 + \alpha, a)\boldsymbol{Z}(\theta_2, 0) = \begin{bmatrix} cos\theta_2 & -sin\theta_2 & 0 & -a \\ sin\alpha\ sin\theta_2 & sin\alpha\ cos\theta_2 & cos\alpha & 0 \\ -cos\alpha\ sin\theta_2 & -cos\alpha\ cos\theta_2 & sin\alpha & 0 \\ 0 & 0 & 0 & 1 \end{bmatrix} \tag{18}$$

The versor is:

$$\boldsymbol{n}_2^2 = \boldsymbol{j}_2^2 = \begin{bmatrix} 0 & 1 & 0 \end{bmatrix} \tag{19}$$

2.2. *Finding the Motion of the Driven Element*

Now, having the components of the normal to the two planes expressed in the coordinate system of the ground, the condition (7) is imposed and leads to the equation:

$$sin\theta_1\ sin\theta_2 + cos\theta_1\ cos\theta_2 - 2\cos^2\alpha\ cos\theta_1\ cos\theta_2 = 0 \tag{20}$$

where the unknown is θ_2. The solution to this equation is:

$$\theta'_2(\theta_1) = atan(\cos 2\alpha / tan\theta_1) \tag{21}$$

The use of the inverse trigonometrical function of a single argument $atan(x)$ may generate errors due to the length of the codomain π. For this reason, it is preferred that the results of trigonometrical equations are expressed by inverse trigonometrical functions of two variables [40] like $atan2(x,y)$ with codomain $[0, 2\pi]$, $angle(x,y)$ with codomain $[0, 2\pi]$ or $\arg(x + iy)$ [41], of codomain $[-\pi, \pi]$:

$$\theta_2(\theta_1) = angle(cos2\alpha / tan\theta_1) \tag{22}$$

Figure 7 compares the variations of the position angle of the driven element, θ_2 as a function of the angle of the driving element θ_1, found with Equations (21) and (22). It can be seen that the plot corresponding to relation (21) presents a jump of 2π which means that, in fact, the driven element is in the same position, but the plot corresponding to relation (21) presents at the middle of the interval a jump of value π which takes the driven element in an opposite position, which doesn't correspond to physical reality.

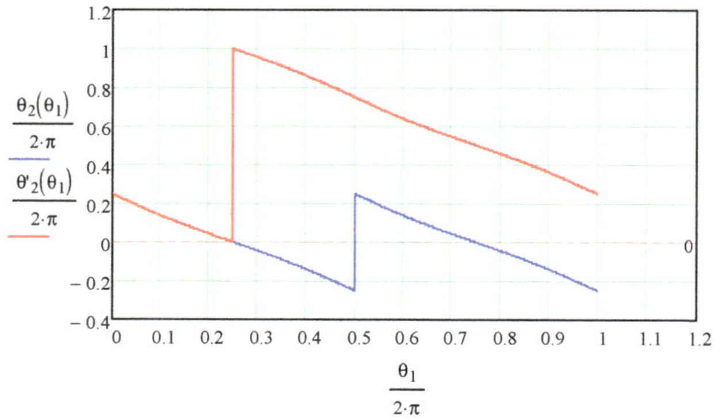

Figure 7. The rotation angle of the driven element.

Thus, the application of an inverse trigonometric function of a single argument in describing the position of the driven element can lead to erroneous conclusions, as shown in Figure 7. At the interval $[0, \pi]$ the two relations give the same position of the driven element while on the domain $[0, \pi]$ between the two positions there is a delay of π. The fact that the correct solution is the one given by the use of an inverse trigonometric function of two arguments will be justified in a subsequent section, by comparing the analytical results with the ones obtained using kinematic analysis software. The negative values of the transmission ratio show that when element 1 rotates in the positive direction of the axis z_1, driven element 2 performs a rotation in the negative direction of the axis z_2. Applying the derivative with respect to time (chain rule) of the relation (21) (or (22)), the transmission ratio of the mechanism can be obtained:

$$i_{1,2} = -\frac{cos2\alpha}{1 - cos^2\theta_1 \, sin^2 2\alpha} \tag{23}$$

and is represented in Figure 8; it can be seen that the absolute value of the transmission ratio varies within the range $[cos(2\alpha), 1/cos2\alpha]$.

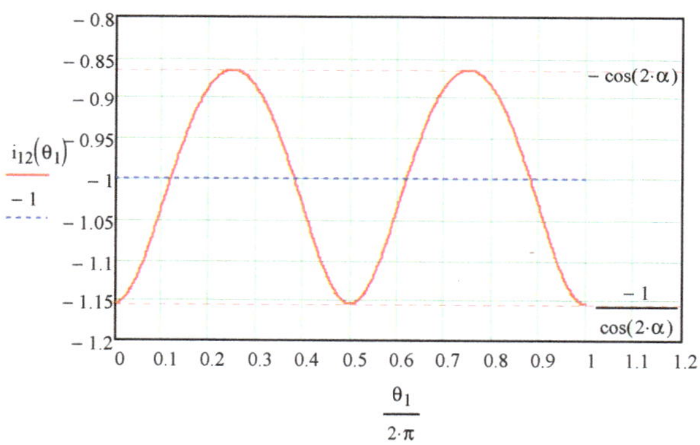

Figure 8. Variation in the transmission ratio of the mechanism.

2.3. Establishing the Trajectory of the Contact Point from the Support Plane

In order to express the conditions (8)–(10), we note: (8)–(10)

$$\boldsymbol{n}_0 = \begin{bmatrix} 0 & -cos\beta & sin\beta \end{bmatrix}^T \tag{24}$$

$$\boldsymbol{r}_{A_1} = \begin{bmatrix} a & 0 & 0 \end{bmatrix}^T \tag{25}$$

$$\boldsymbol{r}_{A_2} = \begin{bmatrix} -a & 0 & 0 \end{bmatrix}^T \tag{26}$$

$$\boldsymbol{r}_O = \begin{bmatrix} 0 & 0 & 0 \end{bmatrix}^T \tag{27}$$

By imposing the conditions (8)–(10), a system of three equations results, where the unknowns are the coordinates of the point $\boldsymbol{B}$:

$$\begin{cases} -y_B cos\beta + z_B sin\beta = 0 \\ -x_B\ sin\theta_1 + a \cdot sin\theta_1 + y_0\ sin\alpha\ cos\theta_1 + z_B\ cos\alpha\ cos\theta_1 = 0 \\ -x_B\ sin\theta_1 - a \cdot sin\theta_2 + y_B\ sin\alpha\ cos\theta_2 - z_B\ cos\alpha\ cos\theta_1 = 0 \end{cases} \tag{28}$$

The solutions of the system are the parametric coordinates of the point B:

$$\begin{cases} x_B = -a\frac{cos(\alpha-\beta)cos^2\theta_1 cos2\alpha - cos(\alpha+\beta)sin^2\theta_1}{cos(\alpha-\beta)cos^2\theta_1 cos2\alpha + cos(\alpha+\beta)sin^2\theta_1} \\ y_B = -a\frac{2sin\theta_1 sin\theta_2 sin\beta}{cos(\alpha-\beta)cos\theta_1 sin\theta_2 + cos(\alpha+\beta)sin\theta_1 cos\theta_2} \\ z_B = -a\frac{2sin\theta_1 sin\theta_2 cos\beta}{cos(\alpha-\beta)cos\theta_1 sin\theta_2 + cos(\alpha+\beta)sin\theta_1 cos\theta_2} \end{cases} \tag{29}$$

Squaring the equations of the system (29) and adding them member by member gives:

$$x_B^2 + y_B^2 + z_B^2 = a^2 \tag{30}$$

which represents the equation of a sphere of radius a and with the center in the origin O of the fixed system. In conclusion, the trajectory of the support point B is a circle of radius a, with the center in origin and placed in the support plane (P_0). The velocity of motion the point B on the circular trajectory is constant, given by:

$$v_B/\omega_1 = 2a \tag{31}$$

2.4. Finding the Motion from the Planar Joint between the Driving and Intermediate Elements

In order to specify the motion from the planar pair between elements 1 and 3, it is required to describe the position of a point from element 3 with respect to element 1 and of the position of the axes of frame 3 with respect to frame 1. The coordinates of the point B from frame 3 in frame 1 are obtained using the relation:

$$\boldsymbol{r}_B^{(1)} = \boldsymbol{T}_{13}\boldsymbol{r}_B^{(3)} \tag{32}$$

where

$$\boldsymbol{T}_{13} = \begin{bmatrix} \boldsymbol{i}_3\cdot\boldsymbol{i}_1 & \boldsymbol{j}_3\cdot\boldsymbol{i}_1 & \boldsymbol{k}_3\cdot\boldsymbol{i}_1 & (\boldsymbol{r}_B - \boldsymbol{r}_{A_1})\cdot\boldsymbol{i}_1 \\ \boldsymbol{i}_3\cdot\boldsymbol{j}_1 & \boldsymbol{j}_3\cdot\boldsymbol{j}_1 & \boldsymbol{k}_3\cdot\boldsymbol{j}_1 & (\boldsymbol{r}_B - \boldsymbol{r}_{A_1})\cdot\boldsymbol{j}_1 \\ \boldsymbol{i}_3\cdot\boldsymbol{k}_1 & \boldsymbol{j}_3\cdot\boldsymbol{k}_1 & \boldsymbol{k}_3\cdot\boldsymbol{k}_1 & (\boldsymbol{r}_B - \boldsymbol{r}_{A_1})\cdot\boldsymbol{k}_1 \\ 0 & 0 & 0 & 1 \end{bmatrix} \tag{33}$$

In relation (33), all vectors are represented by the projections on the axes of the fixed system $Oxyz$ by the relations:

$$\boldsymbol{i}_3 = \begin{bmatrix} -sin\theta_1 \\ sin\alpha\ cos\theta_1 \\ cos\alpha\ cos\theta_1 \end{bmatrix},\ \boldsymbol{j}_3 = \begin{bmatrix} -sin\theta_1 \\ sin\alpha\ cos\theta_2 \\ cos\alpha\ cos\theta_2 \end{bmatrix},\ \boldsymbol{k}_3 = \boldsymbol{i}_3 \times \boldsymbol{j}_3 \tag{34}$$

$$i_1 = \begin{bmatrix} -cos\theta_1 \\ sin\alpha\ cos\theta_1 \\ cos\alpha\ cos\theta_1 \end{bmatrix}, j_1 = \begin{bmatrix} -sin\theta_1 \\ sin\alpha\ cos\theta_1 \\ cos\alpha\ cos\theta_1 \end{bmatrix}, k_1 = \begin{bmatrix} 0 \\ -cos\alpha \\ sin\alpha \end{bmatrix} \quad (35)$$

Relations (34) and (35) are obtained based on the physical meaning of the components of homogenous operators from relations (15) and (19). The components of the vectors $\boldsymbol{r}_B$ and $\boldsymbol{r}_{A1}$ are given by Equations (28) and (25). The coordinate systems 1 and 3 have common axes $\boldsymbol{i}_3$ and $\boldsymbol{j}_1$, respectively. Consequently, the relative motion of system 3 with respect to system 1 is a plane-parallel motion fully specified by the motion of the point B in the plane $A_1x_1z_1$ and by the rotation angle of the axis $\boldsymbol{i}_3$ or of axis $\boldsymbol{k}_3$ with respect to axes A_1x_1 and A_1z_1. Therefore:

$$\boldsymbol{r}_B^1 = \boldsymbol{T}_{13}\boldsymbol{r}_B = \boldsymbol{T}_{13}[0 \quad 0 \quad 0 \quad 1] \quad (36)$$

After the calculus from relation (36) is made, the next relation is obtained:

$$\boldsymbol{r}_B^1 = \begin{bmatrix} x_B^1 \\ y_B^1 \\ z_B^1 \\ 1 \end{bmatrix} = \begin{bmatrix} (r_B - r_A)\cdot \boldsymbol{i}_1 \\ (r_B - r_A)\cdot \boldsymbol{j}_1 \\ (r_B - r_A)\cdot \boldsymbol{k}_1 \\ 1 \end{bmatrix} \quad (37)$$

By direct calculus, it can be shown that of the three components only the component from the axis A_1x_1 is non-zero. It represents the displacement of point B along the straight-line trajectory, represented in Figure 9. By differentiating with respect to time, the velocity of point B results, as shown in Figure 10.

For the rotation between the plane Bx_3z_3 with respect to the plane $A_1x_1z_1$ about the common normal $\boldsymbol{j}_3 \equiv \boldsymbol{j}_1$, the following relation is applied:

$$\theta_{31}(\theta_1) = angle[\boldsymbol{k}_3 \cdot \boldsymbol{k}_1, \boldsymbol{k}_3 \cdot \boldsymbol{i}_1] \quad (38)$$

The variation in this rotation is represented in Figure 11. The Equation (38) is derived numerically with respect to time to obtain the expression of the reduced angular velocity $\omega_{31}(\theta_1)/\omega_1$ of the intermediate element with respect to the driving element. The variation in the angular velocity $\omega_{31}(\theta_1)$ is presented in Figure 12.

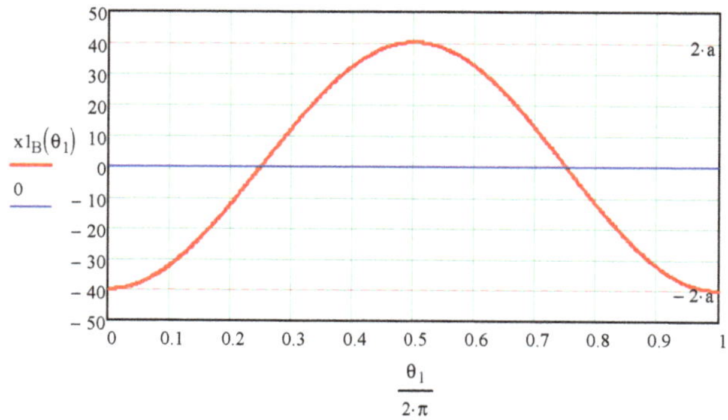

Figure 9. Variation in the displacement of point B along the straight-line trajectory.

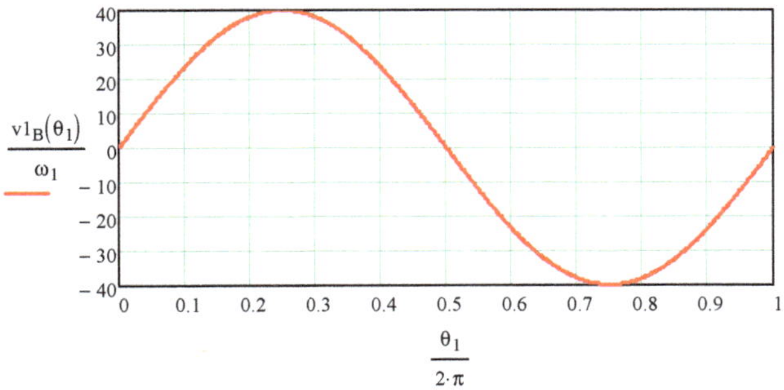

Figure 10. The velocity of point B along the straight-line trajectory.

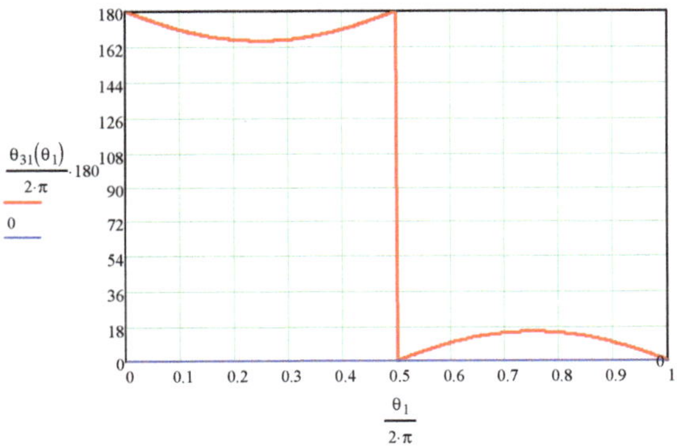

Figure 11. The variation in the rotation angle $\theta_{31}(\theta_1)$.

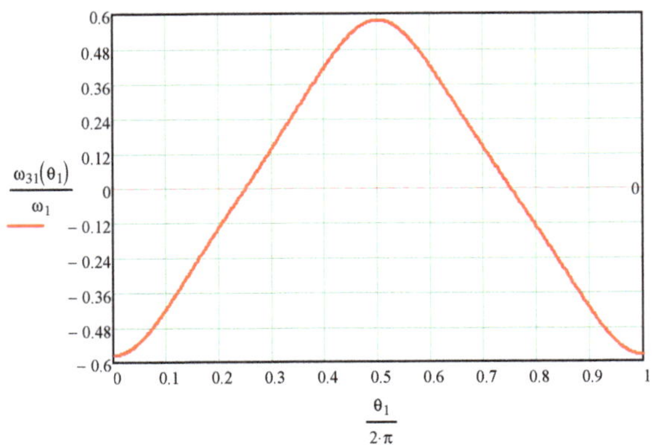

Figure 12. Variation in the angular velocity $\omega_{31}(\theta_1)$.

When the velocity of a point B from the intermediate element 3 is known with respect to the driving element 1 and the angular velocity ω_{31} of the intermediate element with respect to the driving element, using the Euler relation one can find the velocity of any point of element 3 with respect to the driving element:

$$\boldsymbol{v}_M = \boldsymbol{v}_B + \omega_{31} \times \overline{BM} \tag{39}$$

2.5. Establishing the Relative Motion between the Intermediate and Driven Elements

Similarly, the coordinates of point B from system 3 are expressed in frame 2 by the relation:

$$\boldsymbol{r}_B^{(2)} = \boldsymbol{T}_{23}\boldsymbol{r}_B^{(3)} \tag{40}$$

where

$$\boldsymbol{T}_{23} = \begin{bmatrix} \boldsymbol{i}_3 \cdot \boldsymbol{i}_2 & \boldsymbol{j}_3 \cdot \boldsymbol{i}_2 & \boldsymbol{k}_3 \cdot \boldsymbol{i}_2 & (\boldsymbol{r}_B - \boldsymbol{r}_{A_2}) \cdot \boldsymbol{i}_2 \\ \boldsymbol{i}_3 \cdot \boldsymbol{j}_2 & \boldsymbol{j}_3 \cdot \boldsymbol{j}_2 & \boldsymbol{k}_3 \cdot \boldsymbol{j}_2 & (\boldsymbol{r}_B - \boldsymbol{r}_{A_2}) \cdot \boldsymbol{j}_2 \\ \boldsymbol{i}_3 \cdot \boldsymbol{k}_2 & \boldsymbol{j}_3 \cdot \boldsymbol{k}_2 & \boldsymbol{k}_3 \cdot \boldsymbol{k}_2 & (\boldsymbol{r}_B - \boldsymbol{r}_{A_2}) \cdot \boldsymbol{k}_2 \\ 0 & 0 & 0 & 1 \end{bmatrix} \tag{41}$$

And

$$\boldsymbol{i}_2 = \begin{bmatrix} cos\theta_2 \\ sin\alpha\ sin\theta_2 \\ -cos\alpha\ sin\theta_2 \end{bmatrix},\ \boldsymbol{j}_2 = \begin{bmatrix} -sin\theta_2 \\ sin\alpha\ cos\theta_2 \\ -cos\alpha\ cos\theta_2 \end{bmatrix},\ \boldsymbol{k}_2 = \begin{bmatrix} 0 \\ cos\alpha \\ sin\alpha \end{bmatrix} \tag{42}$$

$$\boldsymbol{i}_3 = \begin{bmatrix} -sin\theta_1 \\ sin\alpha\ cos\theta_1 \\ cos\alpha\ cos\theta_1 \end{bmatrix},\ \boldsymbol{j}_3 = \begin{bmatrix} -sin\theta_2 \\ sin\alpha\ cos\theta_2 \\ cos\alpha\ cos\theta_2 \end{bmatrix},\ \boldsymbol{k}_3 = \boldsymbol{i}_3 \times \boldsymbol{j}_3 \tag{43}$$

This relation (43) is written based on Equation (18). Comparing relation (43) with relation (34), one can see that the systems $A_2x_2y_2z_2$ and $Bx_3y_3z_3$ have coinciding axes $\boldsymbol{j}_2$ and $\boldsymbol{j}_3$ and as a consequence, the relative motion between these systems can be fully described by the motion of point B in plane $A_2x_2z_2$ and by the rotation of one of the axes Bx_3 or Bz_3 with respect to the axes of $A_2x_2z_2$.

The trajectory of the point B in plane $A_2x_2z_2$ is found using the relation:

$$\boldsymbol{r}_B^2 = \begin{bmatrix} x_B^2 \\ y_B^2 \\ z_B^2 \\ 1 \end{bmatrix} \boldsymbol{T}_{23}\boldsymbol{r}_B = \boldsymbol{T}_{13}\begin{bmatrix} 0 & 0 & 0 & 1 \end{bmatrix} \tag{44}$$

After calculus is made in relation (44), one can observe that:

$$y_B^2(\theta_1) \equiv 0 \tag{45}$$

The physical meaning of relation (45) is that point B performs a planar trajectory relative to the driven element, as shown in Figure 13.

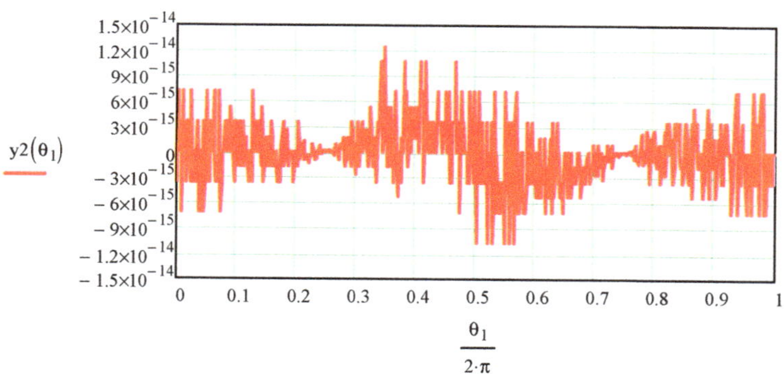

Figure 13. Validation in the planar trajectory of point B with respect to the driven element.

The trajectory described by point B in the plane $A_2x_2z_2$ is plotted in Figure 14 and its shape resembles a lemniscate enclosed by a $4a \times a$ rectangle.

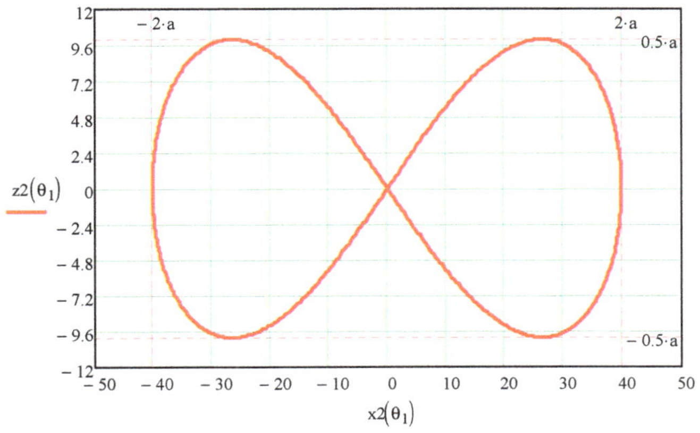

Figure 14. Lemniscate-like trajectory of point B in the plane $A_2x_2z_2$.

In order to obtain the rotation motion of the intermediate element with respect to the final element, the next relation is applied:

$$\theta_{32}(\theta_1) = angle[\boldsymbol{k}_3 \cdot \boldsymbol{k}_2, \boldsymbol{k}_3 \cdot \boldsymbol{i}_2] \tag{46}$$

The variation in this rotation for a complete rotation of the driving element is given in Figure 15. The time derivative of relation (46) leads to the expression of reduced relative angular velocity $\omega_{32}(\theta_1)/\omega_1$, whose variation is presented in Figure 16. From Figures 12 and 16, it can be seen that for a complete rotation of the driving element, both angular velocities ω_{31} and ω_{32} present sign changes attesting that the intermediate element performs oscillatory motions, both with respect to the driving element and the driven element, respectively.

As mentioned previously, there are few references in the literature concerning planar joints. A significant example is given in [16] where the planar joint is modeled using a different method, namely the dual matrix method. However, in fact, this methodology transposes in dual form the condition that the planar pair is equivalated to a succession of prismatic–prismatic–revolute joints, and the H-D method is recovered.

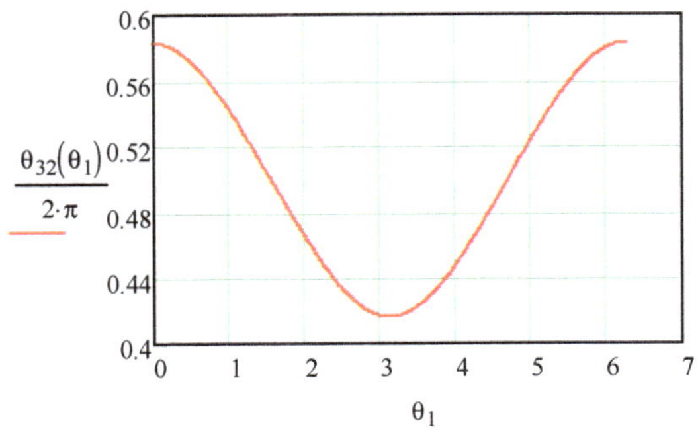

Figure 15. Variation in the rotation of the intermediate element for a complete rotation of the driving element.

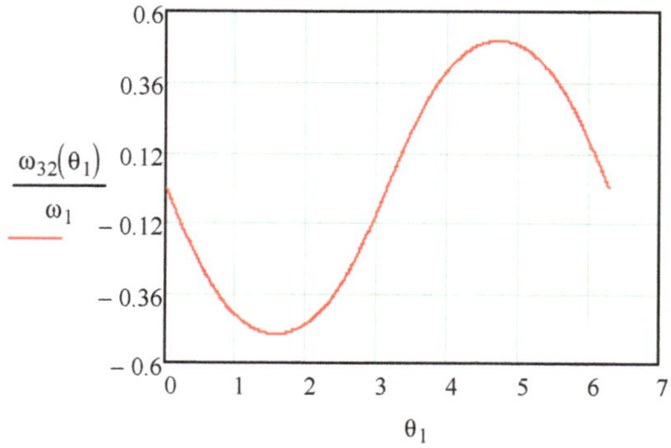

Figure 16. Variation in the reduced relative angular velocity for a complete rotation of the driving element.

3. Corroboration of Theoretical Results with a Numerical Simulation

3.1. Design of the Basic Mechanism

In order to validate the analytical results obtained above, the simplified mechanism was modeled in CATIA software. Specifically, the elements were modeled using the Wireframe and Surface Design modules, and then, the Assembly module was used for the assembly of the device, and the animation was performed in the DMU Kinematics module. The result is presented in Figure 17, where the circular trajectory of point *B* in the support plane and the trajectories of points from two segments belonging to the intermediate element, parallel to coordinate axes, are shown. In Figures 18 and 19 the trajectories of segments Δ_{31} and Δ_{32} are detailed and also compared to the analytical results, obtained in Mathcad, following the relations (33) and (41), respectively. An excellent quantitative concordance is attained from the comparison.

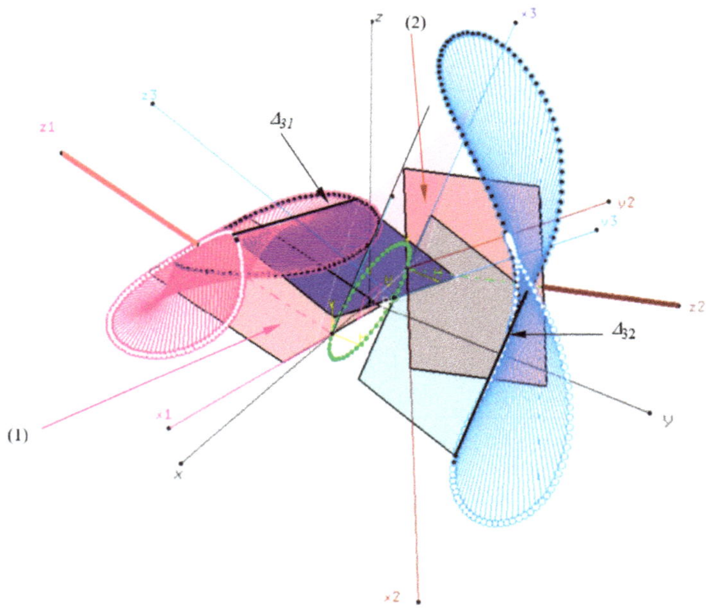

Figure 17. Simplified model of the mechanism: trajectory of point B in the fixed plane (green circle); (1) is the plane of symmetry of driving element; (2) is the plane of symmetry of the driven element; Δ_{31} and Δ_{32} are segments attached to the elements (1) and (2) respectively.

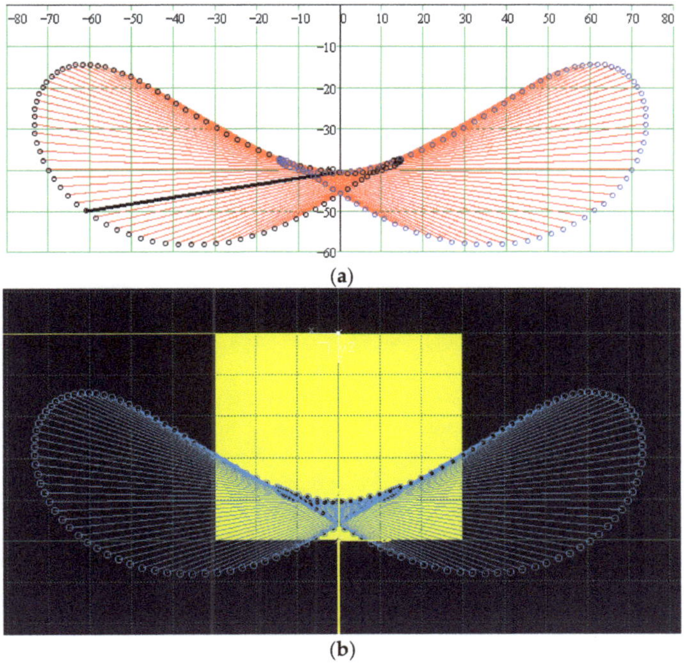

Figure 18. Comparison between relative trajectories of a point situated on a segment of the intermediate element with respect to the driving element: (**a**) analytic trajectories–relations (33), of the points from the lines Δ_{31}; (**b**) CATIA simulation.

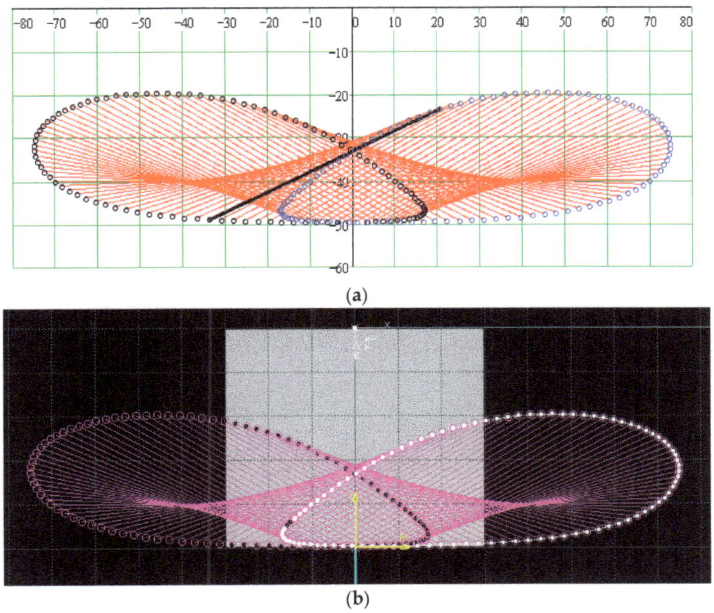

Figure 19. Comparison between relative trajectories of a point situated on a segment Δ_{32} of the intermediate element with respect to the driven element (**a**) analytic trajectory obtained with the relations (41); (**b**) CATIA simulation.

3.2. The Constructive Solution of the Proposed Coupling

To realize the transmission, the elements of the mechanisms should be designed to ensure the creation of the five kinematic pairs: revolute pairs, planar pairs, and the class 1 pair (the support between the intermediate element and the ground). The revolute pairs through which the first element and the final element are linked to the ground are straightforward to produce by mounting radial bearings on the surfaces A_1 and A_2 of the two elements. In Figure 20, the main components of the driving and driven elements are the two identical parts 1 and 2. In the bodies of these parts, two parallelepipedal channels are manufactured, with walls rigorously parallel to the axes of rotation of the parts. The main part of intermediate element 3 is crown 3 on which frontal faces are two parallelepipedal wedges $3b_1$ and $3b_2$, with the planes of symmetry reciprocally perpendicular. These wedges have the same width, theoretically identical to the width of the parallelepipedal channels from parts 1 and 2. By introducing the wedges $3b_1$ and $3b_2$ in the corresponding channels of parts 1 and 2, the two sliding fits are formed, realizing the planar pairs required by the structure of the mechanism. For achieving the pair of class 1, the major impediments are the revolute motions of elements 1 and 2 with respect to the ground. While rotating about the axes of the entrance and exit of the mechanism, respectively, these parts will generate the working spaces of the two elements. The presence of other parts in these working spaces could generate interference, and result in the locking of the mechanism. The proposed constructive solution is based on the fact that the points from the axes of rotation of elements 1 and 2 are fixed and can be considered as belonging to the ground. Additionally, as can be observed in Figure 20, the points inside any cylindrical hole coaxial to one of the two parts may be considered fixed points belonging to the ground. This explains the presence of the cylindrical plungers 1a and 1b, coaxial to the entering and exiting elements respectively, and having at one end a turntable. It is proposed that the pair of class 1 is created between the frontal surfaces of the turntables and the spherical surface 3a of the central body of the intermediate element 3, Figure 21. Obviously, the two contacts would conduct to a degree of mobility of the mechanism $M = 0$. Hence, the conclusion is that the center of sphere 3a must keep the same distance only with respect to one of the turntables.

In Figure 20 the position of the turntable is fixed with the aid of rigid sleeve 1b of a length adequate to maintain the center of the sphere at the desired distance with respect to the body of part 1. Two screw nuts 1c block the plunger in the required position. For element 2, the rigid sleeve is replaced by helical spring 2b (Figure 21b), which, acting on the plunger 2a, will permit the axial displacement of the plunger with respect to the body of part 2. Thus, the class 1 pair is formed between spherical part 3a and the frontal surface of plunger 1a. An adequate running of the mechanism imposes the existence of the class 1 pair at any time. This requirement dictates that spring 2b is mounted with a minimum interference fit, made with screw nuts 2c. The screw nut tightening force can be obtained from dynamic analysis of the cam mechanism formed by the driving element 3a, the cam, and the follower realized by the plunger 2b.

The contact between spherical surface 3a and the frontal faces of plungers 1a and 2a are point Hertzian contacts, where important contact stresses occur that can lead to the rapid deterioration of the contacting surfaces, having as an immediate effect the improper running of the mechanism. This drawback can be mitigated as shown in [42], by introducing a shoe-type part between spherical surface 3a and the frontal face of plunger 1a, as shown in Figure 22.

By introducing the supplementary part between spherical surface 3a and plane surfaces 1a and 3a, all the pairs of the mechanism become lower pairs, having extremely high wear resistance. From the point of view of efficiency, the revolute pair, by which the driving and driven elements are joined to the ground, the employment of roller bearings is a solution. The friction from the higher pair can be decreased by manufacturing shoe part 4a from an antifriction material like graphite-filled bronze and through appropriate lubrication. Regarding the planar pairs, there is no technical solution for replacing the sliding friction with rolling friction. Similar to the case of higher pair, the diminishing of friction wear can be achieved by using antifriction pairs of materials like steel-bronze, PTFE (Teflon)-steel, etc.

The proposed coupling should be further improved because spatial couplings with crossed axes are quite rare, such as the patent of Segreti [43].

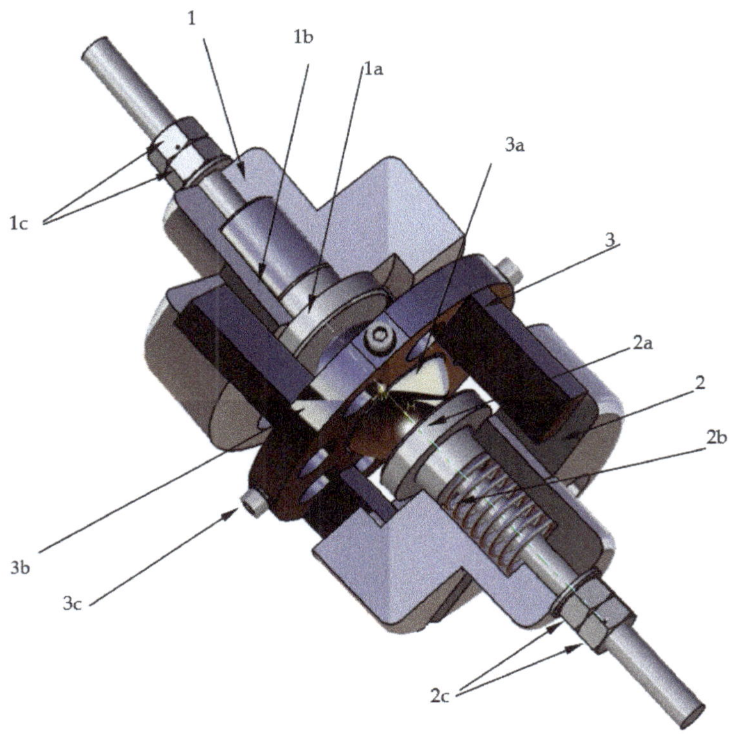

Figure 20. Design of the proposed coupling.

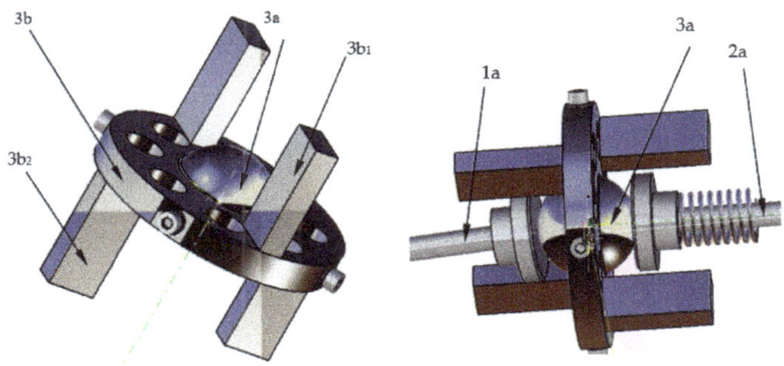

(a) (b)

Figure 21. The intermediate element: (**a**) design; (**b**) assembly for ensuring the contact from class 1 pair.

Figure 22. Solution for diminishing the contact stresses and the wear from the higher pair.

4. Discussions

The proposed coupling mechanism is entirely new among the spatial couplings transmitting the rotation motion between two shafts. The structural solution of the coupling resulted from the condition of transmission of rotation motion between two shafts, one driving and one driven, through an intermediate element. Within the practical solutions, a symmetrical structure of type RP1PR was the chosen option, such as the middle element completing a planar joint to each shaft and a class 1 pair with the ground. The choice of planar joints is based on the constructive straightforwardness and high reliability of these types of pairs. The existence of the class 1 pair between the intermediate element and the ground was imposed by the requirement that the degree of mobility of the mechanism is $M = 1$. To create the class 1 pair, it was required that the axis points of the two shafts are fixed and consequently can be considered as belonging to the ground. A stationary plane was fixed to one of the shafts, on which a spherical surface attached to the driving element is supported. Thus, the condition is met that the center of the spherical surface is permanently in a fixed plane attached to the ground and normal to the axis of the shafts (here, the driving shaft). A solution for diminishing the contact stresses from the sphere-plane concentrated point contact is presented, by placing a part between the spherical and plane surfaces, specially designed to replace the class 1 pair with two lower pairs of class 3: a spherical pair and a planar pair. The kinematic analysis of the planar pair requires obtaining the motions from planar joints, the relative trajectory of a point, and the angular velocity normal to the contacting surfaces. With these elements known, the absolute motion of any element of the transmission can then be expressed. The classical H-D methodology cannot be applied directly. It is shown that the method assumes equivalating the mechanism to another mechanism having a structure composed only of cylindrical, prismatic, and/or revolute pairs. By applying this methodology, complex trigonometrical systems result that can be solved only by numerical methods. For this solving procedure, the initialization demands a set of values corresponding to values close to a possible assembly solution for the actual mechanism, which is an extremely difficult task. The geometrical conditions (expressed in vector form) of constructing the joints from the structure of the mechanism, were applied. The components of the vectors from the relations of condition were expressed via the method of homogenous operators.

The proposed mechanism was also modeled in silico in order to obtain a numerical solution to validate the analytical results, comparing:

- the absolute trajectory of the center of the spherical surface of the intermediate element;
- the relative trajectories of points belonging to two segments from the middle part with respect to the driving element and final element, respectively.

A very good agreement was observed.

5. Conclusions

This work presents a completely new constructive solution of mechanical coupling that permits the transmission of motion between two axes positioned at a random angle in space, containing the succession of revolute–planar–point contact–planar–revolute joints, abbreviated RP1PR.

The kinematical analysis of the mechanism requires finding the motion from the revolute pair of the driven shaft, the trajectory of the spherical surface's center, and the motions from the planar pairs.

The well-known method of Hartenberg and Denavit cannot be applied directly to the mechanism due to the presence in the structure of the planar pair and of the class 1 pair.

In order to overcome these difficulties, the geometrical conditions of creating the pairs from the structure of the mechanism, expressed in vector form were utilized.

With the purpose of validating the resulting theoretical relations, a scheme of the mechanism was modeled in numerical simulation software.

The excellent concordance between analytical and numerical results confirms that the obtained relations are correct.

The constructive solution of the mechanism is presented in a section of the paper, detailing the conception of the kinematical pairs and ways of diminishing contact stresses and wear. Compared to other structural solutions containing non-H-D pairs (spherical joints), the solution is more robust, reliable, and simpler from a technological point of view and more economic. From a constructive perspective, if a spherical joint risks locking, here, the three permitted motions are not limited.

The analytical results that were obtained could be, for future research, the basis for studies on the optimization of dimensions, with the task of reducing wear and improving the efficiency of transmission.

Author Contributions: Conceptualization, S.A., I.D. and M.-C.C.; methodology, I.D. and F.-C.C.; software, I.-C.R. and I.-A.D.; validation, I.-C.R. and M.-C.C.; investigation, I.-C.R. and I.-A.D.; writing—original draft preparation, S.A. and F.-C.C. writing—review and editing, I.D. and F.-C.C.; supervision, S.A. and M.-C.C. All authors have read and agreed to the published version of the manuscript.

Funding: This research received no external funding.

Data Availability Statement: The data presented in this study are available within the article.

Conflicts of Interest: The authors declare no conflict of interest.

References

1. Uicker, J.J., Jr.; Pennock, G.R.; Shigley, J.E. *Theory of Machines and Mechanisms*, 4th ed.; Oxford University Press: New York, NY, USA, 2010; pp. 368–370.
2. Molotnikov, V.; Molotnikova, A. Kinematic Analysis of Mechanisms. In *Theoretical and Applied Mechanics*; Springer Nature: Cham, Switzerland, 2023; pp. 299–310. [CrossRef]
3. Hunt, K.H. *Kinematic Geometry of Mechanisms*; Oxford University Press: Oxford, UK, 1990; pp. 30–51.
4. McCarthy, J.M. *Introduction in Theoretical Kinematics*, 3rd ed.; MIT Press: Cambridge, MA, USA, 2018; pp. 103–108.
5. Roupa, I.; Gonçalves, S.B.; Silva, M.T. Kinematics and dynamics of planar multibody systems with fully Cartesian coordinates and a generic rigid body. *J. Mech. Mach. Theory* **2023**, *180*, 105134. [CrossRef]
6. Inurritegui, A.; Larranaga, J.; Arana, A.; Ulacia, U. Numerical-experimental analysis of highly crowned spherical gear couplings working at high misalignment angles. *J. Mech. Mach. Theory* **2023**, *183*, 105260. [CrossRef]
7. Wu, K.; Liu, Z.; Ding, Q. Vibration responses of rotating elastic coupling with dynamic spatial misalignment. *J. Mech. Mach. Theory* **2020**, *151*, 103916. [CrossRef]
8. Cao, A.; Jing, Z.; Ding, H. A general method for kinematics analysis of two-layer and two-loop deployable linkages with coupling chains. *J. Mech. Mach. Theory* **2020**, *152*, 103945. [CrossRef]
9. Baigunchekov, Z.; Laribi, M.A.; Carbone, G.; Mustafa, A.; Amanov, B.; Zholdassov, Y. Structural-Parametric Synthesis of the RoboMech Class Parallel Mechanism with Two Sliders. *Appl. Sci.* **2021**, *11*, 9831. [CrossRef]
10. Zhang, J.; Ng, N.; Scott, C.E.H.; Blyth, M.J.G.; Haddad, F.S.; Macpherson, G.J.; Patton, J.T.; Clement, N.D. Robotic arm-assisted versus manual unicompartmental knee arthroplasty. *Bone Joint J.* **2022**, *104*, 541–548. [CrossRef] [PubMed]
11. McCarthy, J.M.; Soh, G.S. *Geometric Design of Linkages*; Springer: Berlin/Heidelberg, Germany, 2010; pp. 253–279.
12. Hartenberg, R.; Denavit, J. *Kinematic Synthesis of Linkages*, 1st ed.; McGraw-Hill Inc.: New York, NY, USA, 1964; pp. 343–368.

13. Alaci, S.; Pentiuc, R.D.; Doroftei, I.; Ciornei, F.C. Use of dual numbers in kinematical analysis of spatial mechanisms. Part II: Applying the method for the generalized Cardan mechanism. *IOP MSE* **2019**, *568*, 12032. [CrossRef]
14. Angeles, J. *Spatial Kinematic Chains: Analysis-Synthesis-Optimization*; Springer: Berlin/Heidelberg, Germany, 1982; pp. 189–218.
15. Ciornei, F.C.; Amarandei, D.; Alaci, S.; Romanu, I.C.; Baesu, M. On direct coupling of two shafts. Part 2: Kinematical analysis. *Tehnomus J.* **2017**, *24*, 281–285.
16. Fischer, I. *Dual-Number Methods in Kinematics, Statics and Dynamics*; CRC Press: New York, NY, USA, 1999; pp. 54–95.
17. Alaci, S.; Pentiuc, R.D.; Ciornei, F.C.; Buium, F.; Rusu, O.T. Kinematics analysis of the swash plate mechanism. *IOP MSE* **2019**, *568*, 012017.
18. Angeles, J. *Rational Kinematics*; Springer: New York, NY, USA, 1998; pp. 12–34.
19. Uicker, J.J., Jr.; Denavit, J.; Hartenberg, R.S. An Iterative Method for the Displacement Analysis of Spatial Mechanisms. *J. Appl. Mech.* **1964**, *31*, 309–314. [CrossRef]
20. Selig, J.M. On the Plane Symmetric Bricard Mechanism. In *Advances in Robot Kinematics 2020 (Springer Proceedings in Advanced Robotics Book 15)*; Lenarčič, J., Siciliano, B., Eds.; Springer Nature: Cham, Switzerland, 2021; pp. 73–81.
21. Seherr-Thoss, H.C.; Schmelz, F.; Aucktor, E. *Universal Joints and Driveshafts. Analysis, Design, Applications*, 2nd ed.; Springer: Berlin/Heidelberg, Germany, 2006; pp. 53–79.
22. Inurritegui, A.; Larranaga, J.; Arana, A.; Ulacia, U. Load distribution and tooth root stress of highly crowned spherical gear couplings working at high misalignment angles. *J. Mech. Mach. Theory* **2023**, *179*, 105104. [CrossRef]
23. Luzi, L.; Sancisi, N.; Parenti-Castelli, V. The Potential of the 7R-R Closed Loop Mechanism to Transfer Motion Between Two Shafts with Varying Angular Position. In *Interdisciplinary Applications of Kinematics. Mechanisms and Machine Science*; Kecskeméthy, A., Geu Flores, F., Carrera, E., Elias, D., Eds.; Springer: Cham, Switzerland, 2019; Volume 71, pp. 185–195. [CrossRef]
24. Lobontiu, N.; Hunter, J.; Keefe, J.; Westenskow, J. Tripod mechanisms with novel spatial Cartesian flexible hinges. *J. Mech. Mach. Theory* **2022**, *167*, 104521. [CrossRef]
25. Yoon, K.; Cho, S.-M.; Kim, K.G. Coupling Effect Suppressed Compact Surgical Robot with 7-Axis Multi-Joint Using Wire-Driven Method. *Mathematics* **2022**, *10*, 1698. [CrossRef]
26. Litvin, F.L.; Fuentes, A. *Gear Geometry and Applied Theory*; Cambridge University Press: Cambridge, UK, 2004; pp. 441–474.
27. Vullo, V. *Gears, Volume 1: Geometric and Kinematic Design*; Springer: Cham, Switzerland, 2021; pp. 139–151.
28. Gonzales-Palacios, M.A.; Angeles, J. *Cam Synthesis*; Springer: Dordrecht, The Netherland, 1993; pp. 37–53.
29. Alaci, S.; Ciornei, F.C.; Amarandei, D.; Baesu, M.; Mihaila, D. On direct coupling of two shafts. Part 1: Structural considerations. *Tehnomus J.* **2017**, *24*, 277–280.
30. Akbil, E.; Lee, T.W. On the motion characteristics of tripode joints. Part 1: General case; Part 2: Applications. *ASME J. Mech. Transm. Autom. Des.* **1984**, *106*, 228–241. [CrossRef]
31. Johnson, K.L. *Contact Mechanics*; Cambridge University Press: Cambridge, UK, 1985; pp. 84–106. [CrossRef]
32. Hills, D.A.; Nowell, D.; Sackfield, A. *Mechanics of Elastic Contacts*; Elsevier Butterworth-Heinemann: Oxford, UK, 1993; pp. 198–226.
33. Popov, V.L. *Contact Mechanics and Friction. Physical Principles and Applications*; Springer: Berlin/Heidelberg, Germany, 2010; pp. 55–69.
34. Gladwel, G.M.L. *Contact Problems in the Classical Theory of Elasticity*; Sijthoff & Noordhoff: Hague, The Netherlands, 1980; p. 716.
35. Alaci, S.; Buium, F.; Ciornei, F.-C.; Dobincă, D.-I. Tetrapod coupling. *Mech. Mach. Sci.* **2018**, *57*, 349–356. [CrossRef]
36. Inurritegui, A.; Larranaga, J.; Arana, A.; Ulacia, U. Spherical gear coupling design space analysis for high misalignment applications. *Mech. Mach. Theory* **2022**, *173*, 104837. [CrossRef]
37. Hayes, M.J.D.; Rotzoll, M.; Bucciol, Q.; Copeland, A.A. Planar and spherical four-bar linkage vi−vj algebraic input–output equations. *J. Mech. Mach. Theory* **2023**, *182*, 105222. [CrossRef]
38. *EN ISO 3952-1*; Kinematic Diagrams—Graphical Symbols. Part 1. The European Standard: Geneva, Switzerland, 2019; pp. 1–25.
39. Sclater, N. *Mechanisms and Mechanical Devices Sourcebook*, 5th ed.; McGraw Hill: New York, NY, USA, 2011; pp. 109–110.
40. Yoshikawa, T. *Foundations of Robotics: Analysis and Control*; MIT Press: Cambridge, MA, USA, 2003; pp. 259–262.
41. Maxfield, B. *Engineering with Mathcad*; Butterworth-Heinemann, Elsevier: Oxford, UK, 2006; pp. 287–289.
42. Alaci, S.; Ciornei, F.C.; Filote, C. Considerations upon a New Tripod Joint Solution. *Mechanika* **2013**, *19*, 567–574. [CrossRef]
43. Segreti, A. Mechanism for the Transmission of Rotary Movement between two Shafts having Non-Parallel, Non-Coplanar Axes. U.S. Patent WO 02/103220 A2, 27 December 2002.

mathematics

MDPI

Article

A Comprehensive Evaluation Method of Machining Center Components' Importance Based on Combined Variable Weight

Lan Luan [1,2], Guixiang Shen [1,2] and Yingzhi Zhang [1,2,*]

1 Key Laboratory of Reliability of CNC Equipment, Ministry of Education, Changchun 130022, China; luanlan16@mails.jlu.edu.cn (L.L.); shengx@jlu.edu.cn (G.S.)
2 School of Mechanical and Aerospace Engineering, Jilin University, Changchun 130022, China
* Correspondence: zhangyz@jlu.edu.cn

Abstract: The fault transitivity of machining center components causes their fault propagation indexes to demonstrate dynamic time variability, which affects their importance. The method proposed in this study overcomes the biases of existing methods of evaluating the importance of system components, as they are mostly based on single indexes; the fault propagation probability and fault propagation risk are selected to perform a comprehensive evaluation. This study first establishes a network hierarchical structure model for machining center components, and the degree of influence of fault propagation among the components is calculated. On this basis, the improved adjacent spreading paths (ASP) algorithm is used to calculate the fault propagation index of each component; from the two perspectives of fault propagation probability and fault propagation risk, an evaluation mechanism involving the combined variable weight is used to comprehensively evaluate components' importance. Taking a certain type of machining center as an example, through a comparison with ranking results from other node importance methods, it is verified that the proposed method can more effectively distinguish the differences in the importance of each component, thus illustrating the effectiveness and practical value of this method.

Keywords: machining center; fault propagation probability; fault propagation risk; combined variable weight; importance evaluation

MSC: 60E05; 05C20; 93-08

1. Introduction

As the foundation and one of the most widely used types of equipment in the equipment manufacturing industry, with the development of artificial intelligence and system automation, the structure of machining center systems has gradually become complex, and the components have become more diverse [1]. The complex coupling relationships between components cause fault propagation to occur frequently, which increases investments in fault diagnosis and equipment maintenance [2–4]. Therefore, the comprehensive evaluation of the importance of machining center components at different moments allows the timely and accurate identification of the key components of a system, which is conducive to real-time maintenance and the management of equipment for enterprises, thus reducing the occurrence of cascade failures, improving the service life of the machining center, increasing the utilization and service life of manufacturing equipment, and laying the foundation for the development of predictive maintenance technology.

Research on node importance evaluations has mainly been focused on complex networks, and a variety of related techniques and methods for finding key nodes that affect the structure and function of the network have been proposed, which is the focus in the field of network science [5–9]. The characteristics of a network are extended to hardware systems. By abstracting a hardware system into a topological network, the complexity and statistical characteristics of the system can be described and analyzed, and an algorithm can be designed to identify the key nodes quickly and accurately. Since the ranking of node importance is based on different network models, many node-ranking methods have been derived, and they can be divided into three categories:

(1) Methods of node ranking based on complex network topology characteristics. These methods [10] use a network's characteristics to identify its key nodes, including the connections of a node itself and its connections with adjacent nodes, as well as degree centrality, semi-local centrality, eigenvector centrality, etc. Bonacich, P. [11] proposed "degree centrality" in 1972, arguing that the influence of a node on the whole network depends on the number of nodes with which it is connected. Chen et al. [12] proposed a method for ranking node importance based on "semi-local centrality" by using semi-local information to sort nodes. Martin et al. [13] improved the eigenvector centrality method by proposing a non-retrospective centrality method. This method was relatively simple and easy to understand, but it was only suitable for regular and less complex networks; it was not suitable for problems with high computational complexity, and the results were not accurate enough.

(2) Methods of key network node identification based on node operations. These methods [14] measure the importance of a node according to its impact on the whole network after processing the nodes, such as by shrinking nodes, deleting nodes, inserting nodes, etc. Berberler, Z. N. et al. [15] conducted a node importance analysis in wheel-related networks by using a method of evaluating node importance through node contraction based on network agglomeration in communication networks. Obeidat, A. et al. [16] presented a novel adaptive and dynamic network routing algorithm based on a regenerating genetic algorithm (RGA) with the analysis of network delays, the deletion of links or nodes from the network, and the assessment of the network volume (with numerous routes). Choi, W. Y. [17] proposed a node insertion algorithm for the real-time implementation of a connectivity-based multi-polling mechanism in the MAC protocol for Wi-Fi sensor networks. Although this type of method can be used to evaluate node importance in reverse, it may cause the disconnection of the network after its operation, and the measurement method does not consider the particularities of network topologies, resulting in inaccurate evaluation results.

(3) Methods of node importance evaluation based on iterative optimization algorithms. In an iterative calculation process, such methods [18] judge the importance of nodes according to the scoring values of their neighbors and themselves to ensure that the scoring values can converge quickly, such as in the PageRank algorithm, LeaderRank algorithm, HIT algorithm, etc. Liu, C. et al. proposed a novel algorithm for evaluating node contributions based on TOPSIS and PageRank [19], and Jiang, S. et al. defined an improved gravity centrality for identifying key nodes in multi-layer networks based on multi-PageRank centrality [20]. Jiang, S. et al. [21] used an improved weighted LeaderRank algorithm to measure the importance of components and obtain the sequence of critical components. Vinodha, R. et al. [22] recommended a hypertext induced topic search (HITS) based point of interest (POI) recommendation calculation that could take into account the effects of social connections when recommending POIs to individual users. This type of method takes the number of nodes connected to a node and the importance of adjacent nodes when evaluating the importance of a node into account, and this has a wide range of applications. However, most algorithms are not universal; the convergence speeds of various iterative algorithms are different and the evaluation indexes are singular, which is not conducive to their application and popularization.

In this study, based on a hierarchical structure model of a network of machining center components, a comprehensive method of evaluating component importance using the combined variable weight evaluation mechanism is proposed. Compared with the existing methods, the fault propagation impact degree model based on the characteristics of complex network topology established in this paper can demonstrate the relationship of fault propagation among system components more clearly. Moreover, previous studies have not considered the differences of each component at a different hierarchy, which will inevitably lead to deviation in the fault propagation impact results. Therefore, in this paper, it is more reasonable to evaluate the degree of fault propagation impact between components based on a complex network and an interpretive structure model (ISM). The structural characteristics of the model and fault mechanism of the machining center is considered synthetically, two key indexes of importance are proposed from the perspective of fault propagation, and the problem of bias in the evaluation of a single index is corrected. The fuzzy and dynamic problems in the comprehensive evaluation are solved by using the mechanism of combined variable weights, which makes the evaluation results more realistic and provides them with high use value.

2. Comprehensive Evaluation of the Importance of Machining Center Components Based on the Combined Variable Weight

Firstly, according to the mechanical structure and failure information of machining center components, a hierarchical network structure model based on a complex network and an ISM method was established, the characteristic parameters of the network structure of the components were calculated, and the degree of influence of fault propagation among the components was determined from the perspective of the components themselves and the levels of the associated components. Secondly, considering the correlation with failure time, the Johnson method was applied to correct the rankings of the fault data, and a failure probability model for the whole machine and each component was established. Considering the correlations between failure modes, the analytic hierarchy process (ANP) was used to calculate the degree of influence of the failure mode, and the failure risk of each component was calculated according to its failure mode frequency and failure rate. Integrating the degree of influence of fault propagation among the component units, the fault propagation probability and fault propagation risk of each component were calculated by using an improved ASP algorithm. Finally, from the two perspectives of fault propagation probability and fault propagation risk, the mechanism of the combined variable weight was used to comprehensively evaluate the importance of the components. The specific process of the comprehensive evaluation of the importance of machining center components is shown in Figure 1.

2.1. Construction of the Model of the Degree of Influence of Fault Propagation

The choice of the fault propagation path is influenced by the structural characteristics of the fault propagation model and the reliability level of the nodes in the network [23]. In combination with the historical fault information of the machining center, the correlation of the fault was analyzed, and the machining center was taken as a complex system. According to its structural characteristics and functional modules, the model of the influence of fault propagation was constructed based on the ISM of a complex network and an analysis of the fault mechanism.

2.1.1. Calculation of the Feature Parameters of the Topology Based on the Complex Network

The network model of a machining center is a simple abstract expression of the fault propagation relationships of the components of the machining center system through abstract concepts such as nodes and connecting edges in the network. Each node in the network shows an inequality due to the different physical locations. Therefore, it is possible to reflect the differences in the influence of each node on fault propagation by evaluating the network nodes' characteristic parameters [24]. Combined with the structural characteristics of the machining center and the relevant problems studied, the network topological characteristic parameters selected in this study were the node efficiency and edge betweenness.

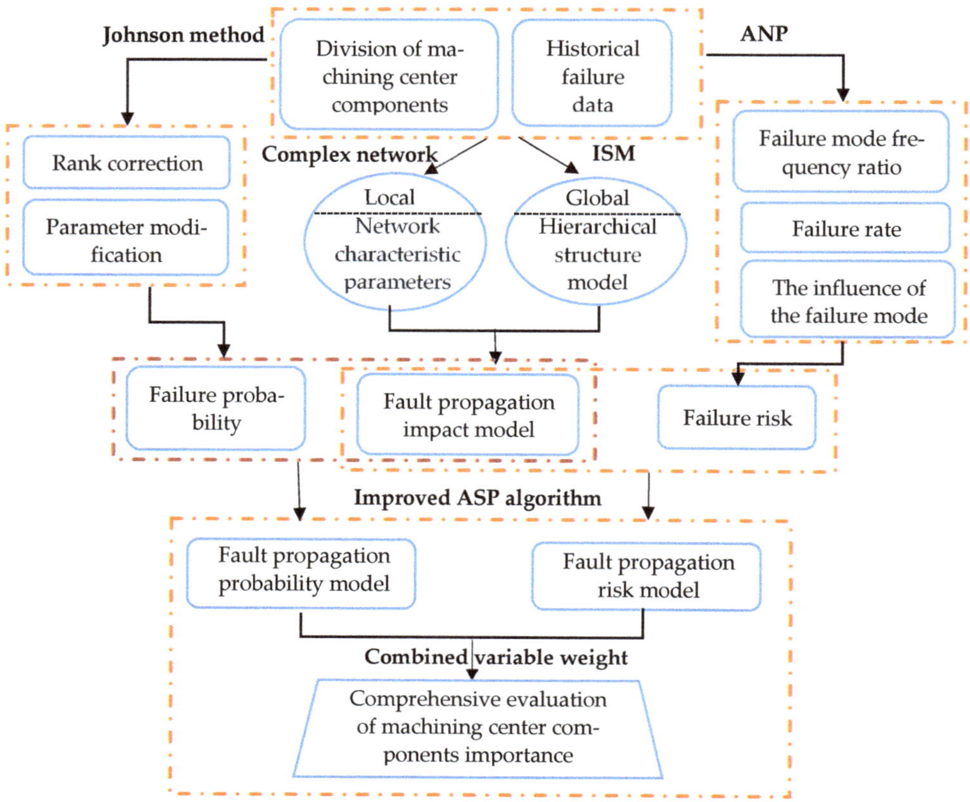

Figure 1. Flowchart of the comprehensive evaluation of the importance of the machining center.

Node efficiency is a metric that indicates the topological properties of a network. The efficiency of a node indicates its average degree of correlation with other nodes. The larger the efficiency value is, the greater the centrality of the node in the network will be. The calculation formula for the efficiency of machining center components I_i is as follows:

$$I_i = \frac{1}{N} \sum_{j=1, i \neq j}^{N} \frac{1}{d_{ij}}, \tag{1}$$

where d_{ij} is the distance between components i and j, and N is the number of machining center components.

Edge betweenness is a dynamic feature indicator of edges in a network diagram. The larger the edge betweenness is, the greater the load of the edge will be, the stronger the contact control effect of the edge on other components will be, the more likely it is to lead to the rapid propagation of faults. The calculation formula for the edge betweenness $L(v_i \to v_j)$ is as follows:

$$L(v_i \to v_j) = \sum_{\substack{v_i, v_j, v_e, v_f \\ (e,f) \neq (i,j)}} \frac{\kappa_{ef} E(v_i, v_j)}{\kappa_{ef}}, \tag{2}$$

where k_{ef} is the number of paths between any components e and f, and $k_{ef} E(v_i, v_j)$ is the number of edges $v(i,j)$ passing by the paths between any components e and f.

2.1.2. Calculation of the Network Hierarchical Weights Based on the ISM Method

The ISM method [25] hierarchically divides all of the elements affecting a system, identifies the interrelationships between the different elements, and forms a relationship matrix and hierarchical structure diagram. The network-level weight is an important index that reflects the differences in component importance between different hierarchies from a quantitative perspective. In this study, the ISM method was used to classify the hierarchy, and the network hierarchical weight of the component to be evaluated was comprehensively evaluated by using the network hierarchy in which the component itself was located and the network hierarchies in which other components connected to the component were located.

The formula for calculating the network hierarchical weight of a component is presented below:

$$H_i = \frac{1/i'}{\sum\limits_{i'=1}^{n} (1/i')}, \tag{3}$$

where H_i represents the network hierarchical weight of component i to be evaluated, and i' represents the network hierarchy in which component i is located.

T_i is used to indicate the degree of influence of the network hierarchical weights of component i to be evaluated; the calculation formula is shown in Equation (4).

$$T_i = Q\sum_{k} H_{k\to i} D_{k\to i} + O\sum_{j} H_{i\to j} D_{i\to j}, \tag{4}$$

where Q and O are, respectively, the in-degree node coefficient and out-degree node coefficient, and $Q + O = 1$. Because the importance of system components is considered from the perspective of fault propagation in this study, this means that the influence of a component's failure on other components is the main consideration. Therefore, the out-degree node of the component is more important than the in-degree node, so $O > Q$, and the weight values of the two indicators can be calculated with the method of weight determination. In this study, the analytic hierarchy process was chosen to calculate $Q = 0.25$ and $O = 0.75$. $H_{k\to i}$ denotes the network-level weights at which all in-degree nodes associated with component i are located; $H_{i\to j}$ denotes the network-level weights at which all out-degree nodes associated with component i are located; $D_{k\to i}$ denotes the number of in-degree nodes associated with component i; $D_{i\to j}$ denotes the number of out-degree nodes associated with component i.

2.1.3. Construction of the Model of the Degree of Influence of Fault Propagation

The contribution matrix of the influence of fault propagation represents the matrix form of the contribution values of all nodes in the network to the fault influences of other neighboring nodes [26]. It reflects the communication control effect between neighboring nodes in the network. That is, the stronger the communication control effect between interconnected nodes, the more likely it is to lead to a rapid propagation of faults. Combined with the edge betweenness that was calculated above, the contribution matrix of the components' influence on fault propagation H_C is defined as follows:

$$H_C = \begin{bmatrix} r_{ij} & \frac{r_{ij}L(v_1\to v_2)}{\sum L(v_i\to v_j)} & \cdots & \frac{r_{ij}L(v_1\to v_n)}{\sum L(v_i\to v_j)} \\ \frac{r_{ij}L(v_2\to v_1)}{\sum L(v_i\to v_j)} & r_{ij} & \cdots & \frac{r_{ij}L(v_2\to v_n)}{\sum L(v_i\to v_j)} \\ \vdots & \vdots & \cdots & \vdots \\ \frac{r_{ij}L(v_n\to v_1)}{\sum L(v_i\to v_j)} & \frac{r_{ij}L(v_n\to v_2)}{\sum L(v_i\to v_j)} & \cdots & r_{ij} \end{bmatrix}, \tag{5}$$

where r_{ij} is the contribution assignment parameter; $r_{ij} = 1$ if the node i has an influence on the node j, otherwise $r_{ij} = 0$. $\sum L(v_i \to v_j)$ is the sum of all edge betweennesses.

In order to determine the position of a component in the whole network and its degree of influence on other components accurately, based on the contribution matrix of components' influence on fault propagation, a determination matrix of components' influence on fault propagation H_E is defined with the efficiency values of the components themselves and the comprehensive weights of their locations.

$$H_E = \begin{bmatrix} r_{11}T_1\frac{I_1}{\sum I_i} & r_{12}T_1\left(\frac{I_1}{\sum I_i} + \frac{L(v_1 \to v_2)}{\sum L(v_i \to v_j)}\right) & \cdots & r_{1n}T_1\left(\frac{I_1}{\sum I_i} + \frac{L(v_1 \to v_n)}{\sum L(v_i \to v_j)}\right) \\ r_{21}T_2\left(\frac{I_2}{\sum I_i} + \frac{L(v_2 \to v_1)}{\sum L(v_i \to v_j)}\right) & r_{22}T_2\frac{I_2}{\sum I_i} & \cdots & r_{2n}T_2\left(\frac{I_2}{\sum I_i} + \frac{L(v_2 \to v_n)}{\sum L(v_i \to v_j)}\right) \\ \vdots & \vdots & \cdots & \vdots \\ r_{n1}T_n\left(\frac{I_n}{\sum I_i} + \frac{L(v_n \to v_1)}{\sum L(v_i \to v_j)}\right) & r_{n2}T_n\left(\frac{I_n}{\sum I_i} + \frac{L(v_n \to v_2)}{\sum L(v_i \to v_j)}\right) & \cdots & r_{nn}T_n\frac{I_n}{\sum I_i} \end{bmatrix}, \quad (6)$$

where $\sum I_i$ is the sum of all component efficiencies.

2.2. Calculation of the Fault Propagation Index Based on an Improved ASP Algorithm

Considering the influence of fault propagation among machining center components, fault propagation probability and fault propagation risk were selected as important parameters for evaluating the influences of components in this study, and a specific process of solving this problem was introduced.

2.2.1. Fault Probability Modeling Based on Time Correlation

The traditional method of fault probability modeling for a machining center and its components does not consider the correlation with the failure time, which leads to some deviation in the model [27]. In order to obtain relatively accurate results, this study establishes a fault probability model of a machining center and its components based on time correlation. First of all, the hypothetical distribution is identified according to data on the operating failure intervals of the component units, and then the least-square method is used to estimate the parameters based on the correction of the rank of the fault data by using Johnson's method. When the number of samples is small, the estimated parameters should undergo an unbiased correction. Finally, a test of the hypothesis was carried out on the obtained probability model, and the fault probability functions of the whole machine and the components were obtained after passing the test. The specific solution process is shown in Figure 2.

2.2.2. Fault Risk Assessment Based on the ANP Method

The fault risk of a machining center component refers to the risk caused by a fault in the component itself, and the calculation formula is as follows:

$$RI_i(t) = \sum_{j=1}^{n} \alpha_{ij}(t)\lambda_i(t)\beta_{ij}, \quad (7)$$

where $RI_i(t)$ represents the fault risk value of component i at time t, n is the number of types of fault modes of component i, $\alpha_{ij}(t)$ represents the ratio of fault mode frequencies of the component unit i at time t due to failure mode j, $\lambda_i(t)$ is the fault rate of component unit i at time t, and β_{ij} represents the impact of the first failure mode j of component unit i.

In order to obtain the fault risk value of a machining center component, it is necessary to calculate its ratio of fault mode frequencies, fault rate, and degree of fault mode influence. The solutions for these three metrics will be highlighted below:

(1) Calculation of the fault mode frequency ratio

The fault modes and causes are analyzed for each component in the machining center, the kinds of fault modes that may occur in the parts or components are found, the fault mechanisms are identified or inferred, the impacts are studied, and then the fault mode frequency ratio of the machining center is obtained.

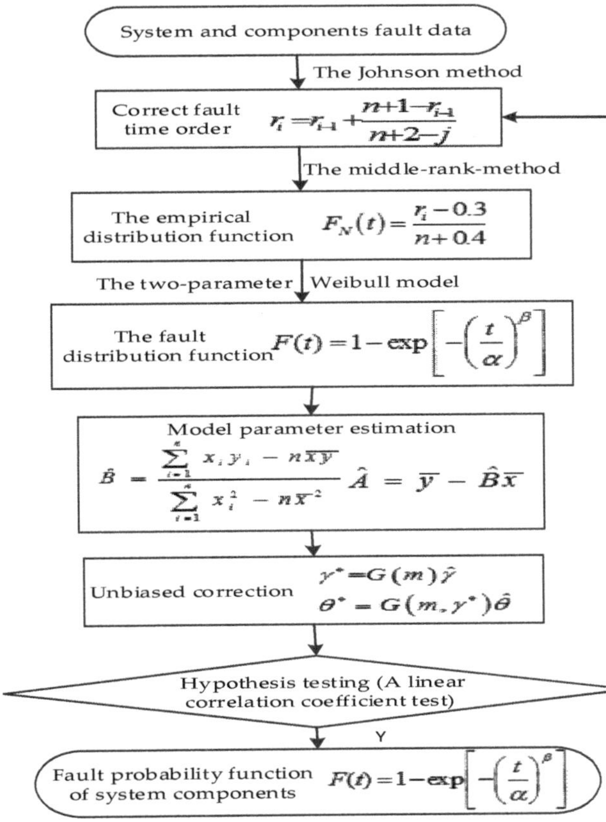

Figure 2. Flowchart of fault probability modeling for machining center components.

(2) Calculation of the fault rate

Since there is a relationship between the failure rate function and the failure probability function, the failure rate function of machining center components at any time can be obtained.

$$F(t) = 1 - \exp\left(-\int_0^t \lambda(t)dt\right). \tag{8}$$

Therefore, the calculation formula of the fault rate function of each component of the machining center is as follows:

$$\lambda(t) = \frac{f(t)}{R(t)} = \frac{\beta}{\alpha^\beta} t^{\beta-1}. \tag{9}$$

(3) Calculation of the degree of influence of a fault mode

By analyzing the fault modes of each component of the machining center, it can be found that the fault modes of different components may be the same or different; the same fault mode may have different impacts on different components, and there are certain correlations and differences among the fault modes. Therefore, the ANP method [28] is introduced to calculate the impact of the fault mode of each component. The steps of the calculation are shown in Figure 3.

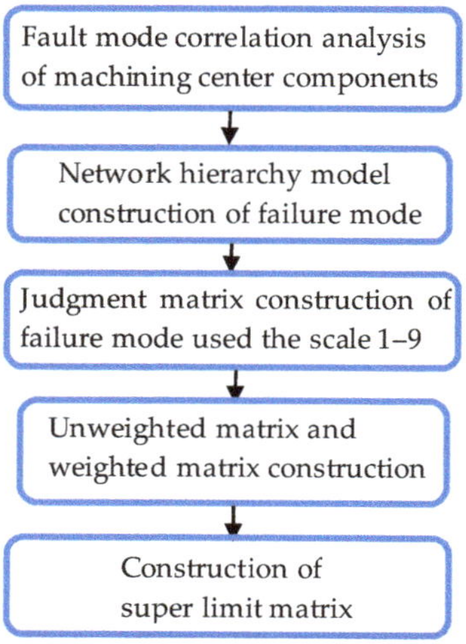

Figure 3. Flowchart of the assessment of fault modes' impacts on machining center components.

2.2.3. Evaluation of Fault Propagation Indexes Based on the Improved ASP Algorithm

In the actual fault propagation process, the fault information of a machining center component depends on its fault indicators and the impacts of upstream component faults. Therefore, in order to examine the fault propagation among components, fault probability and fault risk are combined with the determination matrix of fault propagation effect in a machining center in this study. It is known that a fault in a system component may cause faults in other components that are associated with it. The fault probability and fault risk of a component and the influences of faults among components are combined to represent the fault propagation probability and fault propagation risk among these components.

$$P(v_i, v_j)(t) = F_i(t)H_E(v_i, v_j), \tag{10}$$

$$RP(v_i, v_j)(t) = RI_i(t)H_E(v_i, v_j), \tag{11}$$

where $P(v_i, v_j)(t)$ is the probability of component i propagating a fault to component j at time t; $\mathrm{RP}(v_i, v_j)(t)$ is the risk of component i propagating a fault to component j at time t.

The different locations of machining center components cause the influences of propagation to be different. According to the principle of third-order influence [29], faults in machining center components will not only propagate to the adjacent components, but they may also have an impact on the components within the third order. Therefore, the fault propagation probability and the fault propagation risk are introduced into the improved ASP algorithm. By combining this with the structural model of fault propagation, the values of the probability of fault propagation and the risk of fault propagation can be calculated for each component. The specific calculation process and calculation formula are shown below:

$$fp^{U}{}_{ASP\_i}(t) = fp^{U}{}_{ASP\_ij}(t) + fp^{U}{}_{ASP\_in}(t) + fp^{U}{}_{ASP\_iq}(t), \tag{12}$$

where $fp^{U}{}_{ASP\_i}(t)$ is the Uth fault propagation index of component i at time t. In this study, we choose to use the fault propagation probability and the fault propagation risk as the fault propagation indexes, so $U = 1, 2$. $fp^{U}{}_{ASP\_ij}(t)$ is the success rate of component i in propagating fault information to the one-step-neighboring component j at time t; $fp^{U}{}_{ASP\_in}(t)$ is the success rate of component i in propagating fault information to the two-step neighboring component n at time t; $fp^{U}{}_{ASP\_iq}(t)$ is the success rate of the component i in propagating fault information to the three-step neighboring component q at time t.

The solution process for the fault propagation probability is similar to that for the fault propagation risk. Taking the solving process of fault propagation probability as an example, for the one-step-neighboring components of component i, $fp^1{}_{ASP\_ij}(t)$ is the success rate of component i in propagating fault probability to the one-step-neighboring component j at time t, and calculation formula is shown below:

$$fp^1{}_{ASP\_ij}(t) = \sum_{j\in A(i)} P(v_i, v_j)(t) + \sum_{m\in A(i)} P(v_i, v_m)(t)P(v_m, v_j)(t) + \sum_{r\in A(i)} P(v_i, v_m)(t)P(v_m, v_r)(t)P(v_r, v_j)(t), \quad (13)$$

where $A(i)$ is the set of all one-step-neighboring components of component i; $P(v_i, v_j)(t)$ is the fault propagation probability between components i and j at time t; $P(v_i, v_m)(t)P(v_m, v_j)(t)$ is the propagation probability at time t, where component i passes the fault to component j through component m; $P(v_i, v_m)(t)P(v_m, v_r)(t)P(v_r, v_j)(t)$ is the propagation probability for component i passing the fault to component j through components m and r.

For the two-step-neighboring components of component n,

$$fp^1{}_{ASP\_in}(t) = \sum_{m\in A(i), n\in A^2(i)} P(v_i, v_m)(t)P(v_m, v_n)(t) + \sum_{l\in A^2(i)} P(v_i, v_m)(t)P(v_m, v_l)(t)P(v_l, v_n)(t), \quad (14)$$

where $A^2(i)$ is the set of all two-step-neighboring components of component i; $P(v_i, v_m)(t)P(v_m, v_n)(t)$ is the propagation rate of component i passing the fault to component n through component m; $P(v_i, v_m)(t)P(v_m, v_l)(t)P(v_l, v_n)(t)$ is the propagation rate of component i passing the fault to component n through components m and l.

For the three-step-neighboring components of component q,

$$fp^1{}_{ASP\_iq}(t) = \sum_{m\in A(i), n\in A^2(i), q\in A^3(i)} P(v_i, v_m)(t)P(v_m, v_n)(t)P(v_n, v_q)(t), \quad (15)$$

where $A^3(i)$ is the set of all three-step-neighboring components of component i; $P(v_i, v_m)(t)P(v_m, v_n)(t)P(v_n, v_q)(t)$ is the propagation rate of component i passing the fault to component q through components m and n.

2.3. Mechanism for Evaluating Component Importance Based on the Combined Variable Weight

In order to avoid deviations in the evaluation of the importance of a single index, a comprehensive evaluation of the importance of machining center components was carried out from the two perspectives of fault propagation probability and fault propagation risk. In comprehensive evaluations, subjective weighting and objective weighting methods have advantages and disadvantages. Subjective weighting can better reflect the importance of an index itself, while objective weighting mainly reflects information on the laws of index data. Therefore, a combined weighting method is reasonable and effective.

In this study, the Delphi method was used to calculate the subjective weight, and the entropy weighting method was used to solve the objective weight. Both methods are relatively mature, and they will not be described again here. The subjective weight values for the m evaluation indicators were determined as $\omega_s = (\omega_1, \omega_2, \cdots, \omega_u)$, and the objective weight values were determined as $\omega_o = (\omega'_1, \omega'_2, \cdots, \omega'_u)$. It was assumed that the two weighting methods were of the same importance. After passing a consistency test, equal weights were combined to assign weights, and the constant weight coefficient of each index was obtained. The calculation formula is as follows:

$$\omega_c^U = \left(\omega_c^1, \omega_c^2, \cdots, \omega_c^u\right) = \frac{1}{2}(\omega_1 + \omega'_1, \omega_2 + \omega'_2, \cdots, \omega_u + \omega'_u). \quad (16)$$

Although the combined weighting method can be used to effectively evaluate the comprehensive importance of machining center components on both the subjective and objective levels, the weight coefficients obtained with this method cannot change with the change in the component fault propagation index value. When the value of a certain index is high, but the weight proportion is relatively small, the evaluation result still cannot accurately reflect the actual situation. Therefore, a variable weight formula is introduced to modify the combined variable weights in real time.

$$\omega_b^u(fp_{ASP\_i}^u(t)) = \frac{\omega_c^u}{fp_{ASP\_i}^u(t)_j \sum_{j=1}^{u} \left(\omega_c^u / fp_{ASP\_i}^u(t)\right)}, \tag{17}$$

where $\omega_b^u\left(fp_{ASP\_i}^u(t)\right)$ is the variable weighting coefficient of the uth fault propagation index value of component i at time t; ω_c^u is the constant weighting factor of the uth index, and U is the number of indexes.

The formula for calculating the comprehensive importance of machining center components $CI_i(t)$ is as follows:

$$CI_i(t) = \omega_b^1\left(fp_{ASP\_i}^1(t)\right)fp_{ASP\_i}^1(t) + \omega_b^2\left(fp_{ASP\_i}^2(t)\right)fp_{ASP\_i}^2(t). \tag{18}$$

The calculated results are sorted according to their size to determine the importance ranking of each component. Once a component in the top ranking fails, it has a great impact on other components; attention should be paid to this to provide a strong guarantee for the subsequent development of fault tracing and maintenance strategies.

3. Case Application

We took MDH series horizontal machining centers, which are mainly used to process rotary parts, as research objects. According to the working principle and the functional mapping relationships of the structures of such machining centers, they were divided into 11 components, namely, the spindle system (S), tool magazine (M), feed system (J), CNC system (NC), hydraulic system (D), electrical system (V), pneumatic system (G), lubrication system (L), cooling system (W), auxiliary system (K), and workbench (T). A total of 108 on-site fault details from 36 machining centers of this series were collected and analyzed over the course of one year. After a fault analysis, we determined whether each component fault was an independent fault or a related fault. If it was a related fault, the previous component that caused the component fault was determined through fault analysis, and a network diagram expressing the fault propagation relationship among the components of the machining centers was established as shown in Figure 4.

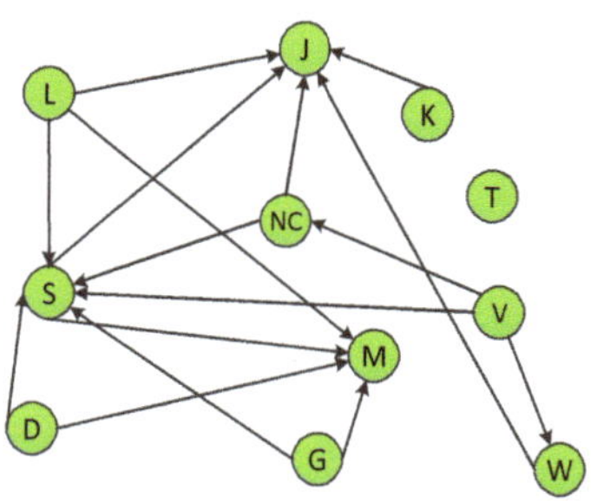

Figure 4. Diagram of the failure propagation network of machining center components. Note: Component T did not have any associations with other components, so subsequent operations did not consider this component.

In order to facilitate quantitative analysis, the failure propagation network diagram of machining center components in Figure 4 is represented by a matrix based on binary logic relationships. Matrix A is an n-order square matrix consisting of 0 and 1 as elements, if the failure of component i directly affects component j, $a_{ij} = 1$, else $a_{ij} = 0$. A corresponding direct correlation matrix was established for the fault correlations of the remaining 10 components:

$$A = \begin{array}{c} \\ S \\ M \\ J \\ NC \\ D \\ V \\ G \\ L \\ W \\ K \end{array} \begin{array}{c} \begin{array}{cccccccccc} S & M & J & NC & D & V & G & L & W & K \end{array} \\ \begin{bmatrix} 0 & 1 & 1 & 0 & 0 & 0 & 0 & 0 & 0 & 0 \\ 0 & 0 & 0 & 0 & 0 & 0 & 0 & 0 & 0 & 0 \\ 0 & 0 & 0 & 0 & 0 & 0 & 0 & 0 & 0 & 0 \\ 1 & 0 & 1 & 0 & 0 & 0 & 0 & 0 & 0 & 0 \\ 1 & 1 & 0 & 0 & 0 & 0 & 0 & 0 & 0 & 0 \\ 1 & 0 & 0 & 1 & 0 & 0 & 0 & 0 & 1 & 0 \\ 1 & 1 & 0 & 0 & 0 & 0 & 0 & 0 & 0 & 0 \\ 1 & 1 & 1 & 0 & 0 & 0 & 0 & 0 & 0 & 0 \\ 0 & 0 & 1 & 0 & 0 & 0 & 0 & 0 & 0 & 0 \\ 0 & 0 & 1 & 0 & 0 & 0 & 0 & 0 & 0 & 0 \end{bmatrix} \end{array}. \quad (19)$$

In order to facilitate path analysis and hierarchical processing, it is necessary to convert matrix A into matrix M. The Warshall algorithm was applied to transform the adjacency matrix A into a reachable matrix M:

$$M = \begin{array}{c} \\ S \\ M \\ J \\ NC \\ D \\ V \\ G \\ L \\ W \\ K \end{array} \begin{array}{c} \begin{array}{cccccccccc} S & M & J & NC & D & V & G & L & W & K \end{array} \\ \begin{bmatrix} 1 & 1 & 1 & 0 & 0 & 0 & 0 & 0 & 0 & 0 \\ 0 & 1 & 0 & 0 & 0 & 0 & 0 & 0 & 0 & 0 \\ 0 & 0 & 1 & 0 & 0 & 0 & 0 & 0 & 0 & 0 \\ 1 & 1 & 1 & 1 & 0 & 0 & 0 & 0 & 0 & 0 \\ 1 & 1 & 1 & 0 & 1 & 0 & 0 & 0 & 0 & 0 \\ 1 & 1 & 1 & 1 & 0 & 1 & 0 & 0 & 1 & 0 \\ 1 & 1 & 1 & 0 & 0 & 0 & 1 & 0 & 0 & 0 \\ 1 & 1 & 1 & 0 & 0 & 0 & 0 & 1 & 0 & 0 \\ 0 & 0 & 1 & 0 & 0 & 0 & 0 & 0 & 1 & 0 \\ 0 & 0 & 1 & 0 & 0 & 0 & 0 & 0 & 0 & 1 \end{bmatrix} \end{array}. \quad (20)$$

According to Formulas (1)–(4), the network topology parameters for each component of the machining center were calculated, as were the weight values of the influence of the network hierarchy, as shown in Tables 1 and 2.

Table 1. Statistics on the edge betweenness of machining center components.

$v(i,j)$	$L(v_i \to v_j)$	$v(i,j)$	$L(v_i \to v_j)$	$v(i,j)$	$L(v_i \to v_j)$	$v(i,j)$	$L(v_i \to v_j)$
S→M	3.5	V→W	0.25	V→S	0.75	D→S	1.5
S→J	3.5	G→S	1.5	V→NC	1.5	D→M	0
NC→S	2.75	G→M	0	W→J	0.25	L→M	0
NC→J	0.25	L→S	1	K→J	0	L→J	0

Table 2. Statistics on the efficiency and network hierarchical weight of components.

Code	I_i	T_i	Code	I_i	T_i
S	0.20	0.220183	V	0.40	0.128440
M	0	0.122324	G	0.20	0.064220
J	0	0.116208	L	0.30	0.091743
NC	0.25	0.100917	W	0.10	0.064220
D	0.20	0.064220	K	0.10	0.027523

The data were brought into Equations (5) and (6) to solve for the contribution matrix and the decision matrix for the influence of fault propagation.

$$H_c = \begin{bmatrix} 0 & 0.208955 & 0.208955 & 0 & 0 & 0 & 0 & 0 & 0 & 0 \\ 0 & 0 & 0 & 0 & 0 & 0 & 0 & 0 & 0 & 0 \\ 0 & 0 & 0 & 0 & 0 & 0 & 0 & 0 & 0 & 0 \\ 0.164179 & 0 & 0.014925 & 0 & 0 & 0 & 0 & 0 & 0 & 0 \\ 0.089552 & 0 & 0 & 0 & 0 & 0 & 0 & 0 & 0 & 0 \\ 0.044776 & 0 & 0 & 0.089552 & 0 & 0 & 0 & 0 & 0.014925 & 0 \\ 0.089552 & 0 & 0 & 0 & 0 & 0 & 0 & 0 & 0 & 0 \\ 0.059701 & 0 & 0 & 0 & 0 & 0 & 0 & 0 & 0 & 0 \\ 0 & 0 & 0.014925 & 0 & 0 & 0 & 0 & 0 & 0 & 0 \\ 0 & 0 & 0 & 0 & 0 & 0 & 0 & 0 & 0 & 0 \end{bmatrix}. \quad (21)$$

$$H_E = \begin{bmatrix} 0.025164 & 0.076057 & 0.076057 & 0 & 0 & 0 & 0 & 0 & 0 & 0 \\ 0 & 0 & 0 & 0 & 0 & 0 & 0 & 0 & 0 & 0 \\ 0 & 0 & 0 & 0 & 0 & 0 & 0 & 0 & 0 & 0 \\ 0.030102 & 0 & 0.015469 & 0.014417 & 0 & 0 & 0 & 0 & 0 & 0 \\ 0.011520 & 0.006459 & 0 & 0 & 0.007339 & 0 & 0 & 0 & 0 & 0 \\ 0.030897 & 0 & 0 & 0.035959 & 0 & 0.029358 & 0 & 0 & 0.027523 & 0 \\ 0.011520 & 0.006459 & 0 & 0 & 0 & 0 & 0.007339 & 0 & 0 & 0 \\ 0.018661 & 0.013841 & 0.013841 & 0 & 0 & 0 & 0 & 0.015727 & 0 & 0 \\ 0 & 0 & 0.004738 & 0 & 0 & 0 & 0 & 0 & 0.003670 & 0 \\ 0 & 0 & 0.001384 & 0 & 0 & 0 & 0 & 0 & 0 & 0.001573 \end{bmatrix}. \quad (22)$$

The model obtained for the degree of influence of fault propagation is shown in Figure 5.

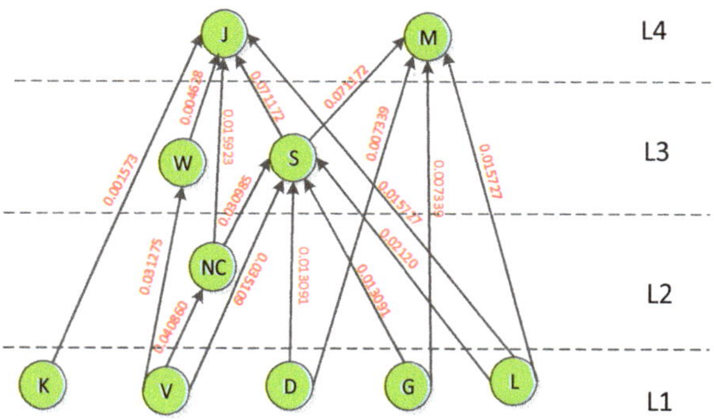

Figure 5. Degree of influence of failure propagation between machining center components.

The collected field failure data of the machining center were statistically analyzed to obtain the frequency diagram of the failure components of the machining centers as shown in Figure 6. The component element code and fault time of the machining centers are shown in Table 3.

Based on the modeling of the failure probability of machining center components shown in Figure 2 and the fault time of machining center components shown in Table 3, the failure probability function was determined for each component of the machining center and the statistical results are shown in Table 4.

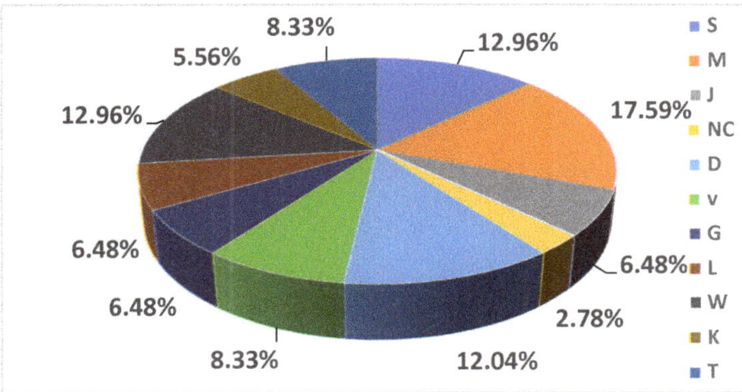

Figure 6. Frequency diagram of failure parts of the machining centers.

Table 3. System component code and failure time statistics table.

Element Code	Fault Time (h)						
D	9.53	19.07	57.21	182.15	200.22	266.96	362.30
	400.44	429.04	896.22	1849.64	2507.51		
S	19.07	28.60	104.88	152.55	209.75	247.89	371.84
	533.92	600.66	610.19	696.00	743.67	781.81	1029.70
M	104.88	143.01	190.68	276.49	343.23	400.44	514.85
	524.38	638.79	657.86	676.93	962.96	1010.63	1239.45
	1411.07	1420.60	2059.40	2269.40	3422.79		
J	123.95	305.10	419.51	448.11	486.25	648.33	686.47
NC	219.29	486.25	1353.87				
V	57.21	85.81	95.34	266.96	362.30	724.60	791.34
	1296.66	1821.04					
G	9.53	128.71	181.15	247.89	419.51	1191.78	1372.93
L	57.21	114.41	705.53	1277.59	1649.42	1792.44	1925.92
W	38.14	104.88	114.41	133.48	162.08	266.96	276.49
	476.71	543.45	791.34	943.89	1058.30		
K	114.41	448.11	505.32	514.85	982.03	1859.18	
T	47.67	57.21	152.55	228.82	247.89	400.44	429.04
	1678.03	2088.00					

Table 4. The fault probability functions of system components in the machining center.

Code	Fault Probability	Code	Fault Probability
S	$F_S(t) = 1 - \exp\left[-\left(\frac{t}{7832.7}\right)^{0.6414}\right]$	V	$F_V(t) = 1 - \exp\left[-\left(\frac{t}{7935.7}\right)^{0.7712}\right]$
M	$F_M(t) = 1 - \exp\left[-\left(\frac{t}{2458.1}\right)^{1.3117}\right]$	G	$F_G(t) = 1 - \exp\left[-\left(\frac{t}{27503.4}\right)^{0.5243}\right]$
J	$F_J(t) = 1 - \exp\left[-\left(\frac{t}{2606.4}\right)^{1.2949}\right]$	L	$F_L(t) = 1 - \exp\left[-\left(\frac{t}{8161.5}\right)^{0.7910}\right]$
NC	$F_{NC}(t) = 1 - \exp\left[-\left(\frac{t}{7912.4}\right)^{0.5422}\right]$	W	$F_W(t) = 1 - \exp\left[-\left(\frac{t}{4145.7}\right)^{0.9101}\right]$
D	$F_D(t) = 1 - \exp\left[-\left(\frac{t}{8905.1}\right)^{0.6556}\right]$	K	$F_K(t) = 1 - \exp\left[-\left(\frac{t}{5960.8}\right)^{0.9314}\right]$

The ANP method was applied to solve the influence of the failure mode of each component, and according to the process of assessing the impacts of the failure modes of machining center components shown in Figure 3. The results are summarized in Table 5.

Table 5. Statistics on the influence of the failure modes of machining center components.

Code	Mode	$\alpha_{ij}(t)$	β_{ij}	Code	Mode	$\alpha_{ij}(t)$	β_{ij}
S	0101	0.142857	0.07288	V	0103	0.777778	0.28312
	0202	0.142857	0.02272		0108	0.111111	0.20851
	0203	0.071429	0.01607		0409	0.111111	0.50837
	0410	0.214286	0.45179	G	0103	0.142857	0.30574
	0503	0.071429	0.10450		0301	0.714286	0.20805
	0603	0.071429	0.03647		0404	0.142857	0.48621
	0605	0.142857	0.03157	L	0101	0.142857	0.41025
	0606	0.071429	0.17020		0103	0.571429	0.35443
	0609	0.071429	0.09381		0301	0.285714	0.23532
M	0101	0.315789	0.23085	W	0101	0.285714	0.21368
	0201	0.052632	0.02538		0103	0.071429	0.27109
	0202	0.105263	0.04964		0301	0.214286	0.08792
	0205	0.105263	0.21235		0302	0.142857	0.06050
	0501	0.052632	0.08795		0601	0.071429	0.14315
	0503	0.157895	0.12623		0610	0.071429	0.18355
	0506	0.052632	0.07042		0805	0.142857	0.04010
	0605	0.105263	0.04268	K	0101	0.500000	0.50000
	0616	0.052632	0.13226		0501	0.500000	0.50000
J	0101	0.285714	0.20472	D	0101	0.153846	0.28747
	0103	0.142857	0.28898		0103	0.153846	0.17769
	0502	0.142857	0.13812		0104	0.076923	0.36466
	0603	0.142857	0.12362		0105	0.076923	0.03580
	0607	0.142857	0.20530		0301	0.461538	0.03171
	0803	0.142857	0.03925		0607	0.076923	0.10267
NC	0102	0.666667	0.50000				
	0501	0.333333	0.50000				

The relationship between the failure probability function and the failure rate function in Formulas (8) and (9) was used to solve the probability of failure and the failure rate of each component of the machining center at any time, and the failure rate value was brought into formula (7) to obtain the failure risk value of each component. In this study, 500 h and 2000 h were used as examples, and the results obtained are shown in Table 6.

Table 6. Statistics on the failure probability and failure risk of machining center components.

Code	$F_i(500)$	$F_i(2000)$	$RI_i(500) \times 10^{-4}$	$RI_i(2000) \times 10^{-4}$
S	0.157533	0.340882	0.031861	0.193801
M	0.160189	0.509823	0.048254	0.743361
J	0.107180	0.563434	0.052543	0.790793
NC	0.174242	0.377515	0.121305	0.643066
D	0.155207	0.298884	0.024791	0.153796
V	0.172201	0.292742	0.054853	0.399435
G	0.115266	0.223705	0.033573	0.173614
L	0.182400	0.312183	0.057049	0.426991
W	0.135228	0.406857	0.036364	0.321034
K	0.147985	0.296352	0.092606	0.842048

By using the improved ASP algorithm, the data in Table 6 were brought into Formulas (12)–(15) to find the value of the fault propagation index of each component, and at the same time, through the solution process of combining the variable weights, the variable weight for each fault propagation index of each component at different moments was obtained. Again, 500 h and 2000 h were used as examples, and the results after normalization are shown in Tables 7 and 8.

Table 7. Statistics of the failure propagation probability and combined variable weight.

Code	$fp^1{}_{ASP\_i}(500)$	$\omega_b^1(fp^1_{ASP\_i}(500))$	$fp^1{}_{ASP\_i}(2000)$	$\omega_b^1(fp^1_{ASP\_i}(2000))$
S	0.342023	0.411216	0.168593	0.375533
M	0	0.520614	0	0.520614
J	0	0.520614	0	0.520614
NC	0.126512	0.703178	0.217187	0.635815
D	0.049059	0.352237	0.026581	0.345499
V	0.284106	0.521667	0.385911	0.586170
G	0.037379	0.491478	0.071993	0.432069
L	0.147825	0.517005	0.110365	0.586613
W	0.009546	0.481495	0.005994	0.454933
K	0.003550	0.683642	0.013376	0.750343

Table 8. Statistics of the failure propagation risk and combined variable weight.

Code	$fp^2{}_{ASP\_i}(500)$	$\omega_b^2(fp^2_{ASP\_i}(500))$	$fp^2{}_{ASP\_i}(2000)$	$\omega_b^2(fp^2_{ASP\_i}(2000))$
S	0.219957	0.588784	0.208086	0.624467
M	0	0.479386	0	0.479386
J	0	0.479386	0	0.479386
NC	0.275976	0.296822	0.227537	0.364185
D	0.024564	0.647763	0.023701	0.654501
V	0.285307	0.478333	0.323120	0.413830
G	0.033266	0.508522	0.026755	0.567931
L	0.145703	0.482995	0.169606	0.413387
W	0.008163	0.518505	0.011208	0.545067
K	0.007064	0.316358	0.009989	0.249657

The results in Tables 7 and 8 were brought into Equation (18) to evaluate the comprehensive importance of each component at 500 h and 200 h and then rank them accordingly. The results are shown in Table 9.

Table 9. Comprehensive importance values and the ranking of machining center components.

Code	CI_i(500)	Rank	CI_i(2000)	Rank
S	0.270152	2	0.271060	2
NC	0.170876	3	0.172858	3
D	0.033192	6	0.032358	5
V	0.284681	1	0.278933	1
G	0.035287	5	0.031696	6
L	0.146800	4	0.146255	4
W	0.008829	7	0.012743	7
K	0.004662	8	0.005202	8
M	0	9	0	9
J	0	10	0	10

The ranking results in Table 4 showed that at 500 h and 2000 h, the electrical system (V) was ranked first in terms of importance, followed by the spindle system (S), which should be taken into account in fault diagnosis and health maintenance.

Since the values of the fault propagation indexes for each component of the machining center dynamically changed at different moments, the fault propagation probability and the fault propagation risk of the system components could be determined at any time by using Formulas (7)–(15). Then, the comprehensive importance values at any time could be determined when different time values were inputted into Formulas (16)–(18). So, the trends of the comprehensive importance of each component are shown in Figure 7.

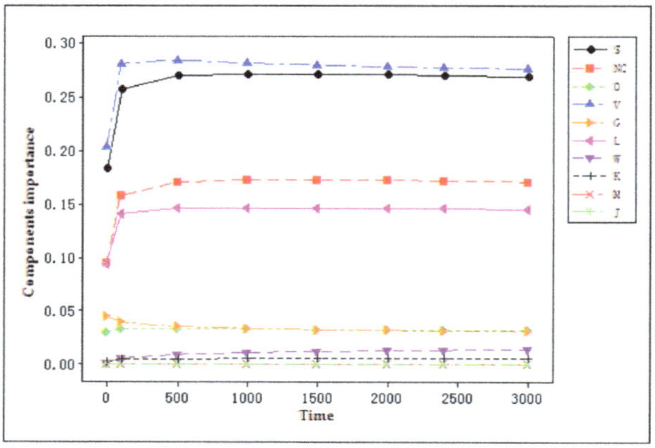

Figure 7. Diagram of the comprehensive importance of machining center components.

4. Comparative Analysis

The method proposed in this study was compared with a method of evaluating the importance of machining center components based on the PageRank algorithm [30]. Referring to the process of calculating the PR value of web nodes with the PageRank algorithm, the system components were regarded as web nodes, and the fault propagation relationships between components were used to replace link relationships between web pages. Unlike in the calculation of web nodes, the degree of influence of component faults was calculated based on the out-degree. According to the above case, based on fault information, MATLAB programming was used to achieve the iterative calculation of the importance of each component of the machining center. The calculation results were compared with the comprehensive importance values at 2000 h, and the statistical values are shown in the following table.

From the ranking results in Table 10, it can be seen that the components with the highest importance values according to the two methods were the electrical system (V) and the spindle system (S), and the ranking results were basically consistent, which verified the correctness and reliability of the method in this study. However, the importance values of the CNC system (NC) and hydraulic system (D) according to the PageRank algorithm were equal, and the values of the cooling system (W) and auxiliary system (K) were also equal, so the differences in the importance of the components were not reflected well. The calculation results verified that the method proposed in this study was more effective than the PageRank method in distinguishing the differences in the importance of each component.

Table 10. Comparison of the importance values of machining center components.

Code	CI_i	Rank	Pr_i	Rank
S	0.229485	2	0.105196	2
M	0	9	0.091134	9
J	0	10	0.091134	10
NC	0.163382	3	0.097193	4
D	0.045910	6	0.097193	5
V	0.423358	1	0.129771	1
G	0.079020	5	0.097193	6
L	0.122867	4	0.103252	3
W	0.009634	8	0.093847	8
K	0.012700	7	0.093847	7

In this study, the comprehensive importance values obtained with the proposed method were compared with the importance evaluation results obtained with a single index. Taking the results calculated for 500 h as an example, Figure 8 was drawn.

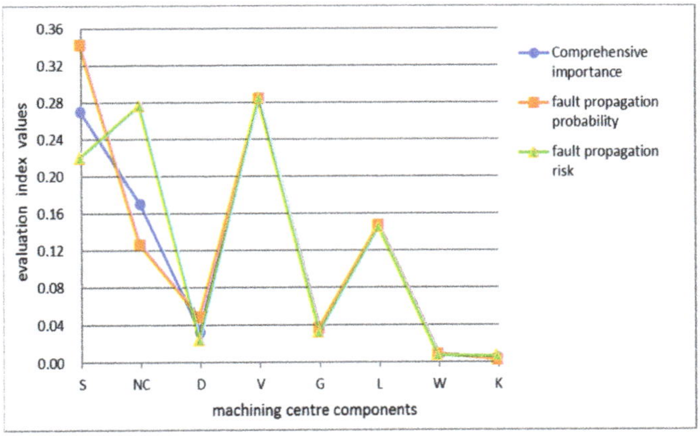

Figure 8. Comparison of the evaluation indicator values of machining center components.

The graph shows that the component with the highest fault propagation probability at 500 h was the spindle system (S), and the spindle system (S) was considered to be the most important component in the importance evaluation using the fault propagation probability. In the graph, we can also see that the component with the highest fault propagation risk was the electrical system (V) at 500 h, and the electrical system (V) was considered to be the most important component in the importance evaluation using the fault propagation risk. The results of evaluating the importance with a single indicator were highly biased. Therefore, the method in this study effectively avoided the one-sidedness and bias of evaluating node importance from a single perspective, and it improved the accuracy of the importance evaluation.

5. Conclusions

In this study, a method of comprehensively assessing importance was proposed, and the main results and conclusions were as follows:

(1) A model of the degree of influence of fault propagation was constructed. The calculation results showed that the spindle system had the greatest fault propagation influence on the tool magazine and feed system components, followed by that of the electrical system on the CNC system, thus clarifying the position of each component in the propagation structure and the influences on other components. The topological structure-based fault propagation impact model of the machining center laid the structural foundation for a comprehensive evaluation of importance.

(2) A comprehensive importance evaluation method was established. The comprehensive importance value of the machining center at 2000 h was obtained, and the ranking result was V > S > NC > L > G > D > K > W > M = J. The component with the highest comprehensive importance was the electrical system, followed by the spindle system, and the two components with the lowest importance were the tool magazine and feed system. The tool magazine and feed system were at the end of the propagation in the fault propagation structure model and did not propagate faults to other components; hence, they had the least importance. The evaluation results for the importance are significant for the identification and maintenance of critical components.

(3) A solution method for combined variable weights was established. The weight value of the first evaluation index of the spindle system at 500 h was 0.411216, the weight value of the first evaluation index of the CNC system was 0.703178, and the weight

value of the spindle system at 2000 h was 0.375533. Through calculation, it was found that the weight values of the importance indexes of different components in different machining centers changed at different times. This effectively solved the problem of a constant weight coefficient not accurately reflecting the variations in index values, and this is conducive to accurately evaluating the importance of each index at different times.

This study presented a comprehensive method of evaluating the importance of components of a machining center, and this can be used to identify the key components of a center at any time. On this basis, fault warning and preventive maintenance can be conducted in a targeted manner, thereby reducing the economic losses and safety hazards of manufacturing enterprises due to equipment faults. However, there are some shortcomings of this study that need to be improved. For example, the mathematical model for evaluating the importance of machining center components was established only from the point of view of fault propagation, without considering other reliability factors of the components themselves, causing certain limitations. Future studies will involve importance evaluations from multiple angles and with multiple indicators, as well as the establishment of a more comprehensive importance evaluation mechanism.

Author Contributions: Conceptualization, L.L. and Y.Z.; methodology, L.L.; software, G.S.; validation, L.L. and G.S.; formal analysis, Y.Z.; investigation, L.L. and G.S.; resources, G.S.; data curation, Y.Z.; writing—original draft preparation, L.L.; writing—review and editing, L.L.; visualization, G.S.; supervision, Y.Z.; project administration, G.S.; funding acquisition, Y.Z. All authors have read and agreed to the published version of the manuscript.

Funding: This research was funded by the Jilin Province Science and Technology Development Plan Project (Grant No. 20190302104GX).

Institutional Review Board Statement: Not applicable.

Informed Consent Statement: Not applicable.

Data Availability Statement: The dataset can be provided upon request.

Conflicts of Interest: The authors declare no conflicts of interest.

References

1. Chen, Y.; Zhang, G.; Ran, Y. Risk Analysis of Coupling Fault Propagation Based on Meta-Action for Computerized Numerical Control (CNC) Machine Tool. *Complexity* **2019**, *2019*, 3237254. [CrossRef]
2. Dey, P.; Mehra, R.; Kazi, F.; Wagh, S.; Singh, N.M. Impact of Topology on the Propagation of Cascading Failure in Power Grid. *IEEE Trans. Smart Grid* **2016**, *7*, 1970–1978. [CrossRef]
3. Mu, L.; Zhang, Y.; Guo, G. A Comprehensive Failure Risk Assessment Method of Machining Center Component Based on Topology Analysis. *Appl. Sci.* **2022**, *12*, 423. [CrossRef]
4. Yang, X.; Ran, Y.; Zhang, G.; Wang, H.; Mu, Z.; Zhi, S. A digital twin-driven hybrid approach for the prediction of performance degradation in transmission unit of CNC machine tool. *Robot. Comput. Manuf.* **2022**, *73*, 102230. [CrossRef]
5. Huang, W.; Li, H.; Yin, Y.; Zhang, Z.; Xie, A.; Zhang, Y.; Cheng, G. Node importance identification of unweighted urban rail transit network: An Adjacency Information Entropy based approach. *Reliab. Eng. Syst. Saf.* **2024**, *242*, 109766. [CrossRef]
6. Zhang, Y.; Mu, L.; Liu, J.; Liu, J.; Tian, Z.; Zhang, Y. Application of fault propagation intensity in fault diagnosis of CNC machine tool. *J. Chin. Inst. Eng.* **2020**, *43*, 153–161. [CrossRef]
7. Wandelt, S.; Xu, Y.; Sun, X. Measuring node importance in air transportation systems: On the quality of complex network estimations. *Reliab. Eng. Syst. Saf.* **2023**, *240*, 109596. [CrossRef]
8. Zhu, J.; Dai, F.; Zhao, F.; Guo, W. Integrating Node Importance and Network Topological Properties for Link Prediction in Complex Network. *Symmetry* **2023**, *15*, 1492. [CrossRef]
9. Chen, T.; Ma, J.; Zhu, Z.; Guo, X. Evaluation Method for Node Importance of Urban Rail Network Considering Traffic Characteristics. *Sustainability* **2023**, *15*, 3582. [CrossRef]
10. Dong, K.; Li, D. Identification of Network Topology Changes Based on r-Power Adjacency Matrix Entropy. *J. Stat. Phys.* **2023**, *190*, 186. [CrossRef]
11. Bonacich, P. Factoring and weighting approaches to status scores and clique identification. *J. Math. Sociol.* **1972**, *2*, 113–120. [CrossRef]

12. Chen, D.-B.; Gao, H.; Lü, L.; Zhou, T. Identifying Influential Nodes in Large-Scale Directed Networks: The Role of Clustering. *PLoS ONE* **2013**, *8*, e77455. [CrossRef]
13. Martin, T.; Zhang, X.; Newman, M.E.J. Localization and centrality in networks. *Phys. Rev. E* **2014**, *90*, 052808. [CrossRef]
14. Wang, Q.; Xie, Z.; Gao, Y. Flexible Networked Machine Integrated Scheduling Algorithm Based on the Dynamic Root Node Operation Set Considering Reverse Scheduling. *Electronics* **2023**, *12*, 526. [CrossRef]
15. Berberler, Z.N.; Yildirim, H.İ.; İltüzer, T.; Tunç, İ. Agglomeration-based node importance analysis in wheel-type networks. *Int. J. Found. Comput. Sci.* **2021**, *32*, 269–288. [CrossRef]
16. Obeidat, A.; Al-Shalabi, M. An Efficient Approach towards Network Routing using Genetic Algorithm. *Int. J. Comput. Commun. Control.* **2022**, *17*, 4815. [CrossRef]
17. Choi, W.-Y. Efficient Node Insertion Algorithm for Connectivity-Based Multipolling MAC Protocol in Wi-Fi Sensor Networks. *Appl. Sci.* **2023**, *13*, 11974. [CrossRef]
18. Tungom, C.E.; Niu, B.; Wang, H. Hierarchical framework for demand prediction and iterative optimization of EV charging network infrastructure under uncertainty with cost and quality-of-service consideration. *Expert Syst. Appl.* **2024**, *237*, 121761. [CrossRef]
19. Liu, C.; Wang, J.; Xia, R. Node importance evaluation in multi-platform avionics architecture based on TOPSIS and PageRank. *EURASIP J. Adv. Signal Process.* **2023**, *2023*, 27. [CrossRef]
20. Lv, L.; Zhang, T.; Hu, P.; Bardou, D.; Niu, S.; Zheng, Z.; Yu, G.; Wu, H. An improved gravity centrality for finding important nodes in multi-layer networks based on multi-PageRank. *Expert Syst. Appl.* **2024**, *238*, 122171. [CrossRef]
21. Jiang, S.; Zhang, X.; Cao, Z. An Improved LeaderRank Algorithm for Identifying Critical Components in Service-Oriented Systems. *J. Phys. Conf. Ser.* **2019**, *1213*, 032012. [CrossRef]
22. Vinodha, R.; Parvathi, R. Content and location based point-of-interest recommendation system using HITS algorithm. *Int. J. Uncertain. Fuzziness Knowl.-Based Syst.* **2023**, *31* (Suppl. S1), 31–45. [CrossRef]
23. Mu, L.; Zhang, Y.; Liu, J.; Zhai, F.; Song, J. Dynamic Analysis Method for Fault Propagation Behaviour of Machining Centres. *Appl. Sci.* **2021**, *11*, 6525. [CrossRef]
24. Zhu, S.; Zhao, X.; Li, N.; Zhou, J.; Lu, J.-A. Identifying partial topology of complex dynamical networks with distributed delay. *Commun. Nonlinear Sci. Numer. Simul.* **2023**, *126*, 107504. [CrossRef]
25. Wankhade, N.; Kundu, G.K. Interpretive Structural Modelling (ISM) Methodology and its application in Supply Chain Research. *Int. J. Innov. Technol. Explor. Eng.* **2020**, *9*, 1101–1109. [CrossRef]
26. Lin, S.; Li, S.; Su, Y. Node Importance Recognition Algorithm Based on the Correlation Degree Transmission Contribution Matrix. *J. Phys. Conf. Ser.* **2023**, *2419*, 012107. [CrossRef]
27. Zhang, Y.; Mu, L.; Shen, G.; Yu, Y.; Han, C. Fault diagnosis strategy of CNC machine tools based on cascading failure. *J. Intell. Manuf.* **2017**, *30*, 2193–2202. [CrossRef]
28. Ergin, A.; Alkan, G. The Selection of Ocean Container Carrier: An Analytic Network Process (ANP) Approach. *J. ETA Marit. Sci.* **2023**, *11*, 159–167. [CrossRef]
29. Luan, L.; Shen, G.; Zhang, Y.; Guo, G. Identification of Key Components of CNC Lathe Based on Dynamic Influence of Fault Propagation. *Appl. Sci.* **2022**, *12*, 6187. [CrossRef]
30. Zhang, Y.-Z.; Liu, J.-T.; Shen, G.-X.; Long, Z.; Sun, S.-G. Reliability Evaluation of Machine Center Components Based on Cascading Failure Analysis. *Chin. J. Mech. Eng.* **2017**, *30*, 933–942. [CrossRef]

mathematics

MDPI

Article

An Analysis of Power Friction Losses in Gear Engagement with Intermediate Rolling Elements and a Free Cage

Egor A. Efremenkov [1], Nikita V. Martyushev [2,*], Svetlana K. Efremenkova [1] and Egor S. Chavrov [1]

[1] Department of Mechanical Engineering, Tomsk Polytechnic University, 634050 Tomsk, Russia; egorefr@tpu.ru (E.A.E.)
[2] Department of Materials Science, Tomsk Polytechnic University, 634050 Tomsk, Russia
* Correspondence: martjushev@tpu.ru

Abstract: Currently, mechanical gears with cycloid engagement are increasingly used in mechanisms along with involute ones. In modern drive mechanisms, using pin gears and gears with intermediate rolling elements (IRE) is widespread, which simultaneously use cycloid gears. To a greater extent, pin gears are now being investigated, but IRE gears have their undeniable advantages. Many works are devoted to the study of cycloid toothing for certain gears, but the efficiency, especially that of IRE gears, has practically not been investigated. Therefore, the analysis of power losses in the engagement of a gear with IRE and a free cage (IREFC) is relevant. In this analysis, the authors of the work have used laws of mechanics, methods of energy flows and a secant normal. Mathematical expressions have been obtained to estimate slip speeds and power friction losses in the engagement of a gear with IREFC, and a formula has been derived to determine the efficiency of a mentioned mechanical transmission. The calculation of slip speeds and power losses at the points of contact of a rolling element with cycloid profiles of wheels for selected initial parameters of a gear with IREFC has been presented. The friction power and the overall efficiency of the entire gear engagement have also been calculated. This work shows that power friction losses at the points of contact of a rolling element with cycloid profiles of tooth wheels of a gear with IREFC are not the same. The friction power in the contact of a rolling element with a cycloid profile of a cam is an order of magnitude higher than the friction power in the contact of a rolling element with a cycloid profile of a crown.

Keywords: friction power; efficiency; cycloid gears; rolling elements; free cage; cycloid engagement; sliding speed; cycloid profile; cycloid wheel; rolling friction; sliding friction

MSC: 65C20

1. Introduction

Mechanical transmissions with cycloid toothing are widely used when designing modern devices and mechanisms. This is explained by the increased resistance of such mechanisms to high loads due to the perception of only contact loads by links in the gearing [1]. Cycloid gears with intermediate rolling elements (IRE) have a set of high technical characteristics; however, the issue of power loss in a cycloid gear with intermediate rolling elements remains insufficiently studied.

Many works are devoted to the study of the engagement of cycloid gears [2–8]. But pin gears, in which there are no intermediate rolling elements, are mainly studied [9–18]. In [9], the efficiency coefficient in the engagement of a pin gear with pins without bushings and with bushings was investigated. It showed that using pins with bushings makes the transmission work smoother, and friction losses decrease. In another work [10], authors developed a nonlinear dynamic model of a needle bearing, taking into account the friction among a cycloid wheel, a needle roller and a bearing cage in a pin gear. The study [11] presented a method for diagnosing damage to a cycloid tooth wheel of pin toothing on a laboratory bench based on a frequency analysis of vibration signals. In [12], the distribution of forces in pin toothing was considered, taking into account the finger deflections of a pin wheel; an improved model of the load distribution of an uncoordinated kinematic cycloid–finger pair was proposed. In works [13,14], the authors considered the operation of a pin cycloid reducer and the influence of various factors on it. The authors of [15] investigated the impact of a gap in the engagement of a cycloid gearing on the distribution of forces, taking into account errors in the assembly, the manufacturing and the modification of a cycloid profile. In another paper [16], the authors proposed a semi-analytical model of the load distribution based on a three-dimensional elastic solution that considers the longitudinal configuration of a cycloid tooth. The model takes into account the contact deformation of a cycloid tooth, and loads are calculated in compliance with the conditions of compatibility and equilibrium. The authors in [17] proposed a new method for modifying the profile of a tooth of a pin gear, based on considering the complex effect of the distribution of the pressure angle, the gap in the engagement and the gap between a tip and a leg of a cycloid tooth. In [18], a new model of cycloid contact in an engagement with several rows of teeth was proposed. This model allows for the studying of the influence of the load on various methods of modifying cycloid teeth, including the accuracy of the pin gear, mechanical characteristics and its efficiency.

When studying cycloid gears with IRE, attention was mainly paid to research of engagement forces and stresses arising in the contact of a cycloid tooth profile with rolling elements [19,20]. The most promising gears with IREB are those with intermediate rolling elements and a free cage (IREFC), and the engagement of this gear was studied mainly to change the accuracy of the profile and the distribution of forces and contact stresses [3,4,21]. Gears with IRE, in general, and a gear with IREFC, in particular, can be used in different mechanisms of shut-off and adjusting fittings, in driving units of transport systems, in rotary drives and in drives of various installations, where it is necessary to use compact mechanisms capable of withstanding significant loads. Such mechanisms can work in an intermittent mode and in an average continuous operating mode. Mechanisms that are based on gears with IRE can operate both indoors and outdoors in various weather conditions. However, despite extensive studies of gears with IRE, the investigation of the friction in an engagement has not been given sufficient attention. Therefore, the analysis of power friction losses in the engagement of gears with IRE is relevant. Power losses in engagement and efficiency can be considered taking into account various factors: materials of contacting links, lubricants, etc. But in this paper, we will consider only the efficiency of the engagement of a gear with IREFC. Therefore, the purpose of this work is to determine the friction losses of engaging the links made of steel, without taking into account losses in lubrication and rolling bearings, on which the links of a gear with IREFC are installed.

Let us consider a gear with IREFC (Figure 1), which consists of an input shaft 1 with an eccentric disc 2 located on it, a tooth wheel 3 with a cycloid profile, which is mounted on the eccentric disc 2 through a rolling bearing 4, a chain of intermediate rolling elements 5 located in a cage 6 and a wheel 7 with internal cycloid teeth fixed motionlessly in a gear housing.

The motion in a gear with IREFC (Figure 1) is transmitted from the input shaft 1 through the eccentric 2 to the chain of rolling elements 5, which, rolling along the cycloid profile of the tooth wheel 7, transmit motion to the tooth wheel 3. Hence, rolling elements are engaged with cycloid profiles of two tooth wheels. Therefore, a gear with IREFC has two contact points of the engagement of rolling elements with tooth wheels, and this is a peculiarity of this gear, which should be taken into account when determining gear efficiency.

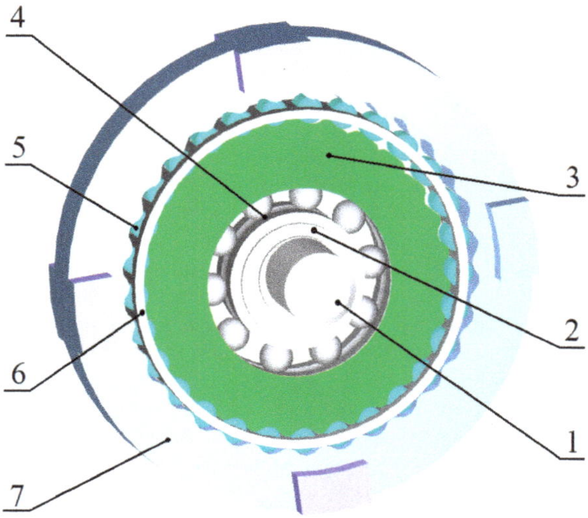

Figure 1. Scheme of a gear with intermediate rolling elements and a free cage: 1—input shaft; 2—eccentric disc; 3—cycloidal wheel-cam; 4—rolling bearing; 5—intermediate rolling elements; 6—cage; 7—cycloidal wheel-crown.

2. Determination of Efficiency and Friction Power at Points of Contact of Rolling Element with Cycloid Profiles of Wheels

Let us determine the efficiency of a gear with IREFC by analogy with rolling bearings. This is justified because, as in the case of rolling bearings, intermediate elements are located between two profiles. The only difference is that bearing rings have straight roller paths (if we consider a reamer) and cycloid wheels have a wavy roller path (in a reamer). But when considering a single rolling element in an enlarged way, the comparison is fair (Figure 2). In general, equations of cycloid profiles for a gear with IREFC are derived in [3].

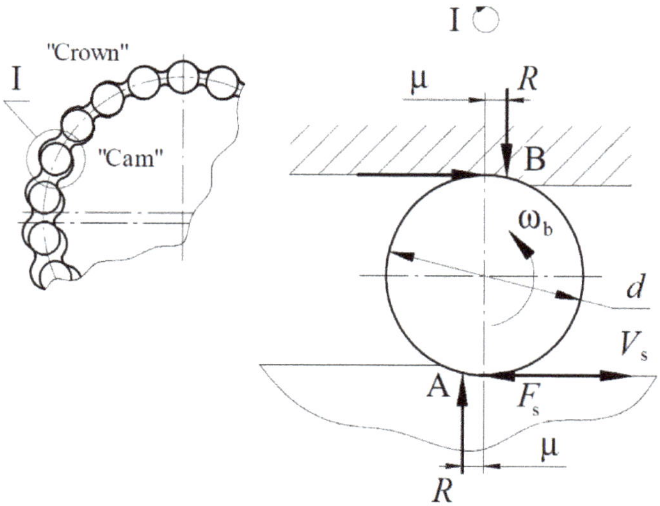

Figure 2. Forces and speeds at the points of contact of a rolling element with a profile of wheels.

Using a method of "energy flows" [22,23], let us consider the engagement of rolling elements with cycloid profiles in a gear with IREFC. The essence of the method is reduced to an analytical representation of efficiency in the form of a power ratio: the power of useful resistances N_{out} to the power of driving forces N_{in}:

$$\eta = \frac{N_{out}}{N_{in}} \tag{1}$$

In the case of a gear with IREFC, the power of useful resistances is N_{out}, which is the power on the tooth wheel 3 (Figure 1), since it is connected to the output shaft of the mechanism. And the power of driving forces N_{in} is the power at the input shaft of the gear supplied to the eccentric disc 2 (Figure 1). The power of useful resistances, i.e., the power spent on performing useful work, is the product of the torque at the output link of the gear (or the output shaft of the mechanism) and the angular velocity of this link. However, it can be presented in a different way. So, the power of useful resistances can be represented as the difference in powers of driving forces N_{in} and friction forces N_{s} arising in the engagement of rolling elements (Figure 2) with two cycloid profiles of gears 3 and 7 (Figure 1).

Then, taking into account the above, Expression (1) will take the following form:

$$\eta = \frac{N_{in} - N_s}{N_{in}} = 1 - \frac{N_s}{N_{in}} \tag{2}$$

The points of contact in the engagement of a gear with IREFC can be schematically represented (Figure 2) similarly to ball guides [23] of a translational or rotational motion. Taking advantage of the similarity of the engagement with a rolling support, the friction power can be represented as the sum of friction powers at the points of contact of rolling elements with cycloid profiles of wheels (Figure 2):

$$N_{\mathrm{s}} = N_{\mathrm{SA}} + N_{\mathrm{SB}} \tag{3}$$

Figure 2 shows that the rolling element is in contact with the cycloid profile of the cam at point A and with the cycloid profile of the crown at point B. According to the principle of operation of a gear with IREFC, a rolling element is rolled along a cycloid profile of a crown without sliding, i.e., only rolling friction is present at point B. When interacting with a cycloid cam profile, a rolling element rolls and slips along this profile; therefore, rolling friction and sliding friction are present at point A. When composing Formula (3), it is necessary to consider the friction power N_{SB} at point B as a single-component power that depends only on rolling friction. At the same time, the friction power N_{SA} should be considered as complex, depending on the rolling friction N_{rf} and the sliding friction N_{sf} of a rolling element along a cycloid cam profile. Therefore, the friction power at point A can be defined as follows:

$$N_{\mathrm{SA}} = N_{rf} + N_{sf}$$

The rolling friction at point A is determined from an expression:

$$N_{rf} = R\mu \cdot \omega_b$$

where

R—the engagement force of a rolling element and a cam, which is also a normal force to contacting surfaces;
μ—the coefficient of the rolling friction;
ω_{b}—the rolling element rotation rate.

The engagement force R is determined by Hooke's law, based on the proportional dependence of force and deformation [3,4].

And the sliding friction at point A is defined as:

$$N_{sf} = F_s \cdot V_s = Rf_s \cdot V_s$$

where

F_s—the friction force in contact with a rolling element and a cycloid cam profile;
F_s—the coefficient of the sliding friction;
V_s—the sliding speed of a rolling element along a cam profile.

Then, the friction power at point A is calculated using the following formula:

$$N_{SA} = R(\mu \cdot \omega_b + f_s \cdot V_s) \tag{4}$$

The friction power at point B, as already mentioned, depends only on rolling friction forces and is determined by a formula:

$$N_{SB} = R\mu\omega_b \tag{5}$$

Engagement forces are determined based on the Hertz theory, assuming a linear relationship between a force and a deformation. A detailed definition of these efforts was described earlier in [3]. Let us choose friction coefficients based on the fact that steel links of high hardness are involved in contact. Supposing this, the coefficient of rolling friction can be assumed to be μ = 0.001 m, and the coefficient of sliding friction is f_s = 0.1 [23]. Speed parameters of a gear with IREFC will be determined based on the geometry of its engagement.

3. The Determination of the Slip Speed in an Engagement

To determine the slip speed in the engagement of a gear with IREFC, let us consider contact points of an arbitrary rolling element with cycloid profiles of wheels (Figure 3). As is known [3], these contact points are located on a general normal to profiles passing through a pitch point of a gear with IREFC. Figure 3 presents an arbitrary rolling element on a circumference of centers r_c. Points of contact with cam A and crown B are indicated on a rolling element. Also in Figure 3, P indicates the pitch point of a gear with IREFC; V^{12} is the speed at a point of contact of a rolling element with a cam profile; V^{32} is the speed of a rolling element with a crown profile.

The slip speed is determined using the secant normal method [24]. Since velocities V^{12} and V^{32} are applied to a rolling element (Figure 3), the slip speed is determined by adding a vector of these speeds:

$$\overline{V_S} = \overline{V}^{12} + \overline{V}^{32} \tag{6}$$

The speeds at points of contact of a rolling element with profiles are analytically determined relative to pitch point P, using a quadratic dependence of the distance from the pitch to contact points on the angle of a rolling element position φ_2. The distance from the pitch point P to the center of the rolling element (Figure 3), expressed through initial parameters of a gear with IREFC, has the form [3]:

$$O'P = L = r_2\sqrt{\chi + 1 - 2\chi\cos\varphi_2} \tag{7}$$

The initial parameters of a gear with IREFC are as follows [3]: the radius of the generating circle r_2, the displacement coefficient χ, the number of rolling elements Z_2 and the radius of the rolling element r_b.

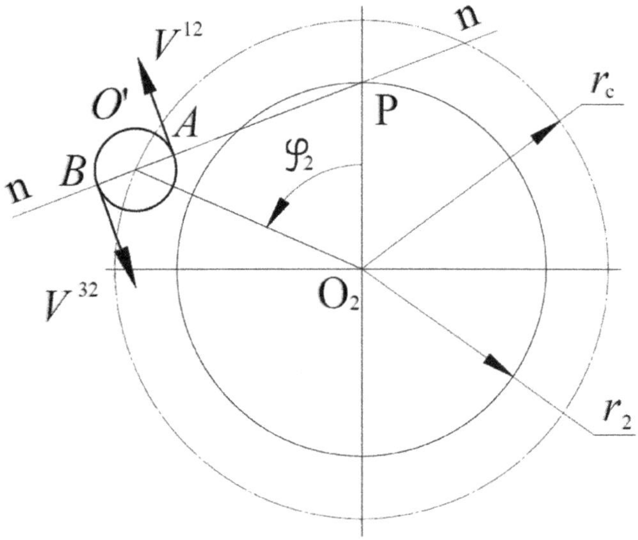

Figure 3. Calculation scheme for determining the slip speed in the engagement of a gear.

Then, the distance from the pitch point P to points of contact A and B (Figure 3), respectively, is equal to:

$$L_A = L - r_b; L_B = L + r_b \tag{8}$$

Cam–cage and cage–crown gear ratios are determined by the following ratios:

$$i_{12} = \frac{\omega_c}{\omega_2}; i_{23} = \frac{\omega_2}{\omega_{cr}} \tag{9}$$

where

ω_c—the angular velocity of the cam;
ω_2—the angular velocity of the cage;
ω_{cr}—the angular velocity of the crown.

Then, the linear velocities at the points of contact of the rolling element with profiles of cycloid wheels through the angular velocity of the cage are expressed, taking into account Formulas (8) and (9), respectively:

$$V^{12} = \omega_2(L - r_b)(i_{12} - 1)V^{23} = \omega_2(L + r_b)(i_{32} - 1) \tag{10}$$

Considering the differential dependence of the velocity on a path and the difference in a traveled path by the point of a rolling element in contact with cycloid profiles of a cam and a crown, we can determine an analytical expression for a slip speed. To do this, let us substitute Expression (10) for linear velocities at contact points into Formula (6) and obtain an analytical expression of the slip speed through gear ratios of contacting links and the angular velocity of a cage:

$$V_s = \omega_c\left[L_A\left(1 - \frac{1}{i_{12}}\right) + L_B\left(\frac{i_{32} - 1}{i_{12}}\right)\right] \tag{11}$$

Replacing angular velocities in Expression (9) with radii of corresponding circles, we will rewrite formulas of gear ratios between links as follows:

$$i_{12} = \frac{r_2}{r_c}$$

$$i_{32} = \frac{r_2}{r_{cr}}$$

In turn, the radii of the generating circles of gears have the following dependence on the initial parameters of a gear with IREFC:

$$r_c = r_2\left(1 - \frac{1}{Z_2}\right)$$

$$r_{cr} = r_2\left(1 + \frac{1}{Z_2}\right)$$

Taking into account the proportional dependence of the radii of the generating circles of links, let us substitute expressions for gear ratios in the following dependence (11):

$$V_s = \omega_c\left[L_A \cdot \frac{1}{Z_2} + L_B\left(\frac{1}{\left(1 + \frac{1}{Z_2}\right)} - 1\right) \cdot \left(1 - \frac{1}{Z_2}\right)\right]$$

and after transformations, we will obtain an analytical expression of the slip speed through the number of intermediate rolling elements and the angular velocity of a cam:

$$V_s = \omega_c\left[\frac{L_A}{Z_2} + \frac{L_B(1 - Z_2)}{Z_2^2 + Z_2}\right] \tag{12}$$

It follows from Formula (12) that the sliding velocity V_S of a rolling element along a cam profile is obtained with a negative sign. This indicates that the angular velocity of a cam rotation is directed in the opposite direction of the sliding velocity of a rolling element.

In Expression (12), the angular velocity of a cam is expressed through the angular velocity of an input shaft (Figure 1):

$$\omega_c = \omega_1 \frac{2}{Z_2 - 1} \tag{13}$$

where ω_1—the angular velocity of the input link (input shaft).

Let us substitute (13) into Equation (12) and obtain an expression of the slip speed in the engagement of a gear with IREFC through the number of teeth and the angular velocity of an input link:

$$V_s = L_A\omega_1\frac{2}{Z_2(Z_2 - 1)} - L_B\omega_1\frac{2}{Z_2(Z_2 + 1)}$$

After the conversion, we will obtain:

$$V_s = \frac{2\omega_1}{Z_2}\left[\frac{L_A}{Z_2 - 1} - \frac{L_B}{Z_2 + 1}\right] \tag{14}$$

The angular velocity of the input link ω_1, as a rule, is equal to the angular velocity of a motor shaft, to which a gear is attached.

4. The Determination of the Total Efficiency in the Engagement of a Gear

After determining the slip speed (14) of a rolling element by a cam profile, it is possible to proceed to derive an analytical expression for friction powers at contact points and to obtain the full efficiency of engaging a gear with IREFC.

Determining the friction power at the points of contact of a rolling element with cycloid profiles of wheels requires determining only the angular velocity of the rolling element ω_b. The angular velocity of the rolling element can be found through the proportional dependence of the radius (r_b) and the linear velocity (V^{23}) at a point of contact with a crown profile:

$$\omega_b = \frac{V^{23}}{r_b} \tag{15}$$

The linear velocity of the rolling element (10) at a point of contact with a cycloid profile of a crown, expressed through the angular velocity (13) of an input link, is analytically determined as:

$$V^{23} = L_B\omega_1 \cdot \frac{2}{Z_2(Z_2+1)} \tag{16}$$

where

Z_2—the number of rolling elements of a gear;
L_B—the distance from the pitch point to the point of contact of a rolling element with a crown profile.

The distance from the pitch point L_B, expressed taking into account (7) and (8), is the following:

$$L_B = r_b + r_2\sqrt{\chi + 1 - 2\chi\cos\varphi_2}$$

Let the angular velocity of a rolling element be expressed with initial parameters and the angular velocity of the input link of a gear with IREFC. For this purpose, Expression (15) of the angular velocity of the rolling element, taking into account (16) and without the consideration of the sign of the relative movement of the links, will be written as follows:

$$\omega_b = L_B \cdot \omega_1 \cdot \frac{2}{r_b Z_2(Z_2+1)} \tag{17}$$

Then, analytical Expression (4) of the friction power at point A, considering (14) and (17), will take the form of:

$$N_{SA} = R\left(\mu L_B \omega_1 \frac{2}{r_b Z_2(Z_2+1)} + f_s \cdot \frac{2\omega_1}{Z_2}\left[\frac{L_A}{Z_2-1} - \frac{L_B}{Z_2+1}\right]\right)$$

and after the conversion, we will finally write an equation for calculating the friction power at point A:

$$N_{SA} = \frac{2R\omega_1}{Z_2}\left(\frac{L_B}{Z_2+1}\left(\frac{\mu}{r_b} - f_s\right) + \frac{f_s L_A}{Z_2-1}\right) \tag{18}$$

Taking into account (13), Expression (5) can be rewritten as:

$$N_{SB} = R\mu \cdot \frac{2L_B \cdot \omega_1}{r_b Z_2(Z_2+1)} \tag{19}$$

Therefore, considering (18) and (19), after the conversion, Expression (3) will have the following view:

$$N_m = \frac{2R\omega_1}{Z_2}\left[\frac{L_B}{Z_2+1}\left(\frac{2\mu}{r_b} - f_s\right) + \frac{f_s L_A}{Z_2-1}\right] \tag{20}$$

In Equation (20), the friction power is expressed through the angular velocity of the input link and represents the quadratic dependence on the number of rolling elements. Then, to determine the efficiency of a gear with IREFC, it is necessary to specify the power of its driving forces. The power of the driving forces is defined as the product of the driving torque (M_{in}), which is the torque on an electric motor shaft, by the angular velocity of the input shaft of an electric motor (the input link of a gear with IREFC), while the angular velocity of the input link will decrease. Then, Expression (2), which determines the efficiency of the gear in question, can be written as an analytical expression:

$$\eta = 1 - \frac{2R}{M_{in} Z_2}\left[\frac{L_B}{Z_2+1}\left(\frac{2\mu}{r_b} - f_s\right) + \frac{f_s L_A}{Z_2-1}\right] \tag{21}$$

The obtained dependence (21) allows for estimating the efficiency of a gear with IREFC in contact with a rolling element with profiles of cycloid wheels. But one must understand that half of the rolling elements are involved in the engagement and transmission of power. In this regard, in order to completely determine the friction losses in the engagement of a gear with IREFC, it is necessary to calculate these losses on each rolling element transmitting power in the engagement:

$$N_{m_i} = \frac{2R_i\omega_1}{Z_2}\left[\frac{L_{B_i}}{Z_2+1}\left(\frac{2\mu}{r_b} - f_s\right) + \frac{f_s L_{A_i}}{Z_2-1}\right] \tag{22}$$

In this case, i covers the values from 1 to $Z_2/2$ in increments of 1, which corresponds to the number of the rolling element, when numbering from a rolling element, located in a depression, to a rolling element, located on a protrusion of a cycloid profile. In view of this, an algebraic sum of expressions will yield the total power of friction losses in the engagement of a gear with IREFC.

And to determine the efficiency of the complete engagement of a gear with IREFC, it is necessary to obtain an algebraic product of the efficiency on each rolling element transmitting power in the engagement of a gear:

$$\eta = \prod_{1}^{Z_2/2}\left(1 - \frac{2R_i}{\mathrm{M_{in}}Z_2}\left[\frac{L_{B_i}}{Z_2+1}\left(\frac{2\mu}{r_b} - f_s\right) + \frac{f_s L_{A_i}}{Z_2-1}\right]\right) \tag{23}$$

The resulting Expression (23) allows for the determining of the efficiency of a gear with IREFC depending on its initial parameters.

5. An Analysis of the Change in the Friction Power on Loaded Rolling Elements of a Gear

Let us consider a gear with IREFC, which has the following initial parameters:

- r_2 = 20 mm;
- Z_2 = 26;
- χ = 1.4;
- r_b = 2 mm.

To determine the engagement losses of a gear, having specified initial parameters, we will also set the power and the speed of an electric motor. Let the power of the electric motor be 1500 watts, and the number of revolutions of the electric motor shaft will be n = 1500 rpm. Then, the angular velocity of the rotation of the input link of a gear with IREFC will be ω_1 = 157.1 s^{-1}, and the torque on the electric motor shaft and, consequently, on the input transmission link will be M_{in} = 9.55 Nm.

According to Formulas (8) and (14), we will calculate the geometric parameters of the L_A and L_B engagement, as well as the value of the slip speed for each rolling element transmitting a load in the engagement of a gear with IREFC. The obtained values for each rolling element are presented in the form of Table 1. Further, after calculating the friction power in the contact of each rolling element with cycloid wheel profiles according to Formula (22), Table 1 can be supplemented. For more information on the distribution of the friction power in the engagement, based on analytical Expressions (18) and (19), we will also provide power values at points A and B.

As already noted, a sign before the value of the slip speed indicates the multidirectionality of the vectors of the linear velocity of the cam relative to the linear velocity of the rolling element at the point of contact with a cycloid profile of the cam. As Table 1 shows, the highest slip speed occurs at the first rolling element, i.e., the one located in a depression. And as the rolling element moves closer to the top of a tooth, the slip speed decreases.

Table 1. Values of geometric, kinematic and energy parameters of the engagement of a gear with IREFC.

No. of the Rolling Element	L_A, m	L_B, m	V_S, 10^{-3}, m/s	N_S, W	N_{SA}, W	N_{SB}, W	R, N
1	0.006	0.01	−1.58	0	0	0	0
2	0.007826	0.011826	−1.51	3.3487	0.1455	0.0013	651.33
3	0.011867	0.015867	−1.37	6.2414	0.1867	0.0024	896.22
4	0.016592	0.020592	−1.2	8.6756	0.1818	0.0033	953.81
5	0.021404	0.025404	−1.02	10.5946	0.1624	0.0039	940.35
6	0.026051	0.030051	−0.86	11.9113	0.1384	0.0044	891.39
7	0.030388	0.034388	−0.7	12.5565	0.1140	0.0046	819.65
8	0.034318	0.038318	−0.56	12.4937	0.0909	0.0046	730.96
9	0.037764	0.041764	−0.44	11.7252	0.0701	0.0043	628.82
10	0.040664	0.044664	−0.33	10.2936	0.0519	0.0037	515.85
11	0.04297	0.04697	−0.25	8.2790	0.0363	0.0030	394.33
12	0.044645	0.048645	−0.19	5.7950	0.0228	0.0021	266.43
13	0.04566	0.04966	−0.16	2.9821	0.0110	0.0011	134.28
14	0.046	0.05	−0.14	0	0	0	0

A change in the friction power in the engagement of rolling elements with cycloid profiles has a nature that differs from a change in the slip speed. On the first and last rolling elements, the friction power is practically absent, which is explained by the lack of forces in the engagement in these places. That is, in these positions, rolling elements do not transmit load or power. The maximum power loss can be attributed to rolling elements, located approximately in the middle of the chain of elements, transmitting the power in the engagement of a gear with IREFC.

Table 1 demonstrates that the friction power at the point of contact of a rolling element with a cam profile is much greater than the friction power at the point of contact with a crown profile.

Having performed the calculation according to Formula (21) for each rolling element and, finally, according to Formula (23), we will obtain a total efficiency of a gear with IREFC with specified initial parameters equal to $\eta = 0.93$.

6. Results and Discussions

By linearly changing the values of the initial parameters of a gear with IREFC, one can see nonlinear changes in the values of the slip speed and the friction power. For example, by changing the radius of the generating circle r_2 from 20 to 30 mm, we can observe a significant change in the slip speed (Figure 4). When $r_2 = 20$ mm, the entire graph of the slip speed lies in a negative range of values (Figure 4a). And when the radius increases to 30 m, the graph moves from an area of negative values to an area of positive values (Figure 4b). However, the friction power in the engagement practically does not change (Figure 5). When $r_2 = 20$ mm, the maximum friction power in the engagement of a gear is $N_S = 12.56$ W, and $N_S = 12.37$ W when $r_2 = 30$ mm. The presented data were determined at the rated power of an electric motor of 1.5 kW, as indicated earlier.

On the other hand, if the radius of the rolling element is changed, when other initial parameters remain unchanged, both the slip speed and the friction power undergo significant changes. For example, if we change r_b from 1.2 to 2.8 mm in increments of 0.4 mm, it is possible to observe a sequential change in the slip speed Vs. in the engagement of a rolling element with a cycloid cam profile (Figure 6) and the friction power N_S on each rolling element in the engagement of a gear with IREFC (Figure 7).

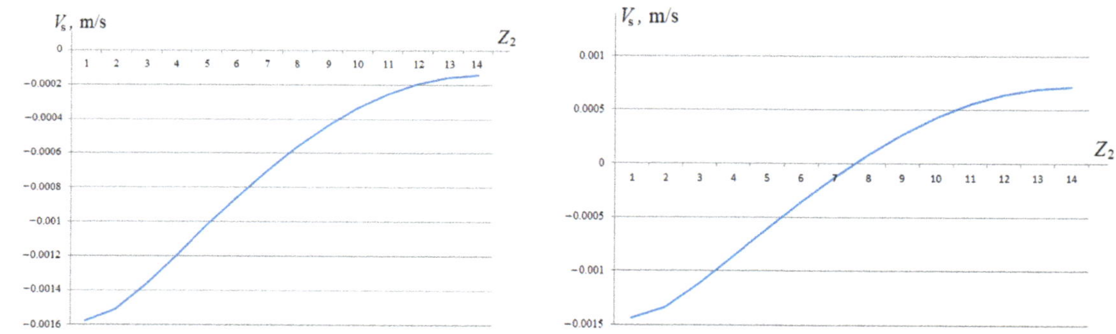

(a) (b)

Figure 4. The change in Vs depending on the position of the rolling element: (**a**) slip speed when r_2 = 20 mm; (**b**) slip speed when r_2 = 30 mm.

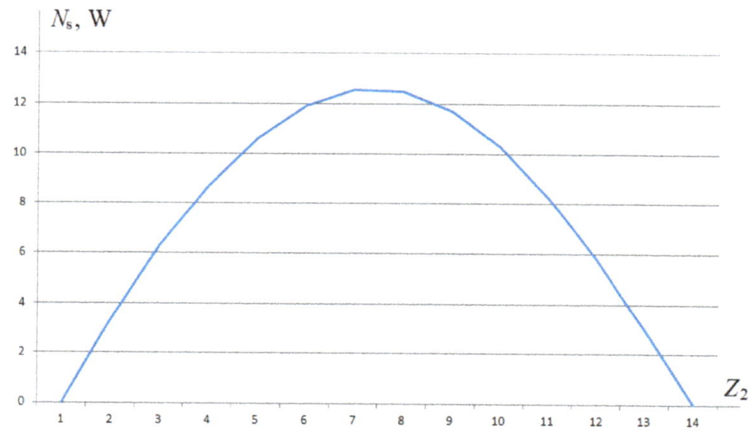

Figure 5. The change in N_S depending on the position of the rolling element.

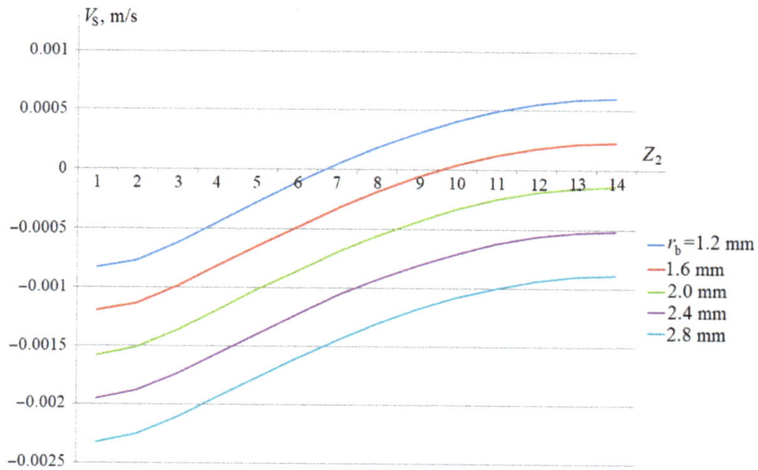

Figure 6. The change in Vs depending on the position of the rolling element when r_b values are different.

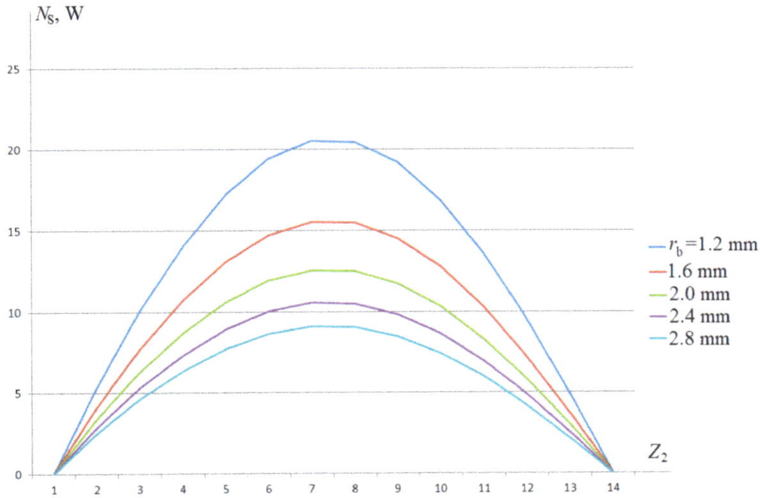

Figure 7. The change in N_S depending on the position of the rolling element at different r_b values.

The graphs of a cosinusoid (Figure 6) show that when the radius of the rolling element increases, the values of the slip speed in the engagement of a rolling element with a cycloid cam profile shift to the negative zone. As already noted, the sign of the slip speed shows the relative direction of its vector. However, this sign has no effect on the determination of the friction power in the engagement, since for this purpose, the slip speed is taken modulo. It should be noted that when changing only the radius r_b, the range of changing the slip speed between the first rolling element and the last one in the power transmission section does not change and is $\Delta V_S = 0.00143$ m/s. Also, the law of changing the slip speed along the cycloid profile of a tooth does not change.

Parabolic graphs (Figure 7) show that when the radius of a rolling element increases, the value of the maximum slip power decreases. When $r_b = 1.2$ mm, the maximum friction power in the gear engagement is $N_S = 20.54$ W, and $N_S = 9.11$ W when $r_b = 2.8$ mm. This is explained by the direct proportional dependence of the power on the force, the speed and the inverse dependence on the geometry of a rolling element. That is, as the radius of a rolling element increases, the circumferential velocity on its surface increases and, accordingly, the slip speed in contact decreases, as can be seen in the graphs of Figure 6. At the same time, the force in contact with a cycloid profile with a rolling element remains unchanged, since the radius of a generating circle is constant (r_2 = const). Therefore, the friction power decreases when the radius of a rolling element increases by 1.6 mm and the maximum friction power decreases by 11.4 W (Figure 8).

For example, when designing mechanisms based on a gear with IREFC, in order to reduce power losses, it is necessary to choose the largest possible diameter of a rolling element. This will allow for reducing the friction power in the gear engagement and therefore increasing the efficiency of the entire mechanism.

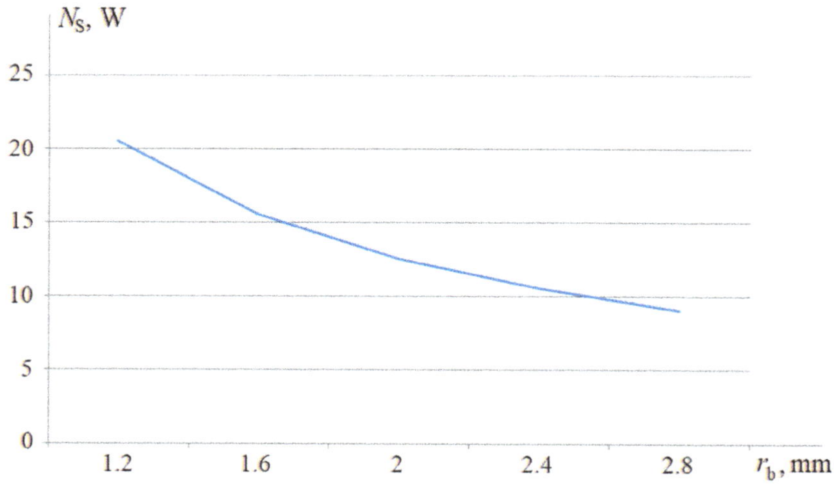

Figure 8. The change in the maximum power N_S depending on r_b in the gear engagement.

7. Conclusions

In conclusion, this work provides analytical expressions for estimating power losses in the engagement of a gear with IREFC, and a formula for determining the efficiency of a specified mechanical transmission has been derived. The calculation of the efficiency, the friction power in the engagement and the power losses at the points of contact of a rolling element with cycloid profiles of wheels for selected initial parameters of a gear with IREFC has been presented.

The authors have shown that the power friction losses at the points of contact of a rolling element with cycloid profiles of tooth wheels of a gear with IREFC are not the same and vary according to the parabolic law. The friction power in the contact of a rolling element with a cycloid profile of a cam is an order of magnitude higher than the friction power in the contact of a rolling element with a cycloid profile of a crown. For example, in contact with the cam, it is 0.091 W, and in contact with the crown, it amounts to 0.0046 W. The authors have also demonstrated that a change in the radius of the generating circle r_2, other things being equal, does not influence the friction power in the engagement of a gear in any way. By changing the radius r_2 1.5 times, we obtain a change in the friction power in the engagement by 0.19 W. On the other hand, a change in the radius of the rolling element r_b influences simultaneously the values of the slip speed in the contact of a cycloid cam profile with a rolling element and the friction power in the gear engagement. This work demonstrates that the slip speed in the engagement varies along a cosinusoid with a possible transition from the fourth quarter to the first quarter of the coordinate plane. Hence, a method for determining the efficiency of engaging a gear with intermediate rolling elements and a free cage was proposed.

The obtained results allow for increasing the accuracy of detection by 1.5% determining the efficiency of a projected gear with IREFC and, therefore, more precisely selecting the power of an electric motor for electromechanical drives based on the mentioned mechanical transmission. The obtained results should be used for designing electromechanical drives, as well as for studying the influence of other initial parameters on the change in power distribution and the efficiency in the engagement of a cycloid gear with intermediate rolling elements and a free cage.

Author Contributions: Conceptualization, E.A.E.; methodology, S.K.E.; software, E.S.C.; validation, E.S.C.; formal analysis, E.S.C.; investigation, S.K.E.; resources, N.V.M.; data curation, E.A.E.; writing—original draft preparation, E.A.E.; writing—review and editing, N.V.M.; visualization, N.V.M. All authors have read and agreed to the published version of the manuscript.

Funding: The research was carried out using the equipment of the Center for Sharing Use «Nanomaterials and Nanotechnologies» of Tomsk Polytechnic University supported by the RF Ministry of Education and Science project #075-15-2021-710.

Institutional Review Board Statement: Not applicable.

Informed Consent Statement: Not applicable.

Data Availability Statement: Data are contained within the article and supplementary materials.

Conflicts of Interest: The authors declare no conflicts of interest.

References

1. Mirko, B.; Matejić, M.; Kostić, N. Dynamic behaviour of a two-stage cycloidal speed reducer of a new design concept. *Teh. Vjesn. Tech. Gaz.* **2018**, *5*, 291–298.
2. Ren, Y.; Bian, W.; Yan, R. Optimization analysis of air gap magnetic field in electromagnetic harmonic movable tooth drive system. *Int. J. Comput. Eng.* **2019**, *4*, 132–135.
3. Efremenkov, E.A.; Efremenkova, S.K. Design of heavily loaded cycloidal transmission with free cage based on contact strength. *Bull. Tomsk Polytech. Univ. Eng. Georesour.* **2021**, *332*, 182–188.
4. Efremenkov, E.A.; Shanin, S.A.; Martyushev, N.V. Development of an Algorithm for Computing the Force and Stress Parameters of a Cycloid Reducer. *Mathematics* **2023**, *11*, 993. [CrossRef]
5. Lustenkov, M.E. Mechanical transmission strength criteria with composite intermediate rolling elements. *Bull. Belarusian-Russ. Univ.* **2015**, *4*, 33–41.
6. Prudnikov, A.P. Planetary Torus Helical Transmission. *IOP Conf. Ser. Mater. Sci. Eng.* **2020**, *795*, 012022. [CrossRef]
7. Ren, Y.; Ma, Y.; Wan, R. Parametric design of inner teeth of center wheel in electromagnetic harmonic movable teeth transmission. *J. Phys. Conf. Ser.* **2021**, *1965*, 012009.
8. Lustenkov, M.E. Planetary Ball Transmissions: Strength Calculations. *Russ. Eng. Res.* **2010**, *30*, 862–866. [CrossRef]
9. Jiang, N.; Wang, S.; Yang, A.; Zhou, W.; Zhang, J. Transmission Efficiency of Cycloid–Pinion System Considering the Assembly Dimensional Chain. *Appl. Sci.* **2022**, *12*, 11917. [CrossRef]
10. Sun, Y.; Zhang, Y.-H.; He, W.-D. Simulation Analysis of Skew Collision of Needle Roller Bearing Used in Precision Cycloid Reducer. *Machines* **2023**, *11*, 419. [CrossRef]
11. Komorska, I.; Olejarczyk, K.; Puchalski, A.; Wikło, M.; Wołczyński, Z. Fault Diagnosing of Cycloidal Gear Reducer Using Statistical Features of Vibration Signal and Multifractal Spectra. *Sensors* **2023**, *23*, 1645. [CrossRef] [PubMed]
12. Li, X.; Tang, L.; He, H.; Sun, L. Design and Load Distribution Analysis of the Mismatched Cycloid-Pin Gear Pair in RV Speed Reducers. *Machines* **2022**, *10*, 672. [CrossRef]
13. Bechhoefer, E. Automated Condition Monitoring of a Cycloid Gearbox. In *Maintenance Management-Current Challenges, New Developments, and Future Directions*; IntechOpen: London, UK, 2022.
14. Grosso, P.; Massaccesi, G.; Cavalaglio Camargo Molano, J.; Mottola, G.; Borghi, D. Signal model of a cycloidal drive for diagnostic purposes. In Proceedings of the ISMA-USD Conference, Leuven, Belgium, 12–14 September 2022; pp. 750–764.
15. Liu, C.; Shi, W.; Xu, L.; Liu, K. A Novel Approach to Calculating the Transmission Accuracy of a Cycloid-Pin Gear Pair Based on Error Tooth Surfaces. *Appl. Sci.* **2021**, *11*, 8671. [CrossRef]
16. Zhang, T.; Li, X.; Wang, Y.; Sun, L. A Semi-Analytical Load Distribution Model for Cycloid Drives with Tooth Profile and Longitudinal Modifications. *Appl. Sci.* **2020**, *10*, 4859. [CrossRef]
17. Li, T.; An, X.; Deng, X.; Li, J.; Li, Y. A New Tooth Profile Modification Method of Cycloidal Gears in Precision Reducers for Robots. *Appl. Sci.* **2020**, *10*, 1266. [CrossRef]
18. Wang, H.; Shi, Z.; Yu, B.; Xu, H. Transmission Performance Analysis of RV Reducers Influenced by Profile Modification and Load. *Appl. Sci.* **2019**, *9*, 4099. [CrossRef]
19. Lustenkov, M.E.; Lustenkova, E.S. Load Capacity of Spherical Roller Transmission with Double-Row Pinion. *IOP Conf. Ser. Mater. Sci. Eng.* **2020**, *795*, 012020. [CrossRef]
20. Lustenkov, M.E.; Moiseenko, A.N. Analysis of contact strength of spherical roller transmission with double-row pinion. *IOP Conf. Ser. Mech. Eng.* **2021**, *1118*, 012006. [CrossRef]
21. Efremenkov, E.A.; Martyushev, N.V.; Skeeba, V.Y.; Grechneva, M.V.; Olisov, A.V.; Ens, A.D. Research on the Possibility of Lowering the Manufacturing Accuracy of Cycloid Transmission Wheels with Intermediate Rolling Elements and a Free Cage. *Appl. Sci.* **2022**, *12*, 5. [CrossRef]

22. Antonov, A.S. *Complex Power Transmissions: Theory of Force Flow and Calculation of Transmission Systems;* Mechanical Engineering, Leningrad Branch: Leningrad, Russia, 1981; 496p.
23. Solovyov, A.I. *Efficiency Coefficient of Mechanisms and Machines;* Mechanical Engineering: Moscow, Russia, 1966; p. 180.
24. An, I.-K.; Belyaev, A.E. *Synthesis of Planetary Gears in Relation to Rotary Hydraulic Machines;* NPI MEPhI: Novouralsk, Russia, 2001; p. 92.

mathematics MDPI

Article

Full Forward Kinematics of Lower-Mobility Planar Parallel Continuum Robots

Oscar Altuzarra, Mónica Urizar *, Kerman Bilbao and Alfonso Hernández

Department of Mechanical Engineering, Bilbao School of Engineering, University of the Basque Country UPV/EHU, Plaza Ingeniero Torres Quevedo, 48013 Bilbao, Spain; oscar.altuzarra@ehu.eus (O.A.); kerman.bilbao@ehu.eus (K.B.); a.hernandez@ehu.eus (A.H.)

* Correspondence: monica.urizar@ehu.eus

Abstract: In rigid lower-mobility parallel manipulators the motion of the end-effector is partially constrained due to a combination of passive kinematic pairs and rigid components. Translational mechanisms, such as the Delta manipulator, are the most common ones among this type of mechanisms. When flexible elements are introduced, as in Parallel Continuum Manipulators, the constraint is no longer rigid, and new challenges arise in performing certain motions depending on the degree of compliance. Mobility analysis shifts from being purely a geometric issue to one that heavily relies on force distribution within the mechanism. Simply converting classical lower-mobility rigid parallel mechanisms into Parallel Continuum Mechanisms may yield unexpected outcomes. This work, making use of a planar parallel continuum Delta manipulator, on the one hand, presents two different approaches to solve the Forward Kinematics of planar continuum manipulators, and, on the other hand, explores some challenges and issues in assessing the resultant workspace for different design alternatives of this kind of flexible manipulators.

Keywords: continuum manipulators; cosserat rods; forward kinematics; workspace; quasi-translational motion; parasitic angle

MSC: 65L05

1. Introduction

Lower-mobility parallel manipulators are a category of closed-loop mechanisms where the motion of the end-effector is restricted to fewer degrees of freedom than the typical three in planar systems or six in the spatial case [1]. These rigid-body mechanisms are constrained by geometric factors, which arise from the configuration and design of passive kinematic joints and are thus independent of the input actuation. These geometric constraints impose relationships between the output parameters, and in simpler cases may completely define some of them. A well-known example is the family of translational manipulators, like the Delta robot [2–4], which maintains a constant oriented end-effector while moving.

In contrast to traditional robots composed of rigid elements, Parallel Continuum Manipulators (PCMs) incorporate flexible elements—such as thin rods, cables, or springs—to connect the rigid end-effector to the actuators [5–7]. These manipulators exhibit characteristics of both conventional parallel kinematic machines and compliant mechanisms [8,9]. The flexibility of components, which undergo significant deformation, plays a key role in their mobility alongside the kinematic joints. Many modern PCMs are adaptations of classical rigid kinematic systems. For instance, substantial research has been conducted on hexapod-like flexible manipulators, as seen in [10–12].

Nevertheless, regarding continuum lower-mobility parallel manipulators, only few studies can be found [13–15]. One of the main differences is that, unlike their rigid counterparts, strict constraints cannot be imposed on flexible manipulators due to the inherent flexibility of the rods. In the context of PCM systems that could serve as alternatives to the classical rigid Delta, this flexibility makes the moving platform to tilt at slight angles rather than follow a purely translational path, resulting in unwanted angular motions, also known as *parasitic motion* [16]. For modelling manipulators with flexible rods, the methods employed in this work are based on Cosserat theory, particularly using the simplified Kirchhoff model. This model, which is designed for slender flexible components, must be combined with the dynamic equilibrium of the entire mechanical system under all applied forces, leading to a nonlinear set of differential equations. A solution for this system is provided in [17], another possibility being applying energetic approaches as in [18,19].

As happened with rigid parallel manipulators, the solving of Forward Kinematics (FK) problem in the case of continuum parallel manipulators may result in multiple different solutions, known as assembly modes. One of the aims of this work is to approach the Forward Kinematics in flexible manipulators. For that, we propose two methodologies: one capable of obtaining all the different solutions, meaning that the Full FK problem is solved, and another approach aimed at obtaining a nearby solution to a certain starting assembly mode configuration. Moreover, a novel strategy combining both methods is presented so as to obtain the workspace of planar continuum robots in a very efficient way.

In general, most classical rigid lower-mobility parallel mechanisms are fully parallel, featuring identical and symmetrical kinematic chains. This symmetry translates into balanced kinematics and workspaces, with both singularities and dexterity distributed symmetrically. However, some asymmetrical mechanisms are also effective. For example, the IGUS commercial planar Keops–Delta manipulator in [20] behaves very well despite its lack of symmetry. Another objective of this work is to demonstrate that simply replacing rigid bars with flexible rods in rigid-body parallel mechanisms may lead to impractical outcomes. To illustrate this, we focus on the planar Keops–Delta continuum parallel robot. Depending on the design alternative of this flexible mechanism, and depending also on the selected assembly mode, the resultant workspace exhibits nearly translational motion, which can be evaluated based on the parasitic inclination angle of the end-effector. This work also discusses key design considerations for creating optimal quasi-translational workspaces.

2. Materials and Methods

In this section, we describe the mathematical procedure and methods used to assess the motion constraints in Parallel Continuum Manipulators. Although general, it is taylored to the case study chosen to illustrate the contribution, a planar quasi-translational flexible mechanism. The schedule followed in this section is structured as follows:

- Overall Analysis Procedure;
- Fundamentals on Deformation Analysis of Rods;
- Methods for Kinematics Analysis;
- Workspace Analysis;
- Mechanisms' Alternative Designs.

2.1. *Overall Analysis Procedure*

Most Parallel Continuum Mechanisms (PCMs) are devised as a flexible alter ego of a classical Parallel Kinematic Machine (PKM). In this sense, flexible hexapods are derived from the classical hexapod [6]. Many successful applications of PKMs are mechanisms with Lower-Mobility, i.e., they have an end-effector with a motion submanifold, as it is the case of the well-known Delta Robot. The planar version of the Delta Robot with linear actuators is shown in Figure 1, alongside its workspace for different input strokes. The rigid parallelogram constrains the end-effector's motion to be a planar translational subgroup.

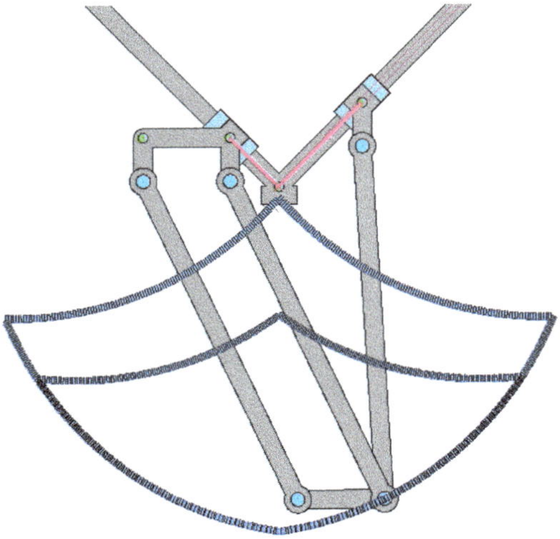

Figure 1. Planar translational rigid mechanism: Workspaces for variable input stroke limits.

A PCM version of the planar Delta robot is shown schematically in Figure 2. Flexible rods replaced rigid bars, and as their deformation adds mobility to the system, the revolute joints at the attachment to linear actuators can be eliminated and simply clamp the first tip of rods to the linear tables.

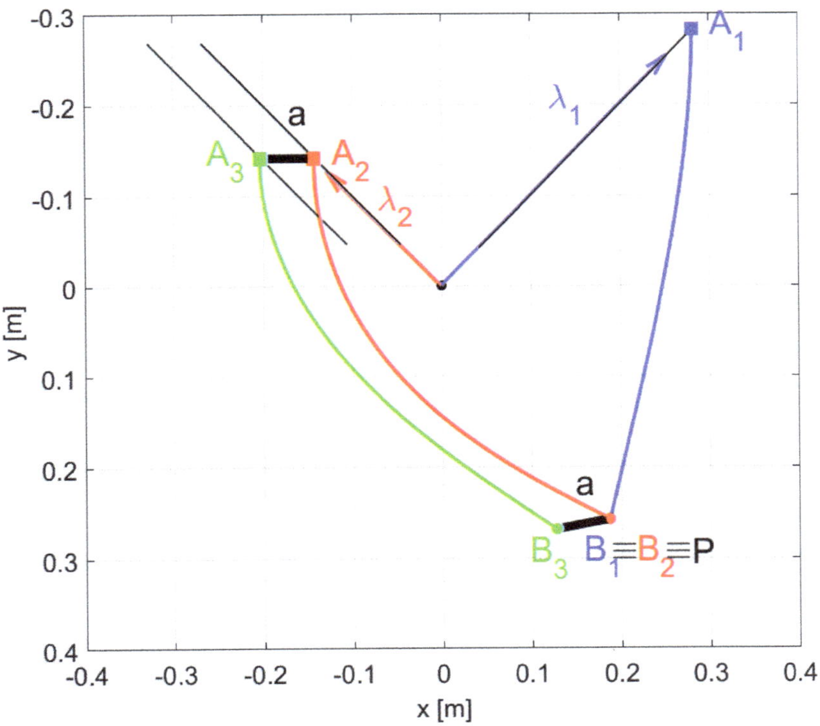

Figure 2. Planar quasi-translational flexible mechanism.

There is no longer a rigid parallelogram to constrain the rotation of the end-effector, as observed in the inclined end-effector in Figure 2, and flexible rods cannot be a generator of a motion subgroup because they do not introduce any geometric constraint. Any restriction of the motion has to be produced by the stiffness behavior of the system as a whole. Moreover, being now a flexible mechanical system, any pose of the system should be at a stable equilibrium configuration, as unstable poses cannot withstand loads. The purpose of this study is to highlight the way different design alternatives generate such restrictions and to what extent.

In order to obtain the design of a flexible parallel mechanism that performs, as much as possible, such a reduced mobility motion, we follow the flowchart in Figure 3. First, several design alternatives are proposed as, for example, the mechanism morphology in Figure 2. For each of those designs, we solve the multiple solutions of the Forward Kinematics (FK) problem. These multiple solutions are called assembly modes.

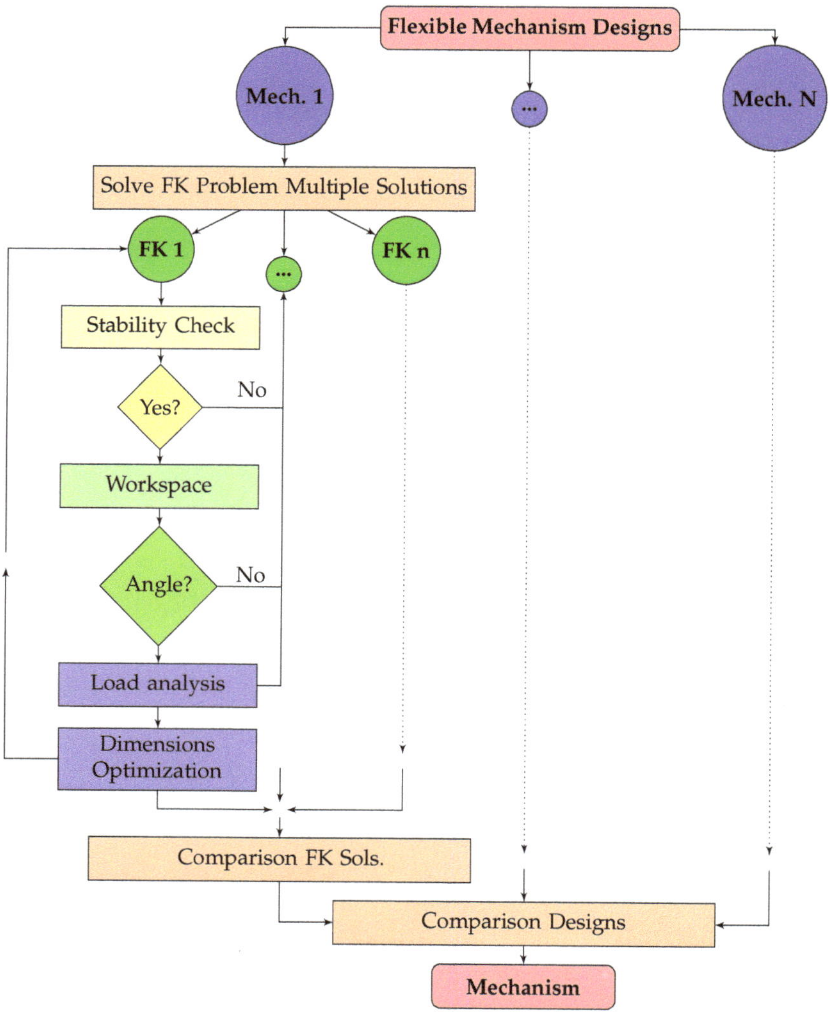

Figure 3. Flowchart for Mechanism's Design Analysis.

For each assembly mode, we check the stability of the solution before finding the available stable workspace. Such workspace needs to be characterized with standard kinematics properties. The most relevant here is the angle of orientation of the end-effector, the objective being to keep this value as close to the horizontal as possible to obtain quasi-translational motions. The variety of applicable loads should be considered to evaluate the consistency of the results, and a dimensional optimization is performed on the design candidates to obtain the best possible result of each one. After that, a comparison of assembly modes is performed for every mechanism design, and the best candidates are compared to finally achieve the best design for quasi-translational motion.

2.2. Fundamentals on Deformation Analysis of Rods

The Kinematic Analysis of closed-loop mechanisms consists in finding the values for some unknown geometric parameters that fulfil a set of geometric constraints. When these mechanisms have flexible elements, such flexibility influences the geometrical conditions due to forces in the system, and then some dynamic equilibrium has to be considered in the problem. The result is that Kinematic Analysis becomes a combination of geometric and force equilibrium conditions.

These flexible mechanisms require a model of deformation for its flexible rods. Here, the choice is the Kirchhoff rod model. The Kirchhoff model neglects the extension of the neutral line and the transverse shear strain, i.e., the deformation of the rod occurs mainly due to bending; then, the complexity of material equations reduces, making more efficient algorithms. A detailed derivation of the following draws on Antman's work [21] (Chapters 4 and 8) on nonlinear elasticity, with adapted notation [22].

The deformed shape of a certain rod can be established by a parametric Cartesian curve $\mathbf{p}(s) \in \mathbb{R}^3$ defining the centroid of each cross-section and the orthonormal rotation matrix $\mathbf{R}(s) \in SO(3)$ to orientate a local frame attached to that section. If we consider the rod plotted in Figure 4, its deformed shape is within the plane XY, and the orientation of a certain cross-section can be expressed as

$$\mathbf{R}(s) = \begin{bmatrix} \cos\theta & -\sin\theta & 0 \\ \sin\theta & \cos\theta & 0 \\ 0 & 0 & 1 \end{bmatrix} \tag{1}$$

Both position and orientation depend on a scalar arc-length parameter s over some finite interval, $s \in [0, L]$, L being the rod's length.

Both position and orientation vary along the arc length according to rates of change, linear $\mathbf{v}(s) \in \mathbb{R}^3$ and angular $\mathbf{u}(s) \in \mathbb{R}^3$. They can be defined in the local frame from the derivatives of $\mathbf{p}(s)$ and $\mathbf{R}(s)$ with respect to parameter s:

$$\begin{aligned} \mathbf{v}(s) &= \mathbf{R}(s)^T \frac{d\mathbf{p}(s)}{ds} = \mathbf{R}(s)^T \mathbf{p}'(s) \\ \mathbf{U}(s) &= \mathbf{R}(s)^T \mathbf{R}'(s) \end{aligned} \tag{2}$$

where $\mathbf{U}(s)$ is a skew-symmetric matrix of the form

$$\mathbf{U}(s) = \begin{bmatrix} 0 & -u_z(s) & u_y(s) \\ u_z(s) & 0 & -u_x(s) \\ -u_y(s) & u_x(s) & 0 \end{bmatrix} \tag{3}$$

In the planar case above, taking the derivative of $\mathbf{R}$ in (1) allows finding

$$\mathbf{U} = \mathbf{R}^T \mathbf{R}' = \begin{bmatrix} 0 & -\theta' & 0 \\ \theta' & 0 & 0 \\ 0 & 0 & 0 \end{bmatrix} = \begin{bmatrix} 0 & -u_z & 0 \\ u_z & 0 & 0 \\ 0 & 0 & 0 \end{bmatrix} \tag{4}$$

Hence, the only component that is not null is $u_z = \theta'$, because there is no bending moment with respect to the local y-axis and there is also no torsion (expressed through u_x).

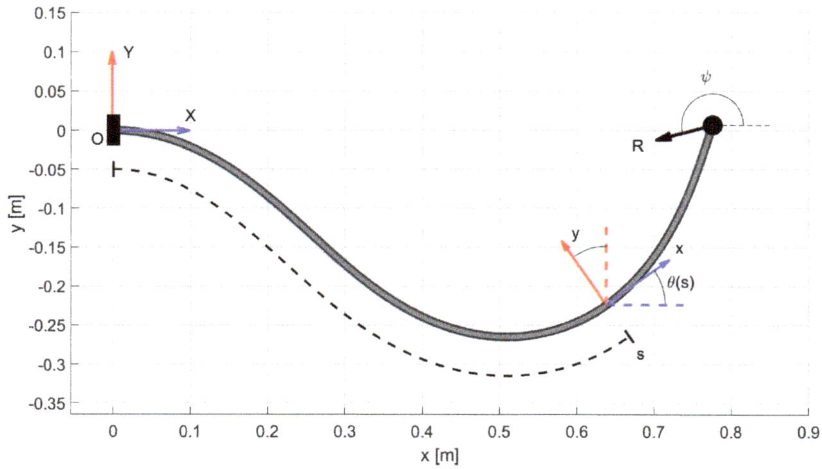

Figure 4. Flexible clamped–hinged planar rod under force R at the end extreme.

When $\mathbf{v}(s)$ and $\mathbf{u}(s)$ are those of the reference, i.e., the unloaded shape of the rod, they are designated as $\mathbf{v}_\circ$ and $\mathbf{u}_\circ$, an initially straight rod has $\mathbf{v}_\circ = [1\ 0\ 0]^T$ and $\mathbf{u}_\circ = \mathbf{0}$. Changes in these magnitudes with respect to the reference values, namely $\Delta\mathbf{v}(s) = \mathbf{v}(s) - \mathbf{v}_\circ(s)$ and $\Delta\mathbf{u}(s) = \mathbf{u}(s) - \mathbf{u}_\circ(s)$, are related to material strain.

Because the stress field is obtained due to the strain field, and the internal force $\mathbf{n}(s)$ and moment $\mathbf{m}(s)$ are due to the stress field, they can be expressed as a function of $\Delta\mathbf{v}(s)$ and $\Delta\mathbf{u}(s)$. Making use of a linear constitutive law relating linear deformation $\mathbf{v}$ to internal forces and angular deformation $\mathbf{u}$ to internal moment, through the use of shear-extension stiffness matrix $\mathbf{K}_{SE}(s)$ and bending-torsion matrix $\mathbf{K}_{BT}(s)$, we obtain

$$\begin{aligned} \mathbf{n}(s) &= \mathbf{R}\mathbf{K}_{SE}(s)\Delta\mathbf{v} \\ \mathbf{m}(s) &= \mathbf{R}\mathbf{K}_{BT}(s)\Delta\mathbf{u} \end{aligned} \tag{5}$$

The equilibrium of forces and moments for each section of the rod, subjected to distributed forces $\mathbf{f}(s)$ and moments $\mathbf{l}(s)$ defined within the infinitesimal interval ds, yields the non-linear ordinary differential equations for the equilibrium of a Cosserat rod which describes the evolution of the internal force $\mathbf{n}(s)$ and moment $\mathbf{m}(s)$ along the arc length:

$$\begin{aligned} \mathbf{n}'(s) + \mathbf{f}(s) &= \mathbf{0} \\ \mathbf{m}'(s) + \mathbf{p}'(s) \times \mathbf{n}(s) + \mathbf{l}(s) &= \mathbf{0} \end{aligned} \tag{6}$$

The Static Model for a flexible rod can be obtained by combining Equations (2) and (6) with Kirchhoff conditions using $\mathbf{m}$ and $\mathbf{n}$ as state variables:

$$\begin{aligned} \mathbf{p}' &= \mathbf{R}\mathbf{e}_1 \\ \mathbf{R}' &= \mathbf{R}\mathbf{U} \\ \mathbf{n}' &= -\mathbf{f} \\ \mathbf{m}' &= -\mathbf{p}' \times \mathbf{n} - \mathbf{l} \end{aligned} \tag{7}$$

where $\mathbf{u} = \mathbf{K}_{BT}^{-1}\mathbf{R}^T\mathbf{m}$.

Hence, for planar rods, neglecting the distributed force and moment ($\mathbf{f}$ and $\mathbf{l}$) along the rod, we obtain

$$\begin{Bmatrix} \frac{dx}{ds} \\ \frac{dy}{ds} \\ \frac{d\theta}{ds} \\ \frac{dn_x}{ds} \\ \frac{dn_y}{ds} \\ \frac{dm_z}{ds} \end{Bmatrix} = \begin{Bmatrix} \cos\theta \\ \sin\theta \\ \frac{m_z}{EI} \\ 0 \\ 0 \\ n_x \sin\theta - n_y \cos\theta \end{Bmatrix} \tag{8}$$

where E is the Young's modulus and I is the moment of area of the cross-section.

The differential equation system in Equation (8) can be solved either by using a direct integration method, such as the 4th-order Runge–Kutta, or analytically by using Elliptic Integrals.

First, regarding direct integration and focusing on the Forward Kinematics (FK) problem of a rod that is clamped at the proximal end $s = 0$ (see Figure 4), the rod suffers a deformation that depends on some boundary conditions. This is a boundary value problem, where the independent variable is s in $[0, L]$. The vector of dependent variables $\mathbf{y}$ and the non-linear function $\mathbf{f}(s,\mathbf{y})$ are

$$\mathbf{y} = \begin{Bmatrix} x \\ y \\ \theta \\ n_x \\ n_y \\ m_z \end{Bmatrix}, \quad \mathbf{f}(s,\mathbf{y}) = \begin{Bmatrix} \cos\theta \\ \sin\theta \\ \frac{m_z}{EI} \\ 0 \\ 0 \\ n_x \sin\theta - n_y \cos\theta \end{Bmatrix} \tag{9}$$

If, for example, the position and orientation at $s = 0$ are data, and the load at the end-tip is known, then the values of $\mathbf{y}$ at both extremes are

$$\mathbf{y}(0) = \begin{Bmatrix} x(0) \\ y(0) \\ \theta(0) \\ n_x(0) \\ n_y(0) \\ m_z(0) \end{Bmatrix} = \begin{Bmatrix} x_0 \\ y_0 \\ \theta_0 \\ ? \\ ? \\ ? \end{Bmatrix}, \quad \mathbf{y}(L) = \begin{Bmatrix} x(L) \\ y(L) \\ \theta(L) \\ n_x(L) \\ n_y(L) \\ m_z(L) \end{Bmatrix} = \begin{Bmatrix} ? \\ ? \\ ? \\ n^x_{ext} \\ n^y_{ext} \\ m^z_{ext} \end{Bmatrix} \tag{10}$$

Since there are 3 unknowns at the initial of the range of integration $s = 0$, we need three starting values, $\mathbf{guess} = \left[n^x_{guess}\ n^y_{guess}\ m^z_{guess} \right]^T$. Then, the initial value problem is solved using the 4th R-K method. A Newton method is used to update guess values until boundary conditions at end-tip $\left[n^x_{ext}\ n^y_{ext}\ m^z_{ext} \right]^T$ are fulfilled. Randomly choosing an initial value of these parameters may result in not reaching any feasible solution. Therefore, it is advisable to start from a known solution that allows us to establish these starting data. Precisely the method explained subsequently, based on the direct analytical integration of the differential equations, allows us to obtain a feasible solution that can be used later as a starting solution.

Second, regarding the analytical integration, the system of differential equations in (8) can be further developed. If only end-point load is applied (load R and orientation ψ as in Figure 4), the internal force is given by $n_x = R\cos\psi$ and $n_y = R\sin\psi$. For constant E and I, with a stress-free reference straight rod, taking into account the Bernoulli–Euler law and substituting into Equation (8), we obtain

$$\left\{\begin{array}{c}\frac{dx}{ds}\\ \frac{dy}{ds}\\ \frac{d^2\theta}{d^2s}\end{array}\right\}=\left\{\begin{array}{c}\cos\theta\\ \sin\theta\\ \frac{R}{EI}\sin(\theta-\psi)\end{array}\right\} \quad (11)$$

Elliptic integrals are the classical mathematical tool to solve Equation (11) [7]. The coordinates of an arbitrary point i along the beam are

$$\begin{aligned} x(\phi_i) &= -\sqrt{\frac{EI}{R}}\cos\psi[2E(k,\phi_i)-2E(k,\phi_1)-F(k,\phi_i)+F(k,\phi_1)]-\sqrt{\frac{EI}{R}}2k\sin\psi[\cos\phi_i-\cos\phi_1] \\ y(\phi_i) &= -\sqrt{\frac{EI}{R}}\sin\psi[2E(k,\phi_i)-2E(k,\phi_1)-F(k,\phi_i)+F(k,\phi_1)]+\sqrt{\frac{EI}{R}}2k\cos\psi[\cos\phi_i-\cos\phi_1] \end{aligned} \quad (12)$$

functions $F(k,\phi)$ and $E(k,\phi)$ being the incomplete elliptic integrals of the first and second kind, respectively. In addition, the value of the end-tip force R must fulfil

$$\sqrt{R}=\frac{\sqrt{EI}}{L}[F(k,\phi_2)-F(k,\phi_1)] \quad (13)$$

Moreover, the bending moment along the rod is given by

$$m_i=2k\sqrt{REI}\cos\phi_i \quad (14)$$

The functions $F(k,\phi)$ and $E(k,\phi)$ depend on the following two parameters:

- **The non-dimensional parameter k**
  This is the **modulus of the function** and it can vary between -1 and 1. In this case, k corresponds roughly but non-linearly to the magnitude of the load R.
- **The variable ϕ**
  It is the **amplitude of the elliptic integral**. It is measured in radians, and it varies continuously along the beam from the first extreme, ϕ_1, to the last extreme, ϕ_2. These amplitudes are defined by the boundary conditions of rod tips.

Hence, (11) is integrated to obtain Equations (12) and (13), i.e., a parametric system that uniquely defines the deformation of the rod in terms of parameters k and ψ for **known boundary conditions** and a **certain buckling mode**.

For a clamped-pinned rod (as in Figure 4), the first clamped tip is defined by a given slope θ_1 for the rod at $s=0$:

$$\phi_1=\arcsin\frac{1}{k}\cos\left(\frac{\psi-\theta_1}{2}\right) \quad (15)$$

Considering a pinned end-tip then, no moment acts at that point. Upon application on Equation (14), the end-tip results to be a point of null curvature, i.e., an inflection point of the deformed curve. This yields $\phi_2=(2q-1)\pi/2$ for $q=1,2,\ldots$ where q is the order of the buckling mode shape.

The possible values of k may depend on ψ, as observed in Equation (15); this condition establishes the grid plotted in Figure 5. Thus, parameters k and ψ belong to the enclosed range of values depicted in Figure 5.

The different problems that can be stated regarding the deformation of a rod under some given conditions result in multiple solutions for each buckling mode. Detailed explanation can be found in [23].

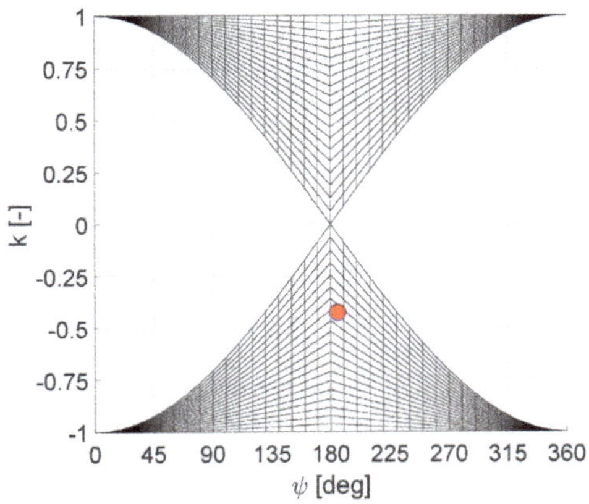

Figure 5. Space of parameters k (modulus of the elliptic integral) and ψ (amplitude).

2.3. *Methods for Kinematic Analysis*

In order to evaluate the kinematic performance of the different continuum mechanism designs, we need to solve the position problem. The Forward Kinematics problem in our planar flexible mechanism consists in determining the pose of the end-effector, i.e., $\mathbf{p}_{\mathcal{P}}$, the position vector of reference point $\mathcal{P}$, and the orientation given by θ_{EE} when input values for each rod λ_i and a load are imposed. Such a problem has multiple solutions, called assembly modes, that in turn generate different *aspects* of the workspace [24]. In the following, we describe two alternatives to solve the FK problem, one generating all the solutions (assembly modes) and another one generating a nearby solution to a starting assembly mode configuration.

As the mechanism has 2 degrees of freedom, hence 2 inputs λ_i, there are 2 independent outputs. Consequently, 2 of the output components of the pose of the rigid moving platform can be controlled (*principal* motions, namely $\mathbf{p}_{\mathcal{P}}$), meanwhile its orientation θ_{EE} depends on the motion, *parasitic* motion.

2.3.1. Forward Kinematics Problem

Let us consider a parallel mechanism of flexible rods like the one in Figure 2. The moving platform is connected to the fixed base by N flexible rods A_iB_i, which are actuated by some inputs. By attaching a moving frame to the end-effector at reference point $\mathcal{P}$, its orientation is defined by the rotation matrix $\mathbf{R}_{EE}$ function of θ_{EE}. Points B_i attached to the moving platform are defined by position vectors $\mathbf{r}_i$ in the moving frame. On the other hand, the initial points of each rod, proximal-ends A_i, are expressed in the fixed frame by position vectors $\mathbf{a}_i$.

To obtain a real pose of the flexible mechanism, two conditions must be fulfilled: a geometrical assembly of the rods with the moving platform and a static equilibrium of the whole system.

The geometrical assembly condition is given by the closed-loop equation for each rod:

$$\mathbf{p}_{\mathcal{P}} + \mathbf{R}_{EE}\mathbf{r}_i = \mathbf{a}_i + \mathbf{p}_i(L_i) \quad i = 1...N \tag{16}$$

$\mathbf{p}_i(L_i)$ being the location of the distal end of each rod i.

In addition, geometrical conditions have to be considered according to the connection of the extremes of the rods to the moving platform. Implementing revolute joints means that a null moment exists. Knowing that $\mathbf{u} = \mathbf{K}_{BT}^{-1}\mathbf{R}^T\mathbf{m}$, we yield

$$\mathbf{u}_i(L_i) = \mathbf{0} \quad i = 1...N \tag{17}$$

In relation to the static equilibrium, the end-effector is subjected to external load $\mathbf{F}_{ext}$ at $\mathcal{P}$ and $\mathbf{M}_{ext}$ and to reaction forces, namely $\mathbf{n}_i(L_i)$, at points B_i because of the rod deformation. Thus, the following static equilibrium can be stated:

$$\begin{aligned} \sum_{i=1}^{N} \mathbf{n}_i(L_i) - \mathbf{F}_{ext} = \mathbf{0} \\ \sum_{i=1}^{N}[(\mathbf{a}_i + \mathbf{p}_i(L_i)) \times \mathbf{n}_i(L_i)] - \mathbf{p}_{\mathcal{P}} \times \mathbf{F}_{ext} - \mathbf{M}_{ext} = \mathbf{0} \end{aligned} \quad (18)$$

To sum up, to pose the position problem, the involved equations are the geometric conditions on the position of the rod extremes (16); the geometric conditions on the attachment points to the moving platform (17); and the static equilibrium conditions (18). For the planar case, this makes a total of $3N + 3$ conditions. These are compiled in the vector of residuals $\mathbf{g}_{res}$,

$$\mathbf{g}_{res} = \left\{ \begin{array}{c} \mathbf{p}_i(L_i) - \mathbf{p}_{\mathcal{P}} - \mathbf{R}_{EE}\mathbf{r}_i + \mathbf{a}_i \\ \mathbf{u}_i(L_i) \\ ine\vdots \\ ine\sum_{i=1}^{N} \mathbf{n}_i(L_i) - \mathbf{F}_{ext} \\ \sum_{i=1}^{N}[(\mathbf{a}_i + \mathbf{p}_i(L_i)) \times \mathbf{n}_i(L_i)] - \mathbf{p}_{\mathcal{P}} \times \mathbf{F}_{ext} - \mathbf{M}_{ext} \end{array} \right\} \quad (19)$$

Direct Integration of Forward Kinematics Problem

The integration involved in each rod to find $\mathbf{p}_i(L_i)$, $\mathbf{u}_i(L_i)$, and $\mathbf{n}_i(L_i)$ can be approached as an initial value problem, as explained in Section 2.2. A vector of dependent variables at $s = 0$ for each rod $\mathbf{y}_i(0)$ is introduced to integrate along the rod L_i using Runge–Kutta. Some of those variables may be known data from boundary conditions, but some other are guess values for unknowns. First tip position and orientation ($x_i(0)$, $y_i(0)$, $\theta_i(0)$) and load ($\mathbf{F}_{ext}$, $\mathbf{M}_{ext}$) are data; internal forces and moments ($\mathbf{n}_i(0)$, $\mathbf{u}_i(0)$) and output components ($\mathbf{p}_{\mathcal{P}}$ and θ_{EE}) are to be guessed ab initio in the FK problem to be optimized for null residuals at the FK solution.

Applying a shooting method to verify the residual vector, guess values are updated in an iterative process until residuals in Equation (19) are below a certain tolerance. The Newton method used in the shooting method requires the evaluation of a Jacobian of the residual vector with respect to the variables, i.e., the guess values. We can consider a special order for guess values, so that the ones corresponding to a rod are together:

$$\mathbf{v}_{guess} = \{\ \mathbf{u}_i(0);\ \mathbf{n}_i(0);\ \ldots;\ \mathbf{p}_{\mathcal{P}};\ \theta_{EE}\ \}^T \quad (20)$$

The Jacobian is then obtained as

$$\mathbf{J}(\mathbf{v}_{guess}) = \frac{\partial \mathbf{g}_{res}(\mathbf{v}_{guess})}{\partial \mathbf{v}_{guess}} \quad (21)$$

The Jacobian related to the FK problem, considering the case $N = 3$, is a sparse matrix $\mathbf{J} \in \mathbb{R}^{12x12}$ of the form

$$\mathbf{J} = \begin{bmatrix} \mathbf{A}_1 & \mathbf{0} & \mathbf{0} & \mathbf{C}_1 & \mathbf{d}_1 \\ \mathbf{0} & \mathbf{A}_2 & \mathbf{0} & \mathbf{C}_2 & \mathbf{d}_2 \\ \mathbf{0} & \mathbf{0} & \mathbf{A}_3 & \mathbf{C}_3 & \mathbf{d}_3 \\ \mathbf{B}_1 & \mathbf{B}_2 & \mathbf{B}_3 & \mathbf{C} & \mathbf{0} \end{bmatrix} \quad (22)$$

The sub-matrices $\mathbf{A}_i \in \mathbb{R}^{3x3}$ are computed by considering the residue associated to the geometrical conditions of rod i and the kinematic variables used as guess values for rod i. To define matrices $\mathbf{B}_i \in \mathbb{R}^{3x3}$, we compute the residue associated to the static conditions of the mechanism and the kinematic variables used as guess values for rod i. Matrices $\mathbf{C}_i \in \mathbb{R}^{3x2}$ are obtained with the residue corresponding to the geometric conditions of each rod i and the coordinates of $\mathcal{P}$ used as guess values. Matrices $\mathbf{d}_i \in \mathbb{R}^{3x1}$ are given by the residue associated to the geometric conditions for rod i and the orientation guess value of the end-effector. And finally, matrix $\mathbf{C} \in \mathbb{R}^{3x2}$ is calculated with the residue of the static conditions and the output position of point $\mathcal{P}$ of the moving platform.

After each iteration j, the guess values have to be updated with

$$\mathbf{v}_{guess}^{j+1} = \mathbf{v}_{guess}^{j} - \mathbf{J}^{-1}\mathbf{g}_{res}^{j} \tag{23}$$

repeating the process until $\mathbf{g}_{res}$ is below a certain established tolerance.

The solution obtained is one that fulfills the geometric conditions for assembly and the static equilibrium of the system; however, there is no guarantee that this equilibrium is stable. An additional check has to be performed to detect the stability of the flexible system. We use the one explained in detail in [12].

The final outcome is a FK solution of the configuration of the mechanism, with neither convergence nor continuity in the assembly mode fully guaranteed, but very efficient and quick when close approximations are used for guess values. The flowchart in Figure 6 shows the summary of the procedure.

Analytical Integration of Forward Kinematics Problem

As explained in Section 2.2, the deformation model of Kirchhoff rods can be analytically integrated in the plane using elliptic integrals. In that case, for a given buckling mode BM_i and a set of values k_i and ψ_i, there is a unique deformed rod shape. Hence, finding a pose of the flexible mechanism means finding the set of m_i, k_i and ψ_i that fulfils the boundary conditions in (19). As such values are within a finite closed space, a numerical search for all solutions is possible. In the following, we employ a non-certified numerical search based in the interpolation of residuals, but certified solutions could also be adopted (see [25]). The choice is made to reduce the computational cost, but a tuning of tolerances is required to verify that no important solutions are missed.

The process of determining the multiple solutions of the FK problem is depicted in the flowchart in Figure 7. Using, again, the mechanism in Figure 2 for reference, given input values of actuators (λ_1 and λ_2) and external load ($\mathbf{F}_{ext}$ and $\mathbf{M}_{ext}$), we can define the first-tip position of rods ($x_i(0)$, $y_i(0)$, and $\theta_i(0)$). Upon definition of a grid on the space of possible values for k_i and ψ_i as shown in Figure 5, we have to take all possible combinations of sets (k_1 ψ_1 k_2 ψ_2 k_3 ψ_3) to obtain rod end-tip positions and forces ($x_i(L)$, $y_i(L)$, R_i) using (12) and (13). These later values are employed in (19) to evaluate the residuals vector of the boundary conditions. A search of null values of those residuals can be performed quickly by interpolation for a fair approximation. These approximate solutions can then be refined using a Newton method to arrive to the final solutions fulfilling conditions. Again, the stability of the equilibrium of these solutions must be verified [11], and those stable solutions are definitively the final multiple solutions of the FK problem.

2.3.2. Workspace Analysis

Once the tools for the FK solution are defined, we can proceed with the finding of workspace of the mechanism. As mentioned above, multiple solutions of the FK problem are found to be the different assembly modes of the mechanism, and each of these in turn generate an *aspect* of the workspace, i.e., a singularity–instability-free region of the workspace [24]. In any case, each pose of the mechanism found is characterized by their kinematics features of interest. In our case, the objective of the study is to evaluate the translational capability of the mechanism, and hence the key factor for further evaluation is the *parasitic angle* of the end-effector.

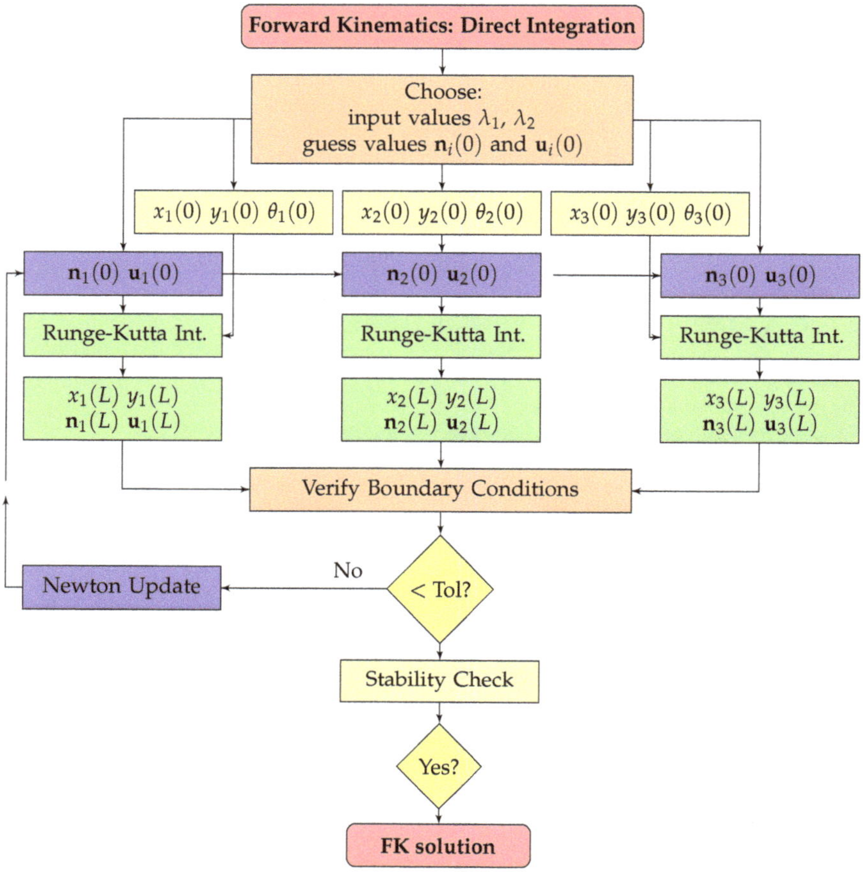

Figure 6. Flowchart for Forward Kinematics Direct Integration Solver.

Two different approaches have been tested for the purpose of a complete finding of *aspects* of the workspace. The first option is depicted in Figure 8, and it is based solely in the FK obtaining of multiple solutions using the elliptic integrals method in Figure 7. The second one (Figure 9) is a combination of the FK multiple solutions solver and the direct integration method in Figure 6.

On the one hand, as shown in Figure 8, we define in the jointspace a discretization λ_1^i and λ_2^i so that we have a finite set of pairs to be analyzed and generate the workspace. Then, we proceed to solve for each pair of inputs the multiple solutions of the FK problem, within a range of buckling modes of interest, generating several stable FK solutions. Those solutions have to be classified into groups corresponding to the different *aspects* depending on the geometric configuration. This classification is not an easy task, and it is one of the drawbacks of this method, along with the computational cost.

As an alternative, we can proceed in a slightly different way with the purpose of reducing the computational cost by following the flowchart in Figure 9. We can choose a starting pair of input values (λ_1^0 and λ_2^0) and apply the procedure to obtain all FK multiple solutions of interest that define the assembly modes. Then, for each of these FK solutions, we can generate a wave propagation to nearby input values (λ_1^i and λ_2^i) solving new poses with the direct integration. When these are stable and non-singular, we propagate the wave again; if not, we stop the propagation there. This approach optimizes the numerical iterations to cover the workspace. The final outcome is again the different *aspects*.

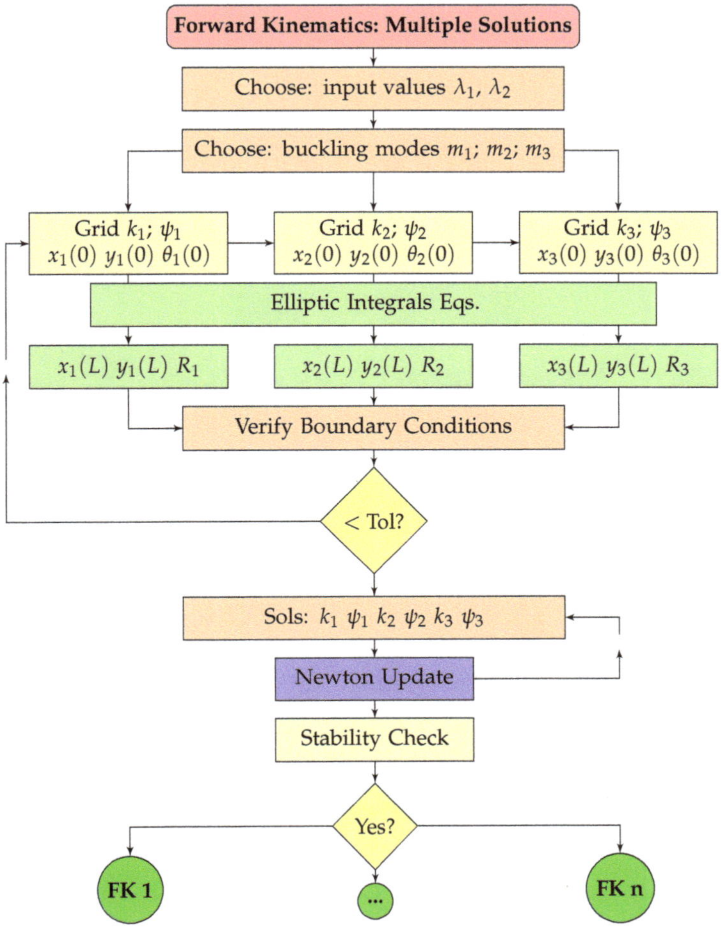

Figure 7. Flowchart for Forward Kinematics Multiple Solution Solver.

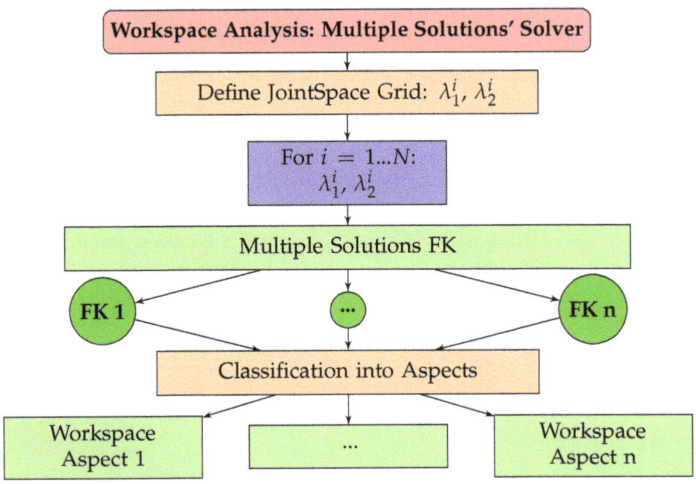

Figure 8. Flowchart for workspace analysis with Multiple Solution Solver.

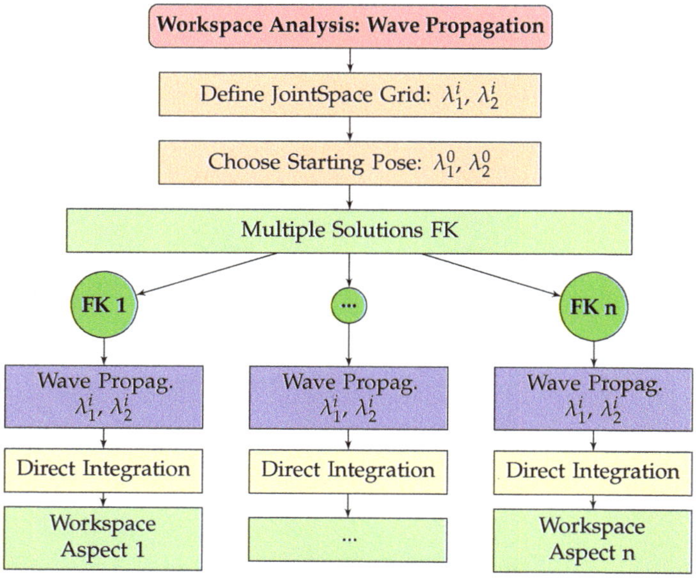

Figure 9. Flowchart for workspace analysis with Wave Propagation.

2.4. *Mechanism's Alternative Designs*

The rigid parallel Delta manipulator depicted in Figure 1 generates a translational movement of the end-effector via the so-called parallelogram joint on the left. This characteristic is independent of the assembly of the rods to the end-effector. Nonetheless, when it comes to the flexible mechanism, this is not the case, and indeed the location of the end-tip of rods at the end-effector greatly affects the resultant motion.

With the aim of achieving a quasi-translational motion, four different designs of the flexible mechanism, in which the placing of the rods differs, have been studied. The four design models are represented in Figure 10. The first two models connect the end-tips with the extremes of the end-effector. On the contrary, the third and fourth design alternatives connect either the red flexible rod (one of the rods forming the parallelogram) or the blue rod (the opposite one) to the central point of the end-effector.

In addition, another alternative (shown in Figure 11) introduces a fourth rod, resulting in an overconstrained mechanism with two parallelograms. The latter model seeks symmetry, a property that is very beneficial.

Whereas the Delta rigid mechanism, such as that in [20], does not benefit from the introduction of a fourth rod due to the added difficulty in the process of assembly as the dimensional tolerances of the components have to be very precise, this is not the case for the flexible overconstrained model.

Moreover, while the diameter of the rods, the size of the end-effector, and the force applied to it do not modify the shape of the workspace nor the parasitic angle in the rigid mechanism, they surely do in the flexible one. All these parameters are taken into account when analyzing and optimizing the mechanism, as shown in the next section.

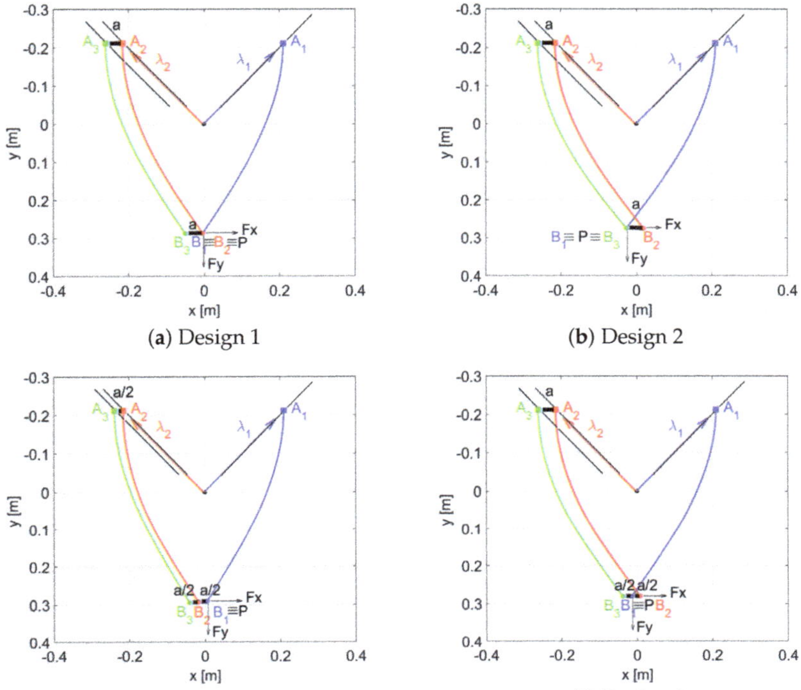

(**a**) Design 1 (**b**) Design 2 (**c**) Design 3 (**d**) Design 4

Figure 10. Four different design models according to the connection of the rods.

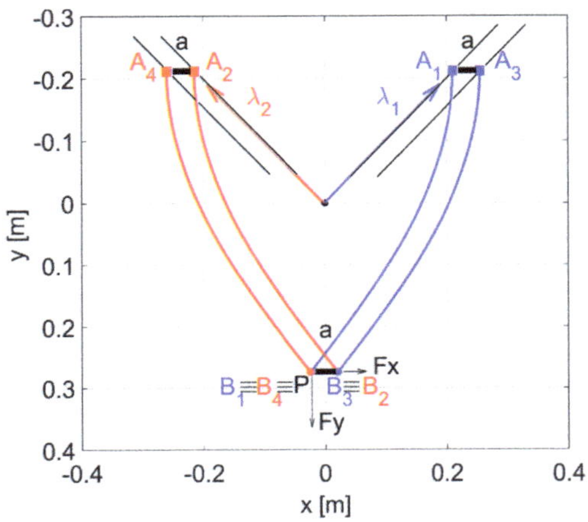

Figure 11. Symmetric overconstrained model.

3. Results

In this section, we describe the results and insights obtained for the different designs, assessing the behavior of the mechanism. The schedule followed is structured as follows:

- Performance Evaluation of Kinematics Analysis;
- Workspace Analysis of Mechanism Alternatives;
- Symmetric Overconstrained Design.

3.1. Performance Evaluation of Kinematics Analysis

The FK problem may offer us a different number of solutions for the same mechanism depending on the values selected for the specified tolerance, the computational time and the number of discretized points selected in the parameter space of k_i and ψ_i. Bear in mind that a certain point in the (k, ψ) parameter space (such as that in Figure 5) establishes the deformed shape of one rod, so the total amount of points results in the combination of the three rods $(k_1, \psi_1, k_2, \psi_2, k_3, \psi_3)$. In this way, Table 1 shows the total number of points to be evaluated for each degree of discretization of the grid in space (k_i, ψ_i), denoted as N_{grid}. Having a high degree of discretization means that a dense discretized mesh is established, formed by a high number of discrete points.

Visualizing the graph represented in Figure 12, it can be observed that the number of different FK solutions found increases as the value of N_{grid} grows and tolerance decreases. However, the computational cost does also become higher in the same direction, so the results end up depending on a compromise between time spent and the number of solutions that are possible to find.

Table 1. Equivalence between N_{grid} and total evaluated points (k, ψ).

Ngrid	Total Evaluated Points (k, ψ)
1	$4^3 = 64$
2	$16^3 = 4096$
3	$36^3 = 46{,}656$
4	$64^3 = 262{,}144$
5	$100^3 = 1{,}000{,}000$
6	$144^3 = 2{,}985{,}984$
7	$196^3 = 7{,}529{,}536$

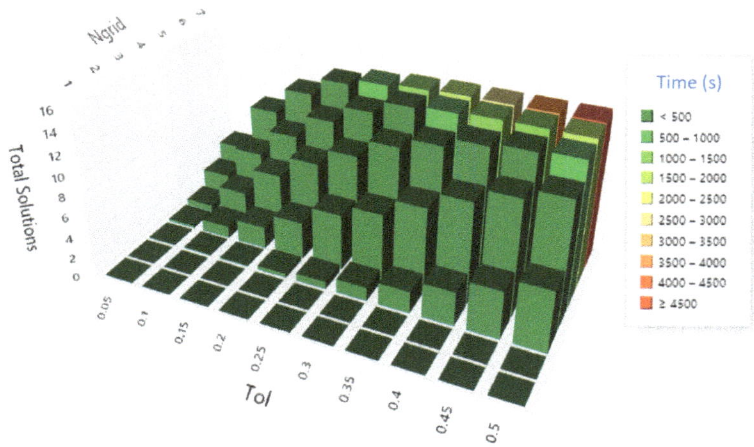

Figure 12. Time–Tolerance–Total Solution number distribution.

For each alternative design model of the mechanism, Table 2 shows the number of solutions (assembly modes) found, as well as the aforementioned indicators of tolerance, computational time, and the discretized mesh for the grid (N_{grid}). This computation was performed with a standard computer and using MATLAB R2023a.

Moreover, focusing on Design model 1, a total of 14 solutions to the FK problem are obtained (Table 2); however, only six of them are stable solutions, those represented in Figure 13.

Table 2. Maximum number of solutions found for different designs considering Buckling mode 1 in every rod.

Design Model	Tol	Ngrid	Number of Solutions	Time Spent (min)
1	0.45	6	14	19.2
2	0.45	6	14	18.7
3	0.5	7	14	68.4
4	0.5	7	15	64.5

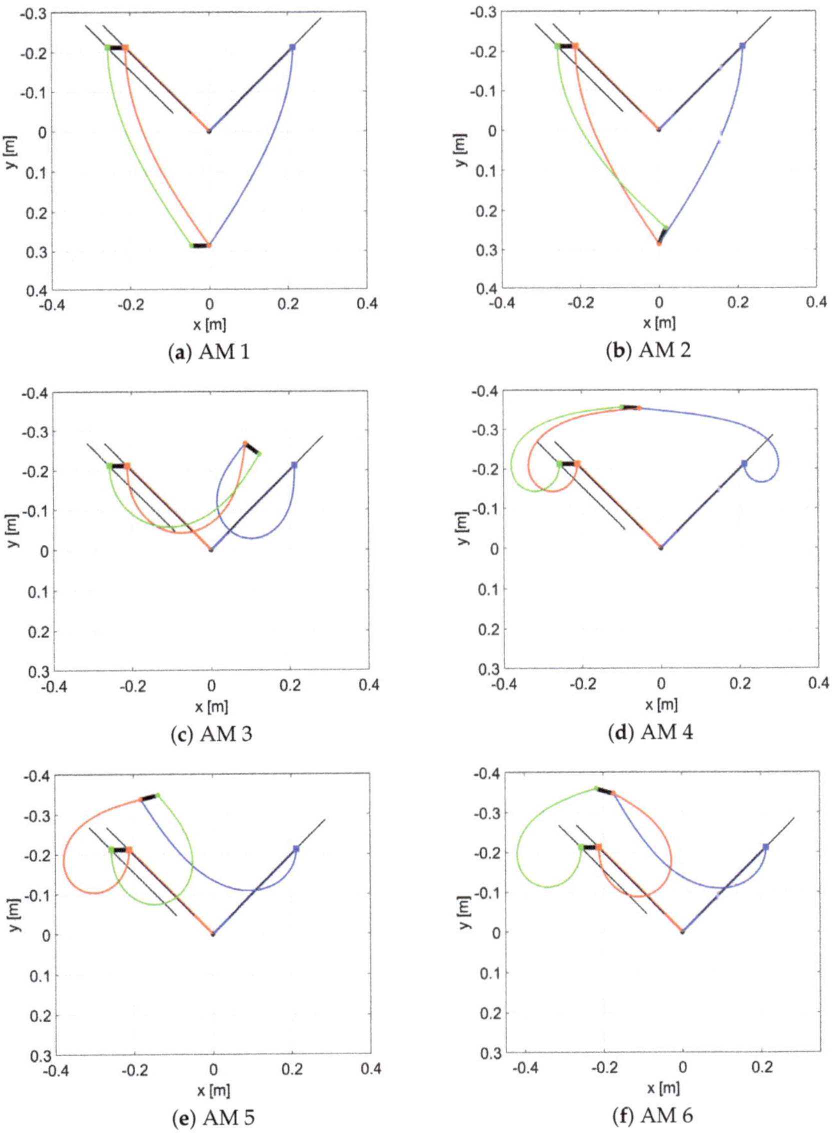

(**a**) AM 1 (**b**) AM 2 (**c**) AM 3 (**d**) AM 4 (**e**) AM 5 (**f**) AM 6

Figure 13. Stable assembly modes for Design model 1.

Looking at the results represented in Figure 13, it is obvious that most solutions do not constitute feasible options in practice due to the existence of collisions among the rods and the linear guides. In this case, the first two assembly modes depicted in Figure 13a,b are the useful solutions. As a consequence of the above results, we focus on obtaining only the assembly modes that are potentially useful, reducing the time required to compute.

In this sense, Figure 14 shows the distribution of useful solutions with respect to tolerance, discretized grid, and computational cost. Accordingly, Table 3 shows the results for the first two design models.

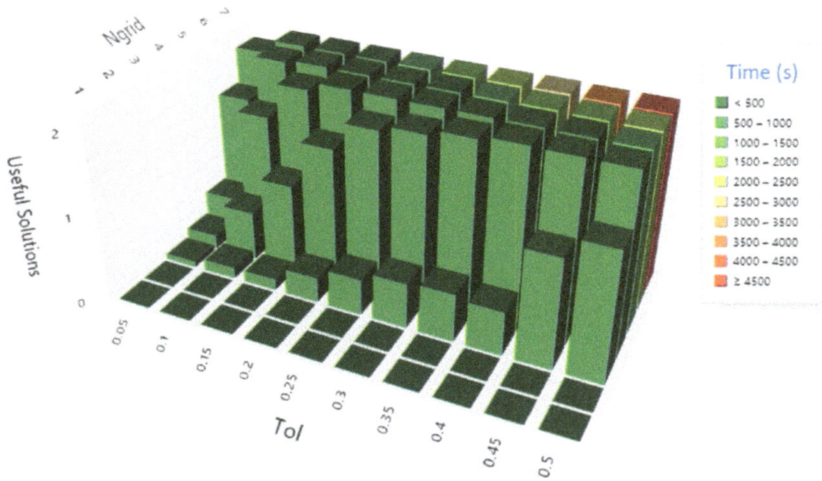

Figure 14. Time–Tolerance–Useful Solution number distribution.

Table 3. Useful solutions found for different designs considering Buckling mode 1 in every rod.

Design Model	Tol	Ngrid	Number of Solutions	Time Spent (min)
1	0.3	5	2	2.4
2	0.2	5	2	1.3

3.2. Workspace Analysis of Mechanism Alternatives

Regarding the workspace corresponding to a certain assembly mode, also known as *aspect*, Table 4 shows a numerical comparison of the time spent for the calculation of the workspaces of the two assembly modes of Design 1 depicted in Figures 13a and 13b, respectively. The two different methods illustrated in Figures 8 and 9 are compared. According to the results given in Table 4, it is clear that the wave propagation method is much more computationally efficient than the multiple solution solver.

Table 4. Design 1: Workspace calculation computational cost comparison

Method	Number of Points in Workspace Grid	Time Spent (min)
Multiple solution solver	31×31	1872
wave propagation	31×31	36

Studying the assembly modes for each of the mechanism's alternative designs, we obtain the following results:

For Design 1 (shown in Figure 10a), the corresponding workspaces of its first two assembly modes are depicted in Figure 15, displayed with a colour scale depending on the parasitic angle of inclination of the end-effector. As it can be seen, the workspace of the first assembly mode (Figure 15a) is bigger and has a smaller range of the parasitic angle. Indeed, the dark green area of the workspace has really low values of the inclination angle, thus performing a quasi-translational motion in that area. On the contrary, the workspace of the second assembly mode (Figure 15b) is not only more limited than the previous one, but also the inclination angle is too high.

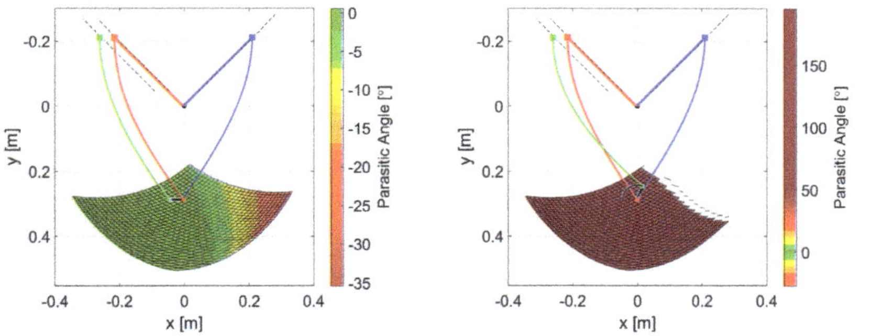

(**a**) AM 1 (**b**) AM 2

Figure 15. Design 1: Workspace for Assembly modes 1 and 2 (no load is applied).

Considering now the first assembly mode, the load influence on the workspace is analyzed. If the maximum payload (50 N) is applied in the Y-direction to point $\mathcal{P}$ of the end-effector, the parasitic angle distribution looks like the one in Figure 16. It can be observed that the workspace subjected to this vertical force is slightly smaller than the previous one with no load, and also there is a variation in the distribution of the parasitic angle.

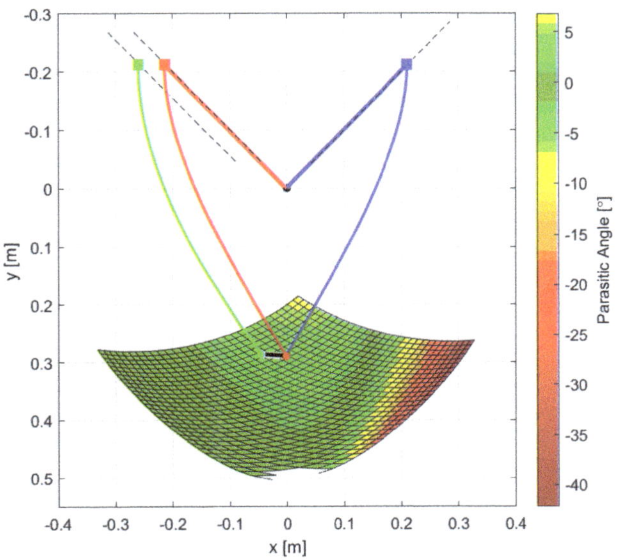

Figure 16. Design 1 (AM 1): Workspace with maximum payload at point $\mathcal{P}$.

The limits of the outer workspace for different load cases are shown in Figure 17.

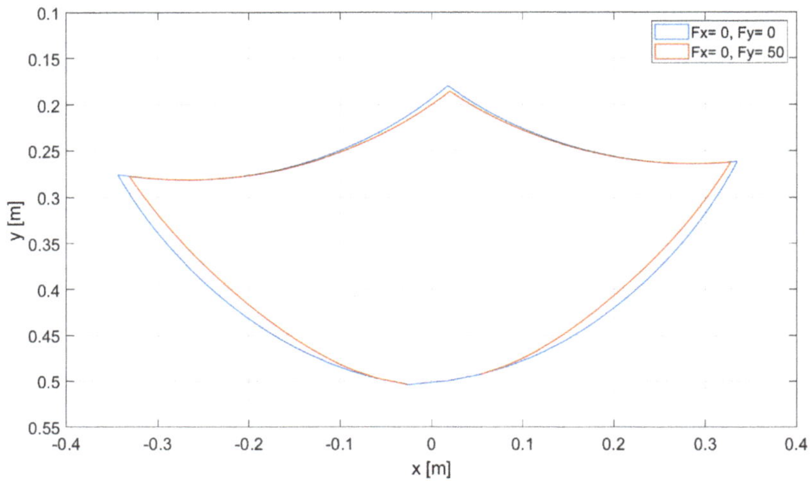

Figure 17. Design 1 (AM 1): Workspace comparison for different loads.

Repeating the same process for the second design alternative of the mechanism (Figure 10b), we obtain the potentially useful solutions shown in Figure 18. Compared to Design 1, it is easy to see that the solutions of the second design do not present any advantage over the first design, as the workspace is smaller and with a higher inclination angle of the end-effector.

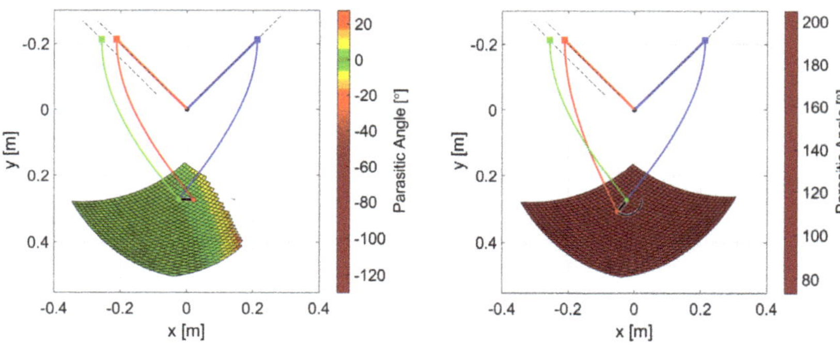

Figure 18. Design 2: Workspace of the potentially useful assembly modes.

Similarly, Designs 3 and 4 lead to worse workspace results compared to the first design, so the results are not included in the paper so as not to lengthen the content unnecessarily.

Dimensional Optimization of Chosen Design

There is the possibility of optimizing Design 1 (in particular its first assembly mode, the one in Figure 15a) to achieve a more suitable workspace. In this sense, searching for the optimum main dimensional parameters, such as the width of the parallelogram (a) and the diameters of the flexible rods (d_i), yields the results shown in Figure 19. Both the workspaces for the initial reference design and the optimized one are shown. For each case, the values of the design parameters and the maximum inclination angle, θ_{EE}, are given in Table 5.

According to the results, increasing the width of the parallelogram (a) and reducing the diameter (d_3) of the third rod (the outer green rod), the inclination angle becomes much more stable and closer to zero in the whole workspace.

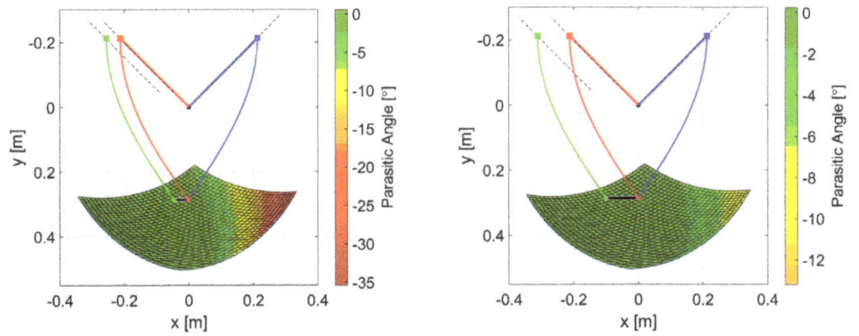

(**a**) Reference design 1 (**b**) Optimized design 1

Figure 19. Design 1: Workspace of the reference and optimized design.

Table 5. Design parameters for reference and Optimized design 1.

Case	a (m)	d_1 (m)	d_2 (m)	d_3 (m)	Max. θ_{EE} (°)
Reference	0.045	0.004	0.004	0.004	35.97
Optimized	0.1	0.004	0.004	0.002	13.44

Regarding the load influence, again considering the maximum payload of 50 N vertically applied to the end-effector, it can be shown in Figure 20 that the optimized design performs better than the reference one.

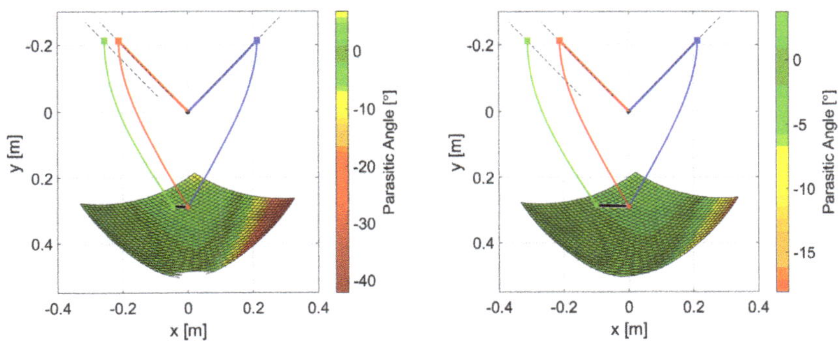

(**a**) Reference design 1 (**b**) Optimized design 1

Figure 20. Workspace subjected to maximum payload in reference and Optimized design 1.

3.3. Symmetric Overconstrained Design

So far, the evaluated designs consist of asymmetric designs, maintaining a similarity to its rigid counterpart, the commercial planar Delta robot from Igus [20]. Next, we analyze the design previously shown in Figure 11 in which, by introducing a fourth rod, we achieve a symmetric overconstrained design. Regarding the design parameter values, the width of the parallelogram, a, is 0.045 m and the diameter of each of the four rods, d_i, is 0.004 m.

The corresponding workspace of this symmetric design is represented in Figure 21. It can be observed that the parasitic angle is almost zero throughout the whole workspace (note that the values of the angle are multiplied by 10^{-5}). This makes it possible for the mechanism to move quasi-translationally independently of its position.

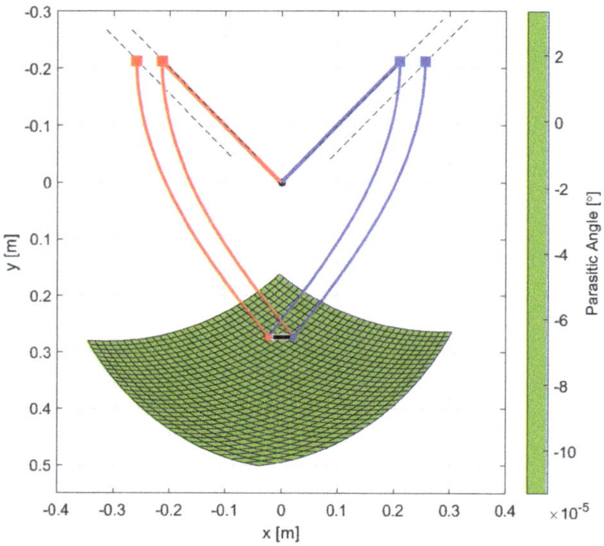

Figure 21. Workspace of the symmetric overconstrained design.

In relation to the load influence, if the maximum payload (50 N) is vertically applied to the end-effector, the workspace takes the shape of Figure 22, having a very small impact on its shape (see also Figure 23) and even decreasing the value of the parasitic angle.

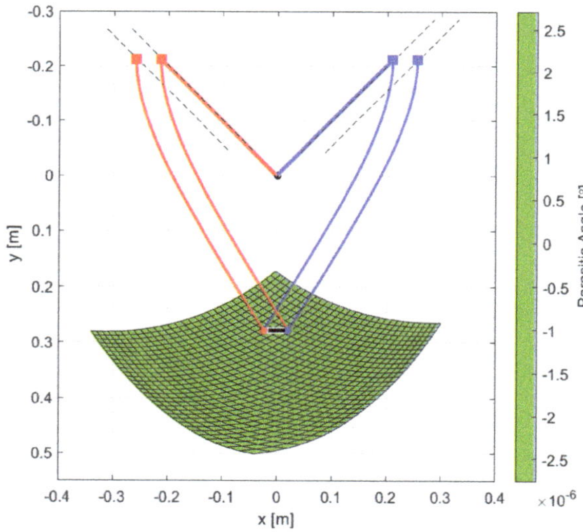

Figure 22. Symmetric design with maximum payload centered at end-effector.

Therefore, if we compare Optimized design 1 and this last symmetric design, we can determine that the symmetric design presents a much more stable workspace in the sense that the parasitic angle is practically null all over it, thus achieving a quasi-translational motion along the whole workspace.

Regarding the load influence, despite having a minimal impact on the extreme limits of the workspace (Figure 23), an even better workspace is achieved as the parasitic angle is smaller than in the unloaded case. As shown in Figure 22, the values of the inclination angle are multiplied by 10^{-6}.

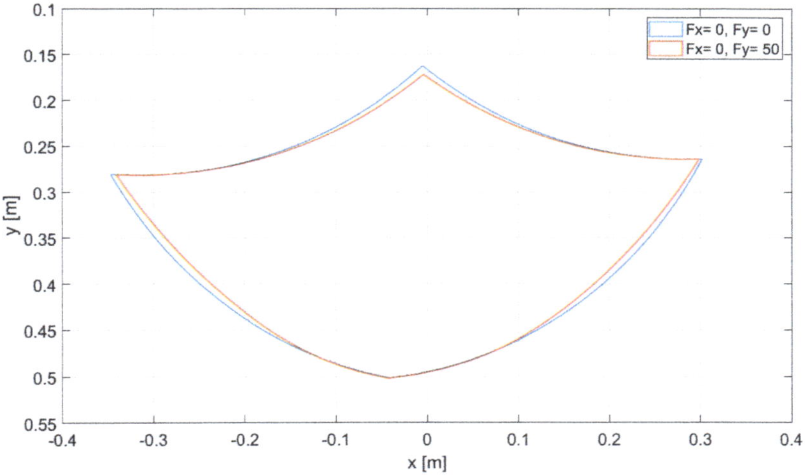

Figure 23. Workspace load influence for symmetric overconstrained design.

4. Discussion

This work proposes two different approaches to solve the Forward Kinematics problem of continuum planar manipulators. One approach is aimed at obtaining one nearby solution of the FK problem, coming from a certain starting solution and making use of a direct Runge–Kutta integration along the length of each rod. The second method covers the full problem in the sense that all possible solutions, assembly modes, are obtained by means of a numeric search in the (k_i, ψ_i) parameter space looking for all the possible combinations of those sets.

By using any of these methods, the workspace can be obtained. In the case of using the multiple solutions solver, all possible workspaces are obtained, that is, each of the so-called aspects corresponding to a given assembly mode. Obviously, the associated computational cost is very high. Therefore, there is a very advantageous alternative that consists in combining the two methods in the following way: once the FK problem is fully solved and we already have all the possible assembly modes, we can focus on one specific assembly mode of interest and then apply the wave propagation strategy to obtain the workspace of that assembly mode. As demonstrated in this work, this latter alternative considerably reduces the computational cost.

As a case study, the planar continuum Keops–Delta manipulator is analyzed with the purpose of achieving a design capable of maintaining the end-effector as much horizontal as possible along its motion throughout the workspace. By comparing various designs, it is demonstrated that the symmetric overconstrained design is the one that presents an optimal workspace in which quasi-translational motion is achieved over the entire area it covers. Furthermore, analyzing how this symmetric design works in the case of applying a vertical load on the end-effector, assuming load values similar to those supported by commercially available Delta robots in pick and place applications, it is verified that the parasitic angle remains practically null, even decreasing its value with respect to the unloaded case.

Future lines of work will approach the dynamic analysis of this type of flexible manipulators. It is also interesting to contrast the real motion that is actually generated in the end-effector with a prototype.

Author Contributions: Conceptualization, O.A. and M.U.; methodology, O.A., M.U., K.B. and A.H.; software, O.A. and K.B.; validation, O.A., M.U., K.B. and A.H.; formal analysis, O.A. and A.H.; investigation, O.A. and M.U.; resources, O.A. and K.B.; data curation, M.U. and K.B.; writing—original draft preparation, O.A. and M.U.; writing—review and editing, K.B. and A.H.; visualization, O.A., M.U., K.B. and A.H.; supervision, O.A. and K.B.; project administration, O.A. and A.H.; funding acquisition, O.A. and A.H. All authors have read and agreed to the published version of the manuscript.

Funding: The authors wish to acknowledge the financial support received from the Spanish Government through the Ministerio de Ciencia e Innovación (Project PID2020-116176GB-I00) financed by MCIN/AEI/10.13039/501100011033 and the support for the research group through Project IT1480-22 provided by the Departamento de Educación from the Regional Basque Government.

Data Availability Statement: The original contributions presented in the study are included in the article, further inquiries can be directed to the corresponding author.

Conflicts of Interest: The authors declare no conflicts of interest. The funders had no role in the design of the study; in the collection, analyses, or interpretation of data; in the writing of the manuscript; or in the decision to publish the results.

Abbreviations

The following abbreviations are used in this manuscript:

PCM	Parallel Continuum Manipulators
PKM	Parallel Kinematic Machine
FK	Forward Kinematics
R-K	Runge–Kutta
AM	Assembly Mode

References

1. Liu, K.; Kong, X.; Yu, J. Operation mode analysis of lower-mobility parallel mechanisms based on dual quaternions. *Mech. Mach. Theory* **2019**, *142*, 103577. [CrossRef]
2. Bouri, M.; Clavel, R. The Linear Delta: Developments and Applications. In Proceedings of the Robotics (ISR), 2010 41st International Symposium on and 2010 6th German Conference on Robotics (ROBOTIK), Munich, Germany, 7–9 June 2010; pp. 1–8.
3. Cheng, H.; Li, W. Reducing the Frame Vibration of Delta Robot in Pick and Place Application: An Acceleration Profile Optimization Approach. *Shock Vib.* **2018**, *2018*, 2945314. [CrossRef]
4. Laribi, M.; Romdhane, L.; Zeghloul, S. Analysis and dimensional synthesis of the DELTA robot for a prescribed workspace. *Mech. Mach. Theory* **2007**, *42*, 859–870. [CrossRef]
5. Lilge, S.; Nuelle, K.; Childs, J.A.; Wen, K.; Rucker, D.C.; Burgner-Kahrs, J. Parallel-Continuum Robots: A Survey. *IEEE Trans. Robot.* **2024**, *40*, 3252–3270. [CrossRef]
6. Bryson, C.E.; Rucker, D.C. Toward parallel continuum manipulators. In Proceedings of the ICRA 2014—IEEE International Conference on Robotics and Automation, Hong Kong, China, 31 May–5 June 2014; pp. 778–785.
7. Chen, G.; Kang, Y.; Liang, Z.; Zhang, Z.; Wang, H. Kinetostatics modeling and analysis of parallel continuum manipulators. *Mech. Mach. Theory* **2021**, *163*, 104380. [CrossRef]
8. Howell, L.L. *Compliant Mechanisms*; John Wiley & Sons: Hoboken, NJ, USA, 2002.
9. Zhu, B.; Zhang, X.; Zhang, H.; Liang, J.; Zang, H.; Li, H.; Wang, R. Design of compliant mechanisms using continuum topology optimization: A review. *Mech. Mach. Theory* **2020**, *143*, 103622. [CrossRef]
10. Black, C.B.; Till, J.; Rucker, D.C. Parallel Continuum Robots: Modeling, Analysis, and Actuation-Based Force Sensing. *IEEE Trans. Robot.* **2018**, *34*, 29–47. [CrossRef]
11. Till, J.; Bryson, C.E.; Chung, S.; Orekhov, A.; Rucker, D.C. Efficient computation of multiple coupled Cosserat rod models for real-time simulation and control of parallel continuum manipulators. In Proceedings of the 2015 IEEE International Conference on Robotics and Automation (ICRA), Seattle, WA, USA, 26–30 May 2015; pp. 5067–5074. [CrossRef]
12. Till, J.; Rucker, D.C. Elastic Stability of Cosserat Rods and Parallel Continuum Robots. *IEEE Trans. Robot.* **2017**, *33*, 718–733. [CrossRef]
13. Wu, G.; Shi, G. Experimental statics calibration of a multi-constraint parallel continuum robot. *Mech. Mach. Theory* **2019**, *136*, 72–85. [CrossRef]
14. Yang, Z.; Zhu, X.; Xu, K. Continuum Delta Robot: A Novel Translational Parallel Robot with Continuum Joints. In Proceedings of the 2018 IEEE/ASME International Conference on Advanced Intelligent Mechatronics (AIM), Auckland, New Zealand, 9–12 July 2018; pp. 748–755. [CrossRef]
15. Lilge, S.; Burgner-Kahrs, J. Kinetostatic Modeling of Tendon-Driven Parallel Continuum Robots. *IEEE Trans. Robot.* **2023**, *39*, 1563–1579. [CrossRef]
16. Altuzarra, O.; Tagliavini, L.; Lei, Y.; Petuya, V.; Ruiz-Erezuma, J.L. On Constraints and Parasitic Motions of a Tripod Parallel Continuum Manipulator. *Machines* **2023**, *11*, 71. [CrossRef]

17. Altuzarra, O.; Urizar, M.; Cichella, M.; Petuya, V. Kinematic Analysis of three degrees of freedom planar parallel continuum mechanisms. *Mech. Mach. Theory* **2023**, *185*, 105311. [CrossRef]
18. Zaccaria, F.; Idá, E.; Briot, S.; Carricato, M. Workspace Computation of Planar Continuum Parallel Robots. *IEEE Robot. Autom. Lett.* **2022**, *7*, 2700–2707. [CrossRef]
19. Briot, S.; Boyer, F. A Geometrically Exact Assumed Strain Modes Approach for the Geometrico- and Kinemato-Static Modelings of Continuum Parallel Robots. *IEEE Trans. Robot.* **2023**, *39*, 1527–1543. [CrossRef]
20. igus® GmbH. IGUS: Technische Dokumentation Technical Documentation. Drylin Delta Robot DLE-ZR-0002. 2022. Available online: https://www.igus.eu/product/21025?C=DE&L=en&artNr=DLE-ZR-0002 (accessed on 4 November 2024).
21. Antman, S.S. *Nonlinear Problems of Elasticity*; Springer: New York, NY, USA, 2005. [CrossRef]
22. Rucker, D.C.; Jones, B.A.; Webster, R.J., III. A Geometrically Exact Model for Externally Loaded Concentric-Tube Continuum Robots. *IEEE Trans. Robot.* **2010**, *26*, 769–780. [CrossRef] [PubMed]
23. Altuzarra, O.; Solanillas, D.M.; Amezua, E.; Petuya, V. Path Analysis for Hybrid Rigid–Flexible Mechanisms. *Mathematics* **2021**, *9*, 869. [CrossRef]
24. Caro, S.; Chablat, D.; Goldsztejn, A.; Ishii, D.; Jermann, C. A branch and prune algorithm for the computation of generalized aspects of parallel robots. *Artif. Intell.* **2014**, *211*, 34–50. [CrossRef]
25. Altuzarra, O.; Merlet, J.P. Certified Kinematics Solution of 2-DOF Planar Parallel Continuum Mechanisms. In *Proceedings of the Advances in Mechanism and Machine Science*; Uhl, T., Ed.; Springer: Cham, Switzerland, 2019; pp. 197–208.

mathematics

Article

Mathematical Dimensional Synthesis of Four-Bar Linkages Based on Cognate Mechanisms

Enrique Soriano-Heras [1,*], Carlos Pérez-Carrera [2] and Higinio Rubio [1]

1 Department of Mechanical Engineering, University Carlos III of Madrid, Avda. de la Universidad, 30, 28911 Madrid, Spain; hrubio@ing.uc3m.es
2 Department of Industrial Engineering, University of Salerno, Via Giovanni Paolo II, 132, 84084 Fisciano, Italy; cperezcarrera@unisa.it
* Correspondence: esoriano@ing.uc3m.es

Abstract

In the field of mechanical engineering, understanding mechanisms is essential for designing and developing devices and systems. Mechanisms, composed of interconnected elements, transform the energy applied to the input link into motion or force in the output link. Mechanisms are found in a wide variety of machines, from industrial machines to household machines. In this paper, a mechanism synthesis method is developed that can model four-bar linkages and build their cognate mechanisms to be able to select the mechanism that best suits the required work. Studying four-bar mechanisms offers a strong foundation for grasping more complex mechanical systems. The concepts and principles learned from four-bar mechanisms are widely applicable to advanced mechanical systems, making them a crucial starting point in mechanical engineering education and research. The mechanism synthesis method proposed in this article is organized into three main sections. The first section provides a comprehensive overview of the theoretical and mathematical foundations required for modeling mechanisms, laying the groundwork for understanding the subsequent calculations. The second section delves into the process of obtaining and analyzing the initial mechanism and constructing cognate mechanisms, detailing the procedures and algorithms used for modeling and calculating the coupling curve. Finally, the third section discusses the practical implementation of the method, including the graphical representation of mechanisms and a comparative analysis of the solutions obtained, assessing dimensional differences, design and manufacturing efficiency, and their suitability for various practical applications. The proposed four-bar mechanism synthesis method serves as a valuable tool for mechanism design, offering versatile and adaptable solutions that can optimize both technical performance and economic viability across a wide range of engineering applications.

Keywords: dimensional synthesis; four-bar linkage; cognate mechanism; path and motion generation; optimization methods

MSC: 70G55

1. Introduction

1.1. General Background and Main Significance of the Present Research Work

The theory of machines and mechanisms constitutes a fundamental pillar of mechanical engineering. It is dedicated to the comprehension of the mechanisms underlying the transformation of energy into controlled motion or force within mechanical systems. This field of study examines the interplay between geometry, movement, applied forces, and the resulting energy changes within a system. The significance of this field lies in its capacity to facilitate the design and optimization of devices and machines across a spectrum of applications, encompassing industrial systems and everyday household appliances. The field is divided into two main approaches: kinematic analysis, which focuses on the study of mechanism motion independent of forces, and mechanism synthesis, which emphasizes the design and creation of new systems tailored to specific functions [1].

The synthesis of mechanical systems plays a pivotal role in the advancement of technology, particularly in meeting the functional and operational specifications that are essential for the development of advanced machinery. By calculating the dimensions and configurations required to achieve the desired motion or force transformations, this approach ensures the effective and efficient operation of machines. Depending on the intended functionality, synthesis methods are classified into three main types: path generation, in which mechanisms are designed so that a specific point follows a desired trajectory; function generation, in which a mechanism's transmission ratio is controlled; and rigid-body guidance, in which a particular element is constrained to follow a defined path [2]. These classifications illustrate the versatility and scope of synthesis methods in addressing a diverse range of engineering challenges. Among the numerous mechanical systems that have been the subject of study, four-bar linkages are distinguished as a foundational class of mechanisms due to their simplicity, versatility, and pervasive utilization. These mechanisms provide an essential foundation for understanding more complex systems, as many principles and concepts initially developed for four-bar linkages can be readily applied to advanced designs [3].

Their applications are diverse, encompassing fields such as robotics, automotive engineering, and manufacturing, and they are therefore indispensable in both academic and industrial contexts. The significance of four-bar mechanisms lies in their adaptability and utility across a wide spectrum of applications, which renders them more versatile than other mechanisms. As an illustration, in the automotive industry, four-bar linkages represent a crucial component of suspension systems, where they facilitate smooth vehicle handling and ride quality by effectively managing wheel motion. In the field of robotics, these mechanisms are often utilized in manipulator arms to achieve precise movement and trajectory control, which is a prerequisite for tasks such as assembly and material handling. In the context of manufacturing machinery, four-bar linkages facilitate the transfer of complex motion, as exemplified by their use in presses and cutting tools, where they provide dependable and consistent operation. Beyond industrial applications, these mechanisms are also employed in everyday devices, including windshield wipers, which depend on their ability to convert rotary input into linear sweeping motion. Their extensive utility can be attributed to their capacity to deliver tailored motion profiles and force transmission within compact and efficient designs, establishing them as a foundational mechanism in mechanical engineering.

The study of four-bar mechanisms is therefore not only essential for engineering education but also serves as a foundation for the resolution of real-world mechanical design problems. Despite notable advancements, the synthesis of mechanisms continues to present a challenge when attempting to achieve an optimal balance between functional performance, economic viability, and manufacturing feasibility. Conventional methodologies frequently yield mechanisms that satisfy the theoretical specifications but are unfeasible for production due to economic constraints, complexity, or material limitations. This gap highlights the necessity for the development of novel synthesis techniques that can surmount these limitations. This research addresses this need by focusing on the systematic design of four-bar linkages and their cognate mechanisms.

1.2. Formulation of the Specific Problem of Interest for This Investigation

The challenge in mechanism design is to reconcile the theoretical precision of synthesis methods with the practical constraints of engineering applications. Although existing techniques permit the design of mechanisms that are optimized for specific trajectories, transmission ratios, or motion profiles, the solutions they produce are not always economically viable or manufacturable. This discrepancy is particularly apparent in applications where precision and efficiency are of paramount importance, yet resources are constrained. For example, the attainment of a desired motion trajectory may necessitate the use of components that are prohibitively expensive or challenging to manufacture [4–6].

One promising avenue for addressing this issue is through the use of cognate mechanisms. Such designs represent an alternative means of achieving the desired functional output, differing from the original in terms of their geometric and dimensional characteristics. Cognate mechanisms offer the advantage of providing additional options for evaluation in terms of cost, manufacturability, and operational constraints [7]. Nevertheless, the construction of cognate mechanisms presents a number of challenges. The current methods for generating these alternatives are limited in scope, relying on predefined mathematical frameworks that lack the flexibility and adaptability required to address the diverse engineering scenarios that may arise [8,9]. Therefore, there is a need to develop an intuitive and original method for the creation of cognate mechanisms. In this context, this research addresses the specific problem of developing a systematic, intuitive, and adaptable method for constructing cognate mechanisms for four-bar linkages. The objective of the proposed method is to address the shortcomings of existing approaches by providing a framework that integrates functional requirements with economic and manufacturing considerations. This investigation aims to bridge the gap between theoretical mechanism design and practical engineering needs, thereby providing a robust tool for engineers tasked with designing optimized mechanical systems.

1.3. Literature Review

The design and analysis of mechanisms have undergone considerable advancement through the application of diverse methodologies, each of which has sought to enhance precision, adaptability, or computational efficiency. The synthesis of four-bar mechanisms and their extensions, such as six-bar and multi-loop systems, has been a central focus of numerous studies, given their relevance to a diverse range of engineering applications. A significant contribution to the field of path generation was made by Wampler et al. [10], who addressed the long-standing problem of determining all four-bar linkages whose coupler curve passes through nine prescribed points. By employing a combination of classical elimination, multihomogeneous variables, and numerical polynomial continuation, they demonstrated the existence of 1442 non-degenerate solutions, accompanied by their Roberts cognates, which yielded a total of 4326 distinct solutions. The development of a computer algorithm for computing all possible solutions for any given nine points represented a significant breakthrough in this field. This computational approach constituted a foundation for subsequent research and applications.

The work by Roth and Freudenstein further extended the use of algebraic methods in kinematic synthesis, emphasizing the necessity for iterative numerical procedures in solving non-linear algebraic equations [11]. The algorithms were particularly efficacious for nine-point path synthesis problems in geared five-bar motion, where four-bar mechanisms could be regarded as a special case. This study demonstrated the utility of numerical methods in expanding the domain of mechanism design while guaranteeing convergence without the necessity of exact initial approximations. In a related vein, Kramer and Sandor introduced the Selective Precision Synthesis (SPS) method, which provides a general framework for the optimal design of planar mechanisms [12]. This approach, which is applicable to the generation of paths, motions, and functions, permitted the specification of different accuracy limits at discrete positions. By integrating non-linear programming and dyadic construction, the SPS method exhibited stability and adaptability that were previously uncommon in traditional Burmester theory or other synthesis techniques. The versatility of the method is evidenced by its capacity to accommodate four-bar, five-bar, multi-loop, and adjustable mechanisms, particularly in the context of interactive computer-aided design environments. In addition to four-bar linkages, six-bar mechanisms have been the subject of considerable research interest due to their enhanced functional capabilities and motion diversity. Plecnik and McCarthy addressed the kinematic synthesis equations for Stephenson III six-bar mechanisms, attaining solutions capable of accommodating up to 11 accuracy points [13]. The use of a numerically general multihomogeneous homotopy facilitated the discovery of thousands of linkage solutions, which were subsequently sorted and analyzed for practical applications such as dynamic wrist splints for stroke survivors. Similarly, Baskar and Plecnik investigated six-bar timed curve generators of the Stephenson type, employing random monodromy loops to compute comprehensive solution sets [14]. This research demonstrated the potential of six-bar mechanisms for modifying force and velocity transmission in specific applications.

The properties and applications of mechanism cognates have also been subjected to extensive investigation. Simionescu and Smith presented a novel proof of the existence of three function cognates for Stephenson II mechanisms and two for Stephenson III mechanisms, along with a new class of overconstrained mechanisms [15]. Their investigation of four-bar and six-bar planar mechanisms revealed pivotal functional characteristics, including the diagonal-type function cognates of four-bar couplers. This study served to reinforce the theoretical and practical relevance of cognates in extending the design possibilities for both simple and complex mechanisms. Han and Liu put forth the Solution Region Synthesis Methodology (SRSM) for path synthesis in planar four-bar mechanisms, with an emphasis on eight-precision-point path generation [16]. Their approach represented an infinite number of solutions within a plane, thereby enabling the elimination of defective solutions and the classification of feasible linkages. This methodology provided an innovative approach to visualizing and optimizing design spaces, particularly when additional constraints or design requirements were imposed. Further studies have explored the integration of diverse linkage types. Mehdigholi and Akbarnejad examined the optimal synthesis of four-bar linkages and their combination with cognates to form Watt's six-bar mechanisms [17]. The aforementioned mechanisms exhibited utility in applications such as legged machinery, where the ability to achieve both straight and parallel motion was crucial for maintaining stability and enhancing efficiency. Meanwhile, Starns and Flugrad [18] illustrated the synthesis of geared five-bar path generators using continuation methods, emphasizing the flexibility provided by variable gear ratios. Their approach permitted designers to investigate a multitude of configurations, thereby enhancing the versatility of geared mechanisms.

The collective evidence presented in these studies illustrates the extensive scope and complexity of research in mechanism synthesis, encompassing a range of methodologies from foundational algebraic approaches to advanced numerical and computational techniques. While four-bar mechanisms remain a fundamental aspect of this field, the investigation of six-bar, multi-loop, and overconstrained mechanisms illustrates the continued evolution of kinematic design methodologies. These developments not only enhance the theoretical comprehension of mechanisms but also furnish practical instruments and insights for confronting intricate engineering quandaries.

1.4. Scope and Contributions of This Investigation

The objective of this investigation is to develop and apply a novel synthesis method for four-bar linkages. By focusing on this specific class of mechanisms, the research aims to address fundamental challenges in mechanical design while offering engineers practical tools for use in their work. The study is structured into three phases: the first is the establishment of the theoretical foundations, the second is the development of the synthesis method, and the third is the evaluation of its practical implementation. Each phase contributes to a comprehensive understanding of the proposed approach and its potential applications.

The theoretical foundations of this study establish the groundwork for modeling and analyzing four-bar linkages, providing the mathematical and geometric principles necessary for mechanism synthesis. Subsequently, these principles are employed to develop a systematic methodology for the generation of cognate mechanisms, encompassing algorithms for the derivation of coupler curves and the evaluation of design alternatives. Finally, the practical implementation of the method is explored. This includes graphical visualization and dimensional comparisons. This investigation makes several contributions to the existing literature. First, it provides a framework for visualizing and comparing alternative mechanisms. This enhances decision-making in the design process, and it addresses a critical gap in the literature. The investigation also presents an intuitive and adaptable approach to constructing cognate mechanisms. This advances the state of knowledge in mechanical engineering research.

2. Materials and Methods

The mechanism synthesis method proposed in this article is structured in three essential parts. First, a detailed description of the theoretical and mathematical foundations on which the method is based is presented, including the equations and expressions necessary for modeling the mechanisms. This part provides the necessary theoretical background and lays the foundation for understanding the subsequent calculations. The second part describes the process of obtaining and analyzing the initial mechanism and the construction of cognate mechanisms. The procedures and algorithms used for modeling the initial mechanism and the calculations for obtaining the coupling curve are detailed here. Finally, the practical implementation of the method is addressed, where the graphical representation of the mechanisms and a comparative study of the solutions obtained are shown. This comparison includes the evaluation of dimensional differences, efficiency in terms of design and manufacturing, and the suitability for different practical applications.

2.1. Theoretical Background

A mechanism is formed by a set of solids joined together with the objective of performing a specific movement. The movement can be either rotational or translational, as shown in Figure 1.

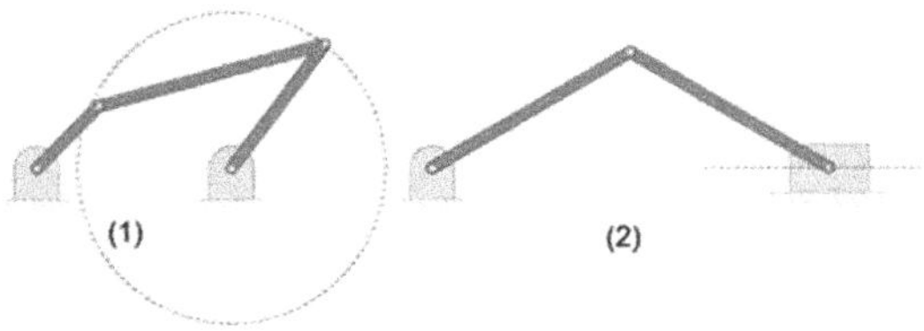

Figure 1. Examples of rotational motion (**1**) and translational motion (**2**).

Mechanisms can take on a variety of configurations and be composed of a wide variety of parts, but the function remains the same: to trace a specific path at a given point in the mechanism by means of the movement of the input link. To simplify these systems, the components of the mechanism are represented symbolically, thus creating a diagram that facilitates a visual understanding of the mechanism.

Mechanisms are composed of three main types of components, as shown in Figure 2:

(1) Links: These are the solid parts of the mechanism that connect to each other to transmit movement. Depending on the number of nodes (connection points between links) the links are classified as binary, ternary, or quaternary.

(2) Joints or rotation pairs: These are the points of connection between two or more links where some movement is allowed between the interconnected links. Reuleaux coined the term lower pair to describe joints with lower contact and the term upper pair to describe joints with point or line contact [19–22].

(3) Supports: These are the fixed points of the mechanism that provide stability and support to the mechanism.

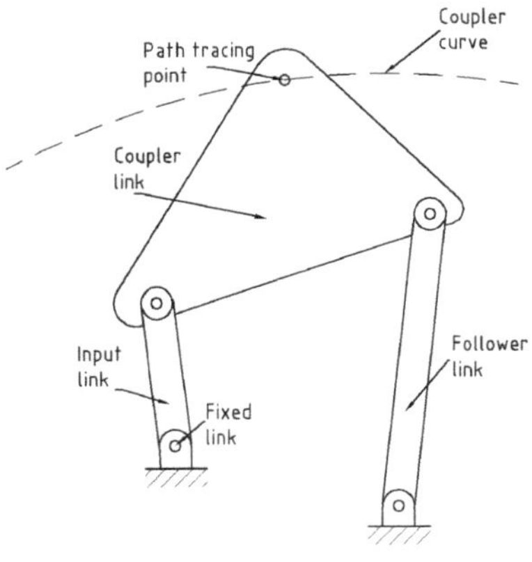

Figure 2. Four-bar planar mechanism.

The types of mechanisms studied in this article are four-bar mechanisms; this means that the mechanism consists of four interconnected solid elements, forming a closed loop whose paths of travel at any point will be contained in the same plane. The mechanisms will consist of two supports and three interconnected links, where one link will be ternary (containing three nodes), known as the coupling triangle, and a fixed link located between the supports. The main function of this type of mechanism is that, when the input link rotates, the coupling point of the ternary link follows the specific desired path, called the coupling path; see Figure 2.

2.1.1. Determination of Degrees of Freedom

A characteristic that determines whether the mechanism being studied can move, or is instead a static structure, is the degrees of freedom (*DOF*) of the mechanism. This characteristic determines the number of independent coordinates necessary to define its position or, in other words, indicates the number of directions in which a mechanism can move.

To determine the *DOF* of a mechanism, the number of links and joints and the interaction between them must be considered. To do this, the Grübler criterion is applied, which states that the degree of freedom of a kinematic chain depends on the number of its links and rotation pairs [23]; see Equation (1).

$$DOF = 3 \cdot (N - 1) - 2 \cdot f_1 - f_2 \tag{1}$$

In Equation (1), N is the number of links, f_1 is the pairs of one degree of freedom and f_2 is the pairs of two degrees of freedom. In the case where $DOF > 1$, the system will be considered as a mechanism, whereas if $DOF = 0$, the system will be considered as a fixed structure.

In the case of the four-bar mechanisms studied in this paper, they have one degree of freedom. This means that the mechanism can only move on a fixed axis or move in a specific linear direction.

2.1.2. Grashof Method

Four-bar mechanisms are differentiated from each other based on their kinematic characteristics. Therefore, these mechanisms are divided into two classes:

(1) Class I: They are defined as crank mechanisms where at least one of its links performs a complete rotation.
(2) Class II: They are defined as rocker mechanisms where none of the elements of the quadrilateral performs a complete rotation.

To classify four-bar mechanisms into one of these two classes, the engineer and professor of applied mechanics Franz Grashof developed a theorem known as "Grashof's Theorem" where, depending on the lengths of the links of the mechanism, one of these two classes could be assigned to the mechanism [24–26].

Grashof's theorem consists of measuring the lengths of the links of the mechanism and observing whether the following condition is met, Equation (2).

$$a + d \leq b + c \tag{2}$$

In Equation (2), a is the length of the shortest link. d is the length of the longest link. b and c are the lengths of the other two links; see Figure 3.

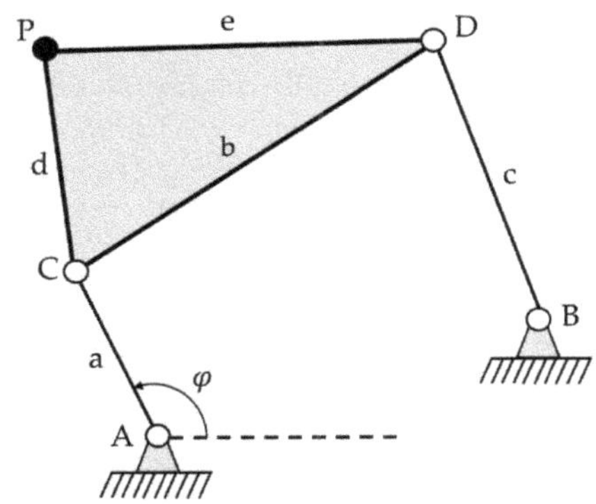

Figure 3. Parameters of a four-bar mechanism.

Thus, if the mechanism is found to be Grashof compliant, at least one of the links will be able to make a complete rotation with respect to the fixed link. This type of kinematic chain belongs to class I. If, on the other hand, the mechanism does not comply with Grashof, then no link will be able to make a complete rotation. This type of kinematic chain is said to be class II.

2.1.3. Mechanism Modeling by Natural Coordinates

Natural coordinates are those variables that completely describe the configuration and position of a mechanism and are related by geometric considerations. These relationships are expressed by constraint equations. The number of constraint equations is determined by the *DOF* and the dependent coordinates of the mechanism, which is obtained by applying Equation (3) [27–31].

$$m = n - F \tag{3}$$

In Equation (3), m indicates the number of constraint equations, n indicates the number of dependent coordinates, and F indicates the degrees of freedom of the mechanism.

As indicated in the previous section, the four-bar mechanism to be modeled consists of one degree of freedom defined by the angular coordinate φ and six dependent coordinates that refer to the position of the kinematic pairs of the mechanism. Applying Equation (3), it is obtained that six constraint equations are necessary to define the position of the mechanism; see Figure 3.

The constraint equations defining the mechanism are obtained by applying the vector loop theorem by adding the input link length and angle. The constraint equations for a four-bar coupler triangle mechanism, as shown in Figure 3, are Equation (4).

$$\begin{gathered}
(C_x - A_x) - a\cos(\varphi) = 0 \\
(C_y - A_y) - a\sin(\varphi) = 0 \\
(D_x - C_x)^2 + (D_y - C_y)^2 - b^2 = 0 \\
(D_x - B_x)^2 + (D_y - B_y)^2 - c^2 = 0 \\
(P_x - C_x)^2 + (P_y - C_y)^2 - d^2 = 0 \\
(P_x - D_x)^2 + (P_y - D_y)^2 - e^2 = 0
\end{gathered} \tag{4}$$

In Equation (4), A and B indicate the fixed supports of the mechanism, and a, b, c, d, and e indicate the lengths of the bars. These nine independent parameters, represented in Figure 3, are not easy to determine since in most cases, non-linear equations must be solved.

2.1.4. Methods for Constructing Cognate Mechanisms

The term "Cognate" was used to describe a mechanism, of different geometry, that generates the same coupler trajectory [32,33]. Sometimes, a good solution to a mechanism synthesis problem that satisfies the realization of the desired path presents dimensional problems such as inappropriate support positions or excessive mechanism size. To solve these cases, the use of a cognate of the mechanism can be useful.

Samuel Roberts and Chebyshev [34] proposed a theorem based on graphical methods for the construction of cognate mechanisms which is currently known as the "Roberts–Chebyshev theorem". This theorem states that three planar quadrilateral mechanisms share the same coupling point P; therefore, they will share the same path motion on their coupling curves, Figure 4. The Roberts–Chebyshev theorem is based on the use of diagrams and geometric representations to construct and visualize cognate mechanisms and is known for its simplicity and direct application through drawings. This method has the disadvantage of being a laborious method and requires the user to have good skills in interpreting and applying the necessary graphical techniques.

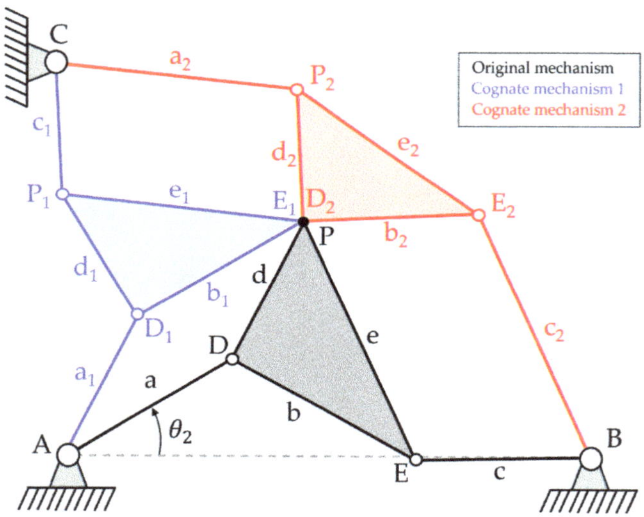

Figure 4. Example of original mechanism and its cognates.

Another useful method for constructing cognate mechanisms is the method proposed by Samantha Sherman et al. [8,9], which is based on the Roberts–Chebyshev theorem but contains a more analytical and mathematical approach. The core of this method lies in permuting the rotations of the links of the initial mechanism. This involves exchanging the positions and connections of the rotations to create a new mechanism that preserves the characteristics of the original mechanism. This method is only applicable to one-degree-of-freedom mechanisms that satisfy Grashof's principle. As discussed above, this method uses a more analytical and mathematical approach, using kinematic equations and permutations of rotations to identify cognates. This leads to a greater understanding of advanced mathematics and kinematics. It also offers greater flexibility and can be applied to a wider variety of mechanisms, including those with a larger number of bars. The method proposed by Samantha can be useful in environments where accuracy and mathematical validation are crucial, but it may be the case that the exchange of rotations does not correspond to a cognate mechanism, creating an inconsistency in the resulting linear equations resulting in laborious work consuming a significant amount of time. This method also relies on graphical interpretation and the need for simulation to verify the results.

The method of constructing cognate mechanisms that this paper proposed aims to be more accessible, without the need to apply complex mathematical concepts, as well as being easier to implement in an application, such as MATLAB (latest v. R2024b), making it useful for practical applications.

2.2. Proposed Method of Constructing Cognate Mechanisms

To develop the construction method, the initial data must first be known. As shown in Figure 5, the data required for modeling the original mechanism are dimensional parameters, such as the position of the two supports and the lengths of the links that define the original mechanism, and the cognate mechanisms will be obtained.

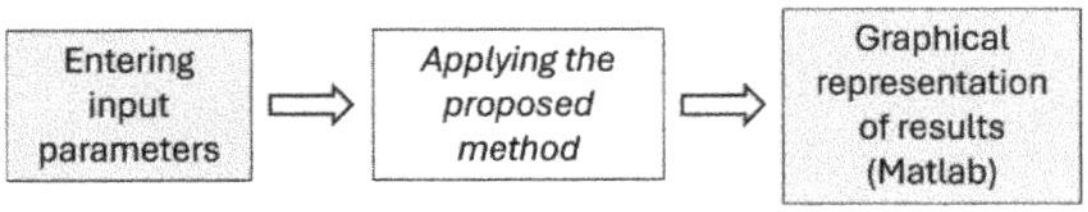

Figure 5. Method development.

With the dimensional parameters of the mechanism entered, the proposed method will perform the following tasks by means of MATLAB:

(1) Modeling of the four-bar mechanism, classification of this according to whether it complies with Grashof or not, and plotting of the trajectory of the coupling point.
(2) Construction of the cognate mechanism 1, classification based on the Grashof condition, and plotting of the trajectory of the coupling point.
(3) Construction of the cognate mechanism 2, classification based on the Grashof condition, and plotting of the trajectory of the coupling point.

The flow chart in Figure 6 shows the processes followed by the proposed method to be able to size the original mechanism and build its cognate mechanisms. The purpose of this method is to be able to graphically represent the mechanisms together with the layout of the coupling curves that they perform. To do this, the synthesis method follows a sequential execution in which the initial mechanism is previously sized, and the trajectory is calculated, then the cognate mechanism 1 is built by relating its parameters to the original mechanism, and, finally, cognate mechanism 2 is built by relating its parameters to the previous mechanisms.

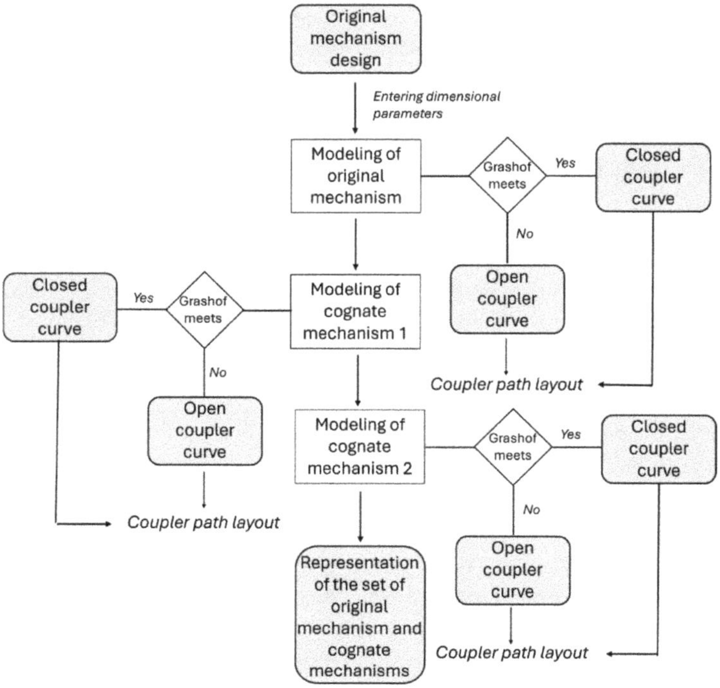

Figure 6. Flow chart of the proposed mechanism synthesis method.

The method, once implemented in MATLAB, will provide a graphical representation in Cartesian coordinates of each mechanism. This will include the curve traced by each mechanism at the coupling point, as well as a joint graphical representation of the mechanisms. This visualization will allow the dimensional differences between the different mechanisms to be evaluated and compared.

2.2.1. Dimensioning of the Original Mechanism

The method starts by introducing the dimensional parameters of a quadrilateral articulated mechanism as shown in Figure 7. The parameters to be introduced are the following:

(1) The separation distance "l" between the supports A and B, expressed in units of length.
(2) The lengths of the links a, b, c, d, and e, expressed in units of length.
(3) The coefficients "t1" and "t2", whose values are 1 or −1 and indicate the configuration of the mechanism, as shown in Figure 8.
(4) The input angle θ_2 expressed in degrees to be able to represent the mechanism in a fixed position.

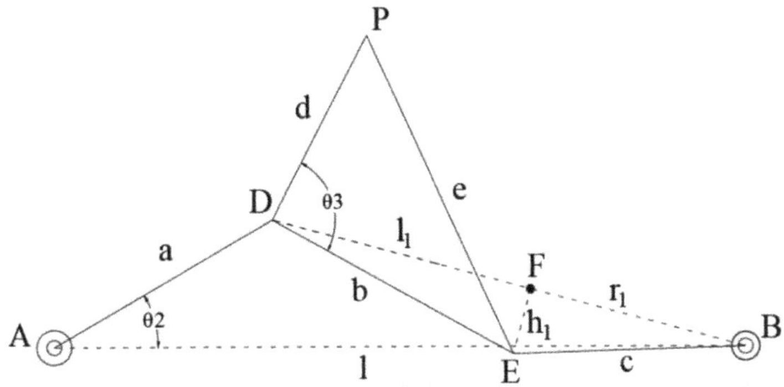

Figure 7. Original mechanism parameters.

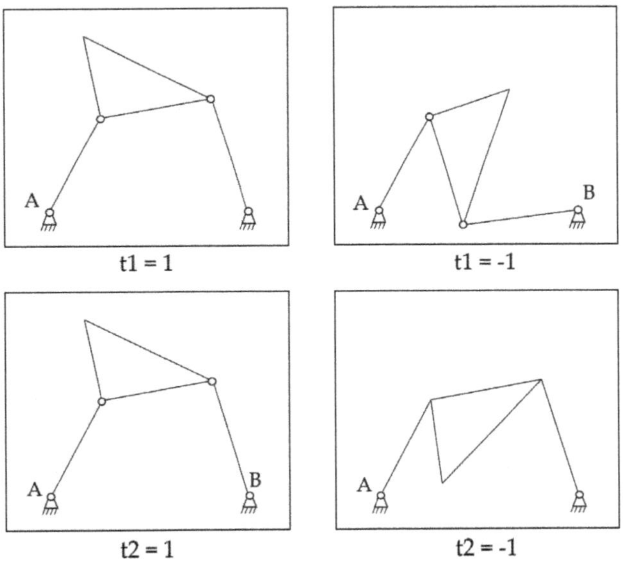

Figure 8. Mechanism configurations.

Once the lengths of the links have been entered, it is checked whether the mechanism complies with Grashof using Equation (2). Thus, the mechanism will be classified as a mechanism where the input link performs the complete rotation if it complies with Grashof; if it does not comply with Grashof, it will be classified as a mechanism where the input link rotation is limited. Knowing this is necessary because mechanisms that do not perform the complete rotation will have values of angles that they will not be able to reach.

To solve this problem, a geometric constraint, Equation (5), is added that decides whether the mechanism can be modeled. This constraint means that if the distance from point D to point B, defined as s (Figure 7) is greater than the sum of the lengths of links b and c, the mechanism cannot be modeled. Thus, if an angle is introduced that the mechanism is not able to reach geometrically, that mechanism will not be represented.

$$s \leq (b + c) \tag{5}$$

To model the mechanism, it is necessary to calculate the natural coordinates of the points of connection between links that define the position of the mechanism for the given input angle. These coordinates are obtained by developing the restriction equations that define the four-bar mechanisms.

To facilitate the calculations, it is decided that the fixed support A will be located at the origin of the coordinates and the fixed support B will be located on the same horizontal line as the support A, separated by the distance "l" that will be introduced as an input parameter (Figure 7). Knowing the length of link a, the coordinates of point D can be obtained with the Equation (6).

$$D = \begin{bmatrix} A_x + a\cos(\theta_2) \\ A_y + a\sin(\theta_2) \end{bmatrix} \tag{6}$$

To obtain the coordinates of point E (Figure 7) a line "s" corresponding to the segment $\overline{DB}$ is previously drawn, the length of which is obtained by calculating its module; see Equation (7).

$$s = \|B - C\| = \sqrt{(B_x - D_x)^2 + (B_y - D_y)^2} \tag{7}$$

From point E, a line is drawn that cuts "s" perpendicularly, whose intersection point is defined as F and divides the segment "s" into r_1 and l_1. In this way, there are two right triangles, $D\hat{E}F$ and $F\hat{E}B$, in which, applying Pythagoras and knowing that $s = l_1 + r_1$, the Equations (8) and (9) are obtained.

$$l_1 = \frac{b^2 + s^2 - c^2}{2s} \tag{8}$$

$$h_1 = t_1\sqrt{b^2 - l_1^2} \tag{9}$$

In this way, the coordinates of point F are obtained from Equation (10), where they are defined by the position of point C and the relation of the vector $\overline{BD}$.

$$F = D + \frac{l_1}{s}(B - D) \tag{10}$$

Point E will be defined by Equation (11), where $\overline{FD}$ is obtained from Equation (12).

$$E = F + \overline{FD} \tag{11}$$

$$\overline{FD} = \frac{h_1}{s}(B - D) \tag{12}$$

Therefore, Equation (13) defines the coordinates of point E.

$$E = D + \frac{l_1}{s}(B - D) + \frac{h_1}{s}(B - D) \tag{13}$$

In the same way, Equations (14)–(16) that define point P are deduced.

$$l_2 = \frac{d^2 + b^2 - e^2}{2b} \tag{14}$$

$$h_2 = t_2\sqrt{d^2 - l_2^2} \tag{15}$$

$$P = C + \frac{l_2}{b}(E - D) + \frac{h_2}{b}(E - D) \tag{16}$$

With the obtained expressions, the natural coordinate vector that defines the position of the four-bar mechanism is constructed; see Equation (17).

$$q = \begin{bmatrix} D \\ E \\ P \end{bmatrix} = \begin{bmatrix} D_x \\ D_y \\ E_x \\ E_y \\ P_x \\ P_y \end{bmatrix} = \begin{bmatrix} A_x + a\cos(\theta_2) \\ A_y + a\sin(\theta_2) \\ D_x + \frac{l_1}{s}(B_x - D_x) + \frac{h_1}{s}(B_y - D_y) \\ D_y + \frac{l_1}{s}(B_y - D_y) + \frac{h_1}{s}(B_x - D_x) \\ D_x + \frac{l_2}{b}(E - D_x) + \frac{h_2}{b}(D_y - E_y) \\ D_y + \frac{l_2}{b}(E_y - D_y) + \frac{h_2}{b}(D_x - E_x) \end{bmatrix} \tag{17}$$

As explained at the beginning of the section, if these restriction equations are calculated for an angle that the mechanism is not able to reach, these equations will have no solution.

2.2.2. Generation of the Trajectory of Mechanisms

To calculate the trajectory, an iteration is performed on the obtained expressions where the value of the introduced angle is increased and, in turn, the value of the coordinates of point P is represented. In the case of mechanisms that do not comply with Grashof and do not perform a complete rotation, the representation will be limited to the angle values that the mechanism can reproduce.

In the case of the original mechanism, it is decided to represent the trajectory by calculating the parametric Equations (18) and (19) that define the natural coordinates of point P for an introduced input angle θ_2 (see Figure 9).

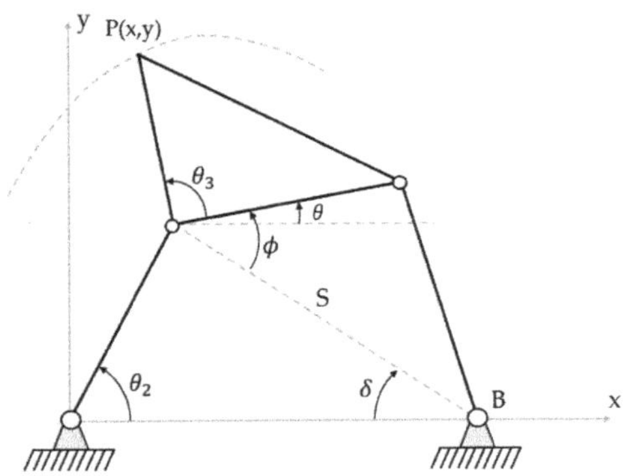

Figure 9. Path of a mechanism.

$$x = a{\cdot}cos\theta_2 + d{\cdot}\cos(\phi + \delta - \theta_2) \tag{18}$$

$$y = a{\cdot}sin\theta_2 + d{\cdot}sen(\phi + \delta - \theta_2) \tag{19}$$

These coordinates are obtained by previously calculating the angles that define the position of the points of the mechanism. These angles, shown in Figure 10, are calculated with the Equations (20)–(22).

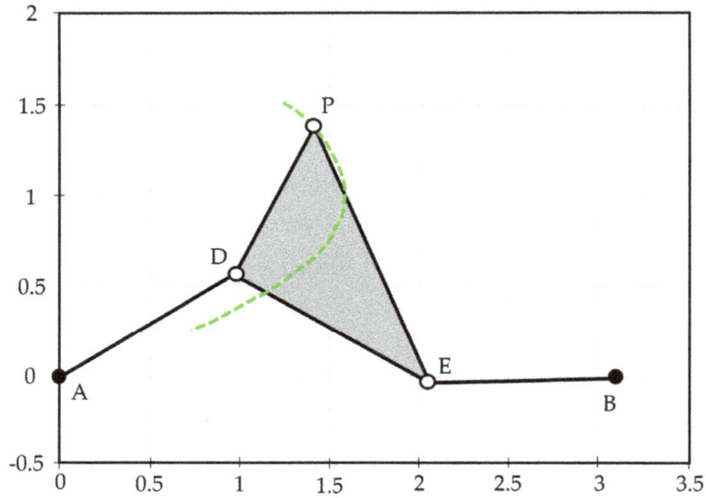

Figure 10. Original mechanism solution.

$$\delta = asin\left(\frac{a \cdot sen(\theta_2)}{s}\right) \tag{20}$$

$$\phi = t1 \cdot acos\left(\frac{s^2 + b^2 - c^2}{2 \cdot s \cdot b}\right) \tag{21}$$

$$\theta = \phi - \delta \tag{22}$$

As with the modeling of the mechanism, to obtain the trajectory of point P, it is necessary to indicate which of the two configurations of point D the mechanism will have; to do this, the value 1 or -1 is introduced into the input for the parameter $t1$ (Figure 8).

2.2.3. Construction of Cognate Mechanisms

To build the cognate mechanisms of the original mechanism, it is first necessary to obtain the point where cognate 1 and cognate 2 will be supported. This point is called support C, as shown in Figure 4, and its function is to serve as a second fixed support for the cognate mechanisms.

As a characteristic of this support C (Figure 4), the triangle formed by the points $A\hat{C}B$ is similar to the coupling triangle formed by the points $D\hat{P}E$. Having the length between the supports A and B, and the lengths of the links d, c, and e, Equation (23) of similarity between triangles can be applied to obtain the length from the support A to the support C, which will be called mAC.

$$mAC = \frac{d}{b} \cdot l \tag{23}$$

Once the length of the segment mAC has been obtained, it is necessary to determinate the angle formed by the lines AB and AC that coincides with the angle formed by the links d and b. This angle is called θ_3 and is obtained by applying the cosine theorem; see Equation (24) and Figure 7.

$$\theta_3 = acos\left(\frac{d^2 + b^2 - e^2}{2 \cdot d \cdot b}\right) \tag{24}$$

With the length mAC and the angle θ_3, the coordinates of point C are obtained.

$$C = \begin{bmatrix} A_x + \overline{AC}\, cos(\theta_3) \\ A_y + \overline{AC}\, sin(\theta_3) \end{bmatrix} \tag{25}$$

To facilitate understanding, the original mechanism will be the mechanism shown in Figure 7, for which all its dimensional parameters will be known. The objective will be to obtain the dimensional parameters of cognate mechanism 1 and the dimensional parameters of cognate mechanism 2. Once these parameters are obtained, it will be easy to represent them graphically by means of MATLAB software.

Cognate one is constructed from the relationship between it and the original mechanism. As explained in Chebyshev's method [34], the segment $\overline{DP}$ of length d coincides with the segment $\overline{AD_1}$ of length a_1, that is, $d = a_1$. Therefore, the coordinates of point D_1 can be calculated with the Equation (26); see Figure 4.

$$D_1 = \begin{bmatrix} A_x + d\cdot \cos(\theta_3 + \theta) \\ A_y + d\cdot \sin(\theta_3 + \theta) \end{bmatrix} \tag{26}$$

Since segment a_1 coincides with segment d, the coupling point P_1 is obtained from Equation (27).

$$P_1 = \begin{bmatrix} D_{1x} + a\cdot \cos(\theta_2) \\ D_{1y} + a\cdot \sin(\theta_2) \end{bmatrix} \tag{27}$$

The segment b_1 of the coupling triangle $D_1\hat{P}_1E_1$ is obtained from the similarity relation of this with the coupling triangle $D\hat{P}E$; see Equation (28).

$$b_1 = \frac{d}{b}\cdot d_1 \tag{28}$$

Another relationship between the original mechanism and cognate one is that the lengths $d_1 = a$; thus, Equation (28) can be replaced by Equation (29).

$$b_1 = \frac{d}{b}\cdot a \tag{29}$$

The length of segment e_1 is obtained by applying the cosine theorem to the coupling triangle of cognate one; see Equation (30).

$$e_1 = \sqrt{d_1^2 + b_1^2 - (2\cdot d_1\cdot b_1\cdot \cos(\theta_2 + \theta_3))} \tag{30}$$

The coordinates of point E_1 are obtained based on the angles that define the position of the mechanism. The link $\overline{D_1P}$ forms the same angle, θ_2, as the link formed by points $\overline{AD}$, so the link $\overline{D_1P}$ will form an angle $(\theta_2 + \theta_3)$; see Equation (31).

$$E_1 = \begin{bmatrix} D_{1x} + b_1\cdot \cos(\theta_3 + \theta_2) \\ D_{1y} + b_1\cdot \sin(\theta_3 + \theta_2) \end{bmatrix} \tag{31}$$

Finally, the length c_1 is obtained from the module formed by the segment E_1C; see Equation (32).

$$c_1 = \sqrt{(E_{1x} - C_{1x})^2 + (E_{1y} - C_{1y})^2} \tag{32}$$

Once the lengths of the links of cognate mechanism one have been obtained, the Grashof condition is applied to classify the mechanism; see Equation (33).

$$a_1 + mAC \leq b_1 + c_1 \tag{33}$$

In Equation (33), mAC is the modulus of the vector $\overline{AC}$.

As with the original mechanism, if the mechanism does not comply with Grashof, the rotation of the input angle will be limited, so a restriction is imposed to be able to represent the mechanism with the angles it can reach; see Equation (34).

$$s_1 \leq (b_1 + c_1) \tag{34}$$

If the geometric condition expressed in Equation (34) is not met, cognate mechanism one will not be represented since the separation distance $\overline{D_1C}$ exceeds the sum of the lengths of the links b_1 and c_1.

The construction of cognate mechanism two is done through the relations that it shares with the original mechanism and cognate mechanism one. Following the Roberts–Chebyshev theorem [34] and the parameters in Figure 5, Equations (35)–(38), which define the relations between the lengths of the links of these mechanisms are obtained. Treating the links as vectors, it can be said that the vector $\overline{CD_2}$ coincides with the vector $\overline{E_1P}$ but transferred to point C and the vector $\overline{D_2P_2}$ coincides with the vector $\overline{E_1C}$ but transferred to point D_2.

$$a_2 = e_1 \tag{35}$$

$$e_2 = c \tag{36}$$

$$c_2 = e \tag{37}$$

$$d_2 = c_1 \tag{38}$$

Since the coupling triangle of cognate mechanism two is similar to the coupling triangle of the original mechanism, their parameters can be related to apply triangle similarity. Thus, the link length b_2 is obtained; see Equation (39).

$$b_2 = \frac{e}{b} \cdot e_2 \tag{39}$$

To obtain the coordinates of point E_2, the vector $\overline{EP}$ is transferred to support B, resulting in Equations (40) and (41).

$$\overline{EP} = \left[(P_x - E_x) \quad (P_y - E_y) \right] \tag{40}$$

$$E_2 = \left[(B_x - EP_x) \quad (B_y - EP_y) \right] \tag{41}$$

The coordinates of point D_2 are obtained by transferring the segment $\overline{E_1P}$ to point C; see Equations (42) and (43).

$$\overline{CD_2} = P - E_1 \tag{42}$$

$$D_2 = C + \overline{CD_2} \tag{43}$$

To obtain the coordinates of point P_2, the vector $\overline{E_1C}$ is transferred to point D_2; see Equation (44).

$$P_2 = D_2 + \overline{E_1C} \tag{44}$$

Once the lengths of the links of cognate mechanism two have been calculated, we proceed to check whether the mechanism meets the Grashof condition, shown in Equation (45), to classify the mechanism according to whether the input link a_2 has full rotation or has limited rotation.

$$a_2 + mBC \leq b_2 + c_2 \tag{45}$$

To obtain the trajectory of point P_2, iterations are performed with the expressions obtained by recalculating and representing point P_2 for each value of the input angle. As the mechanism is related to the original mechanism, the trajectory will be represented for each increment of angle θ_2. In the case that the mechanism does not comply with Grashof and a_2 cannot perform a complete rotation, the geometric restriction in Equation (46) must be checked. Thus, if for a given angle, the restriction is not fulfilled, the mechanism will not be represented.

$$s_2 \leq (b_2 + c_2) \tag{46}$$

As with the condition in Equation (34) for cognate one, if the module $\overline{D_2B}$ exceeds the sum of the lengths b_2 and c_2, the mechanism will not be able to reach that position and will therefore not be represented. The trajectory will only be traced with the angles that the mechanism can reach.

It is important to note that both cognate mechanism one and cognate mechanism two are built based on the relationships they share with the original mechanism. This means that if the input angle of the original mechanism is modified, the position of the original mechanism and the cognate mechanisms will be modified. However, not all angles valid for modeling the original mechanism will necessarily be valid for building the cognate mechanisms, since each mechanism has its geometric requirements, even if they trace the same path. In addition, if a length parameter of the original mechanism is modified, it will directly affect the design of the cognate mechanisms.

3. Results

In this section, we will show an example of how the developed method works as programmed in MATLAB. To do this, the mechanism that appears as the original mechanism in Figure 4 will be modeled. In this case, the mechanism is oriented with the supports positioned on the same horizontal line. In the case that the supports have an angle of inclination, the mechanism will be interpreted and represented with the supports on the same horizontal line, since the angle of inclination does not influence the results.

The input parameters introduced are shown in Table 1 for the original mechanism column. For the representation of the original mechanism, the input angle is $\theta_2 = 30^\circ$.

First, the mechanism is classified according to the Grashof condition. By observing the lengths of the links and applying Equation (2), it is determined that the mechanism does not satisfy Grashof. This means that the input link "a" will not perform a complete rotation and must pass through the geometric restriction; refer to Equation (5). In this way, it is determined whether the mechanism can be represented based on whether it satisfies the condition for the given angle.

Table 1. Values of dimensional parameters in units of length.

Dimensional Parameters			
Parameter	**Original Mechanism**	**Cognate 1**	**Cognate 2**
A (x, y)	(0, 0)	(0, 0)	-
B (x, y)	(1,0)	-	(1, 0)
C (x, y)	-	(−0.05, 2.31)	(−0.05, 2.31)
l (cm)	3.10	-	-
a (cm)	1.13	0.92	1.43
b (cm)	1.23	1.13	1.04
c (cm)	1.04	0.78	1.56
d (cm)	0.92	0.84	0.78
e (cm)	1.56	1.43	1.32

The trajectory of the mechanism will be represented by calculating Equations (18) and (19). The mechanism does not perform a complete rotation. It only traces the curve for the values of the input angle that the original mechanism can reach.

Figure 10 shows the original mechanism with the calculated points, and the trajectory curve of the coupling point P is drawn in green. The black-filled points mark the supports A and B where the mechanism rests. It can be observed that point P coincides with one of the points of the trajectory, ensuring that it passes through any point of the curve for different input angles. The ends of the curve mark the limits of the angle that the mechanism can reach due to its geometric restrictions.

Before starting with the construction of the cognate mechanisms, the coordinates of point C are obtained with Equation (25), which will serve as a second support for cognate one and as a first support for cognate two. To obtain cognate mechanism one, the existing relationships between the cognate and the original mechanism are observed, such as the similarity of coupling triangles and the similarity in the lengths of the links. Once the relationship expressions have been obtained, the lengths of the links and the coordinates of the points of cognate one are calculated.

After calculating the expressions that define cognate 1, the parameters that appear for the cognate mechanism one in Table 1 are obtained. Some lengths coincide with the original mechanism due to the relationships they share. It can also be observed that the coordinates of point P_1 coincide with the coordinates of point P for the given angle. This gives an indication that the trajectories coincide.

Figure 11 shows the graphic representation of cognate mechanism one drawn in blue and the curve of the trajectory of point P_1 obtained. In the figure, it can be observed that cognate mechanism one is different from the original mechanism in terms of dimensions, but it shows certain similarities with the original mechanism. The coupling triangle of cognate mechanism one can be seen to be similar to the coupling triangle of the original mechanism; in addition, the two mechanisms share the support point A. Regarding the trajectory, it can be observed that the layout of the trajectory of cognate one is not the same as the layout of the trajectory of the original mechanism, but they do coincide in being the same curve. This is because, due to geometric restrictions, the two mechanisms are limited to plotting the points of the curve that their input angles allow, causing the layout of the trajectory of cognate one to be the continuation of the layout of the trajectory of the original mechanism.

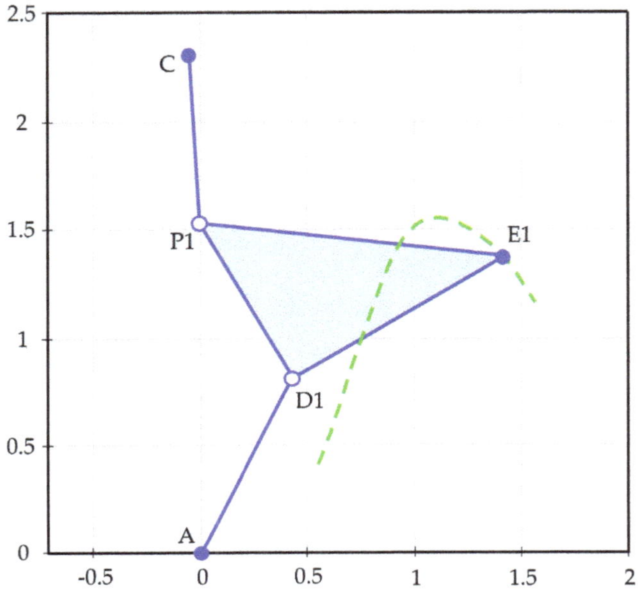

Figure 11. Cognate mechanism 1 solution.

To construct cognate mechanism two, the existing relationships between it and the original mechanism and cognate mechanism one are used. As with cognate one, the coupling triangles are similar, so the dimensions of the coupling triangle of cognate two can be easily calculated. In this case, the input link is located at support C and shares support B with the original mechanism. As a solution, after calculating the expressions that relate them, the dimensional parameters of cognate mechanism two are obtained, which appear for cognate mechanism two in Table 1.

Since the Grashof condition is not met, the geometrical constraint must be applied to determine if the mechanism can be represented for the given angle. As for the dimensional parameters obtained, it can be observed that cognate mechanism two contains lengths that coincide with the lengths of the links of cognate mechanism one and the original mechanism. In addition, the coordinates of point P_2 coincide with those of point P, which indicates that, for the introduced angle, the coupling point of the original mechanism and that of the cognate mechanisms coincide.

Figure 12 shows the representation of cognate mechanism two in red next to the trajectory curve of cognate P_2, where it can be observed that this cognate resembles cognate one and the original mechanism, but its dimensions and movements are different. As for the trajectory of cognate mechanism two, it coincides with the trajectory of the original mechanism, also being limited because the input link "CD" does not perform the complete rotation.

As a final solution, the mechanisms are represented graphically as a whole as they appear in Figure 13, with the original mechanism in black, cognate mechanism one in blue, and cognate mechanism two in red. The trajectory that appears in green is the superposition of the curves of the coupling point made by the three mechanisms.

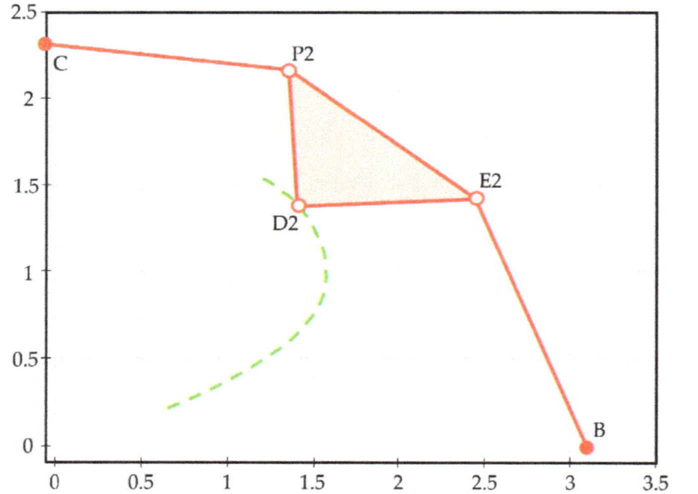

Figure 12. Cognate mechanism 2 solution.

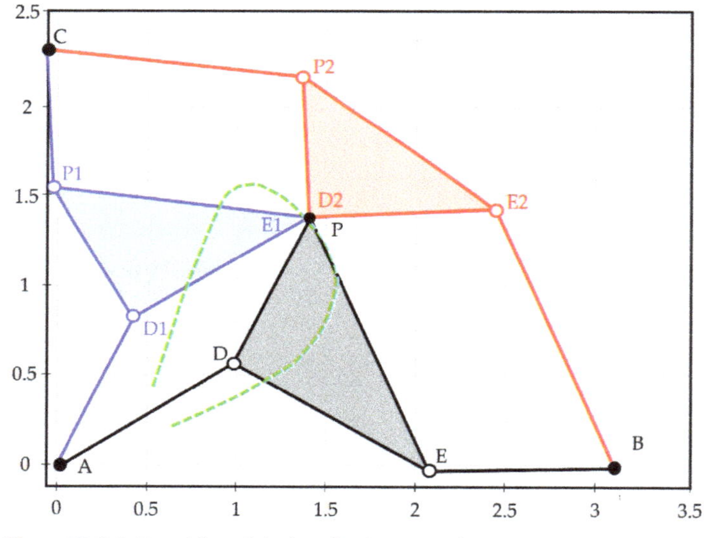

Figure 13. Solution of the original mechanism set and cognates.

In Figure 13, it can be seen how the coupling point P of the three mechanisms coincides for the given angle. If the value of the input angle θ_2 was modified, the position of the three mechanisms would be modified, with the coupling point coinciding with a point on the trajectory. To elucidate the rotational points within the mechanism, it is imperative to acknowledge that although the diagram may visually depict additional segments, only four revolute joints delineate the kinematic structure of the mechanism. Specifically, the four rotational points are as follows: (1) point A, (2) point B, (3) the intersection between segments (AD) and (DE), and (4) the intersection between segments (DE) and (EB). The triangle (*DPE*), although present within the diagram, acts as a rigid structure that does not deform during motion. Therefore, it does not introduce additional rotational points or independent links. This distinction guarantees that the mechanism is correctly classified as a four-bar linkage. This same distinction applies to the other two cognate mechanisms. As for the dimensions, the similarity between the coupling triangles can be seen, where each mechanism has the coupling point located at a different point of the triangle. Observing the graphic representation in Figure 13 and the calculated dimensional parameters in Table 1, it can be seen how some dimensions obtained from the links of the cognates coincide with the dimensions of the links of the original mechanism. This shows that, to obtain a pair of mechanisms that follow the same trajectory at the coupling point as an initial mechanism, there must be dimensional relationships between these and the original mechanism. Moreover, the geometric properties of the cognates were analyzed, and it was observed that the coupling triangle for these mechanisms exhibited dimensional similarities to those of the original mechanism.

$$\frac{b_i}{b_j} = \frac{d_i}{d_j} = \frac{e_i}{e_j} \quad i,j = 1,2,3 \tag{47}$$

Furthermore, the calculated dimensions of the links are in accordance with the anticipated dimensional relationships derived from the original mechanism, thereby reinforcing the theoretical foundation of the method. Furthermore, as illustrated in Figure 14, the synthesis process was employed to construct a second cognate mechanism, thereby providing additional validation of the proposed method's robustness. The objective of this new mechanism was to replicate the coupler point trajectory of the original mechanism.

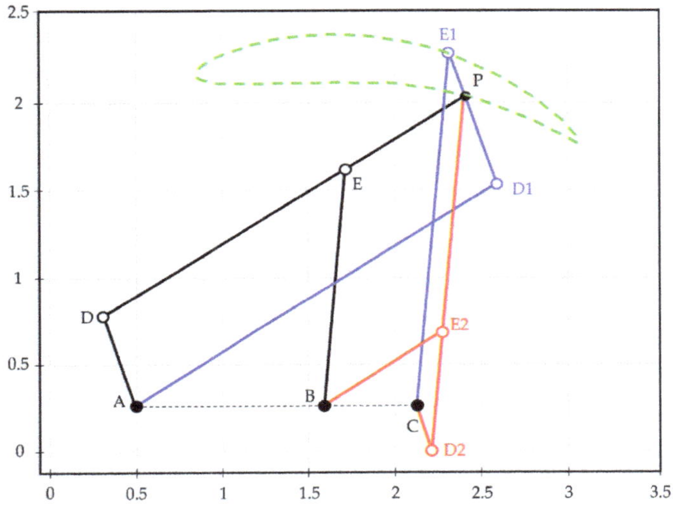

Figure 14. Solution of the new mechanism set and cognates.

The results demonstrated that the coupler point of the second cognate mechanism follows the same trajectory as the initial mechanism for any value of the input angle θ_2 (see Figure 9), which is consistent with the theoretical expectations of cognate mechanism synthesis. This supplementary confirmation serves to illustrate the dependability and precision of the proposed methodology in the generation of cognates that satisfy the requisite kinematic specifications, thus ensuring identical coupler point trajectories.

4. Conclusions

This paper presents a synthesis method developed specifically for four-bar linkages. Despite their apparent simplicity, four-bar linkages offer remarkable flexibility and versatility, making them a fundamental class of mechanisms in engineering applications. These mechanisms serve as the foundation for numerous devices and systems, including robotic manipulators, automotive suspensions, and manufacturing equipment, due to their ability to achieve tailored motion profiles and efficient force transmission. The method presented is concerned with the construction of cognate mechanisms, which are alternative configurations that replicate the motion of the original mechanism while introducing variability in geometric constraints, thereby enhancing design flexibility.

The proposed method is effective in that it generates cognate mechanisms that share the same coupler curve as the original linkage. This guarantees that the desired motion characteristics are maintained, while the geometric variations of the cognates provide the opportunity to optimize the mechanism to align with specific design and manufacturing constraints. The developed method incorporates a robust algorithm implemented in MATLAB, which offers a user-friendly interface for modeling and analyzing these mechanisms. The graphical representations generated by the algorithm illustrate the coupler point trajectories and highlight the dimensional discrepancies between the original and cognate mechanisms. This visualization is essential for enhancing comprehension of the operational characteristics of each mechanism and for facilitating informed design decisions. One of the key advantages of this methodology is its capacity to facilitate the input of dimensional parameters for the initial mechanism in a streamlined manner. The MATLAB-based implementation facilitates the process of precise parameter calibration, allowing for real-time adjustments that enhance efficiency in the design and optimization phases. This accessibility broadens the applicability of the method to a more diverse audience, including those with less technical expertise, while maintaining precision and reliability.

Although the proposed algorithm has been shown to be effective in generating cognate mechanisms for four-bar linkages, it is not without limitations. The primary limitation of this approach is its specificity to four-bar linkages, as the mathematical models and algorithms employed are tailored exclusively to this class of mechanisms. Extending this approach to encompass additional types of mechanisms, such as five-bar linkages or spatial mechanisms, represents a logical next step that could further enhance its applicability across engineering disciplines. Such an extension would entail the development of novel mathematical models and algorithms capable of accommodating the heightened complexity of these systems while maintaining the fundamental tenets of cognate synthesis.

Another promising avenue of research is the integration of multi-objective optimization techniques into the synthesis process. Such an approach would enable designers to simultaneously consider multiple criteria, including the minimization of manufacturing costs, the maximization of mechanical efficiency, and the assurance of reliability under operational loads. The incorporation of these considerations could render the method even more valuable in practical applications. Furthermore, the integration of advanced visualization tools, such as interactive three-dimensional models or augmented reality interfaces, could enhance the usability and effectiveness of the algorithm in both educational and professional contexts. Although this research focuses on the geometric and kinematic aspects of mechanism design, future studies could investigate the dynamic performance of the synthesized cognate mechanisms. It is essential to understand how these mechanisms behave under varying loads, speeds, and environmental conditions to ensure their viability in real-world applications. Incorporating these dynamic analyses into the synthesis method would provide a more comprehensive tool for engineers and researchers.

Author Contributions: This research paper was principally devised and developed by the first author, E.S.-H. The detailed review by the second and third authors, C.P.-C. and H.R., considerably improved the quality of the work. The manuscript was written with contributions from all authors. All authors have read and agreed to the published version of the manuscript.

Funding: This research received no external funding.

Data Availability Statement: Data will be made available on request.

Conflicts of Interest: The authors declare no conflicts of interest.

References

1. Raven, F.H. Velocity and Acceleration Analysis of Plane and Space Mechanisms by Means of Independent-Position Equations. *J. Appl. Mech.* **1958**, *25*, 1–6. [CrossRef]
2. Lee, W.-T.; Russell, K. Developments in quantitative dimensional synthesis (1970–present): Four-bar path and function generation. *Inverse Probl. Sci. Eng.* **2018**, *26*, 1280–1304. [CrossRef]
3. Pathak, V.K.; Singh, R.; Sharma, A.; Kumar, R.; Chakraborty, D. A Historical Review on the Computational Techniques for Mechanism Synthesis: Developments Up to 2022. *Arch. Comput. Methods Eng.* **2023**, *30*, 1131–1156. [CrossRef]
4. Li, X.; Wei, S.; Liao, Q.; Zhang, Y. A novel analytical method for four-bar path generation synthesis based on Fourier series. *Mech. Mach. Theory* **2020**, *144*, 103671. [CrossRef]
5. Hernández, A.; Muñoyerro, A.; Urízar, M.; Amezua, E. Comprehensive approach for the dimensional synthesis of a four-bar linkage based on path assessment and reformulating the error function. *Mech. Mach. Theory* **2021**, *156*, 104126. [CrossRef]
6. Kang, Y.-H.; Lin, J.-W.; You, W.-C. Comparative Study on the Synthesis of Path-Generating Four-Bar Linkages Using Metaheuristic Optimization Algorithms. *Appl. Sci.* **2022**, *12*, 7368. [CrossRef]
7. Lakshminarayana, K.; Butchi Raju, K.C. Function-cognate mechanisms: General theory and application. *Mech. Mach. Theory* **1985**, *20*, 389–397. [CrossRef]
8. Sherman, S.N.; Hauenstein, J.D.; Wampler, C.W. A General Method for Constructing Planar Cognate Mechanisms. *J. Mech. Robot.* **2021**, *13*, 031009. [CrossRef]
9. Sherman, S.N.; Hauenstein, J.D.; Wampler, C.W. Advances in the Theory of Planar Curve Cognates. *J. Mech. Robot.* **2022**, *14*, 031005. [CrossRef]
10. Wampler, C.W.; Morgan, A.P.; Sommese, A.J. Complete Solution of the Nine-Point Path Synthesis Problem for Four-Bar Linkages. *J. Mech. Des.* **1992**, *114*, 153–159. [CrossRef]
11. Roth, B.; Freudenstein, F. Synthesis of Path-Generating Mechanisms by Numerical Methods. *J. Eng. Ind.* **1963**, *85*, 298–304. [CrossRef]
12. Kramer, S.N.; Sandor, G.N. Selective Precision Synthesis—A General Method of Optimization for Planar Mechanisms. *J. Eng. Ind.* **1975**, *97*, 689–701. [CrossRef]
13. Plecnik, M.M.; McCarthy, J.M. Kinematic synthesis of Stephenson III six-bar function generators. *Mech. Mach. Theory* **2016**, *97*, 112–126. [CrossRef]
14. Baskar, A.; Plecnik, M. Synthesis of Six-Bar Timed Curve Generators of Stephenson-Type Using Random Monodromy Loops. *J. Mech. Robot.* **2021**, *13*, 011005. [CrossRef]
15. Simionescu, P.A.; Smith, M.R. Four- and six-bar function cognates and overconstrained mechanisms. *Mech. Mach. Theory* **2001**, *36*, 913–924. [CrossRef]
16. Han, J.; Liu, W. On the Solution of Eight-Precision-Point Path Synthesis of Planar Four-Bar Mechanisms Based on the Solution Region Methodology. *J. Mech. Robot.* **2019**, *11*, 064504. [CrossRef]
17. Mehdigholi, H.; Akbarnejad, S. Optimization of Watt's Six-Bar Linkage to Generate Straight and Parallel Leg Motion. *Int. J. Adv. Robot. Syst.* **2012**, *9*, 22. [CrossRef]
18. Starns, G.; Flugrad, D.R. Five-Bar Path Generation Synthesis by Continuation Methods. *J. Mech. Des.* **1993**, *115*, 988–994. [CrossRef]
19. Moon, F.C. Franz Reuleaux: Contributions to 19th century kinematics and theory of machines. *Appl. Mech. Rev.* **2003**, *56*, 261–285. [CrossRef]
20. Reuleaux, F. *The Kinematics of Machinery: Outlines of a Theory of Machines*; Publications, D., Ed.; Courier Corporation: Mineloa, NY, USA, 2013.
21. Shiwalkar, P.B.; Ceccarelli, M. History of Planar Linkage Coupler Point Loci for Tracing Special Coupler Curves. In *Explorations in the History and Heritage of Machines and Mechanisms. HMM 2024. History of Mechanism and Machine Science, Volume 47*; Ceccarelli, M., Aslan Seyhan, I., Eds.; Springer: Cham, Switzerland, 2024; pp. 213–226.
22. Koetsier, T. *A History of Kinematics from Zeno to Einstein;* History of Mechanism and Machine Science; Springer Nature: Cham, Switzerland, 2024; Volume 46.

23. Grübler, M. Die Relativbewegungen von drei und mehr komplanen Ebenen. In *Getriebelehre*; Springer: Berlin/Heidelberg, Germany, 1917; pp. 55–62.
24. Grashof, F. *Theoretische Maschinenlehre*; Leopold Voss: Leipzig, Germany, 1875.
25. Hartenberg, R.; Danavit, J. *Kinematic Synthesis of Linkages*; McGraw-Hill: New York, NY, USA, 1964.
26. Ting, K.-L. Mobility Criteria of Single-Loop N-Bar Linkages. *J. Mech. Transm. Autom. Des.* **1989**, *111*, 504–507. [CrossRef]
27. Mitsi, S. Position analysis in polynomial form of planar mechanisms with a closed chain of the Assur group of class 4 L'analyse de position sous forme polynomiale des mecanismes plans avec une chaine fermee du groupe d'Assur de 4-eme classe. *Mech. Mach. Theory* **1999**, *34*, 1195–1209. [CrossRef]
28. Rojas, N.; Thomas, F. Distance-based position analysis of the three seven-link Assur kinematic chains. *Mech. Mach. Theory* **2011**, *46*, 112–126. [CrossRef]
29. Rojas, N.; Dollar, A.M.; Thomas, F. A unified position analysis of the Dixon and the generalized Peaucellier linkages. *Mech. Mach. Theory* **2015**, *94*, 28–40. [CrossRef]
30. Romero-Núñez, N.N.; Flórez Serrano, E.G. Análisis de posición de un mecanismo de Stephenson tipo I utilizando coordenadas naturales. *DYNA* **2018**, *85*, 91–97. [CrossRef]
31. Soriano-Heras, E.; Blaya-Haro, F.; Molino, C.; de Agustín del Burgo, J.M. Rapid prototyping prosthetic hand acting by a low-cost shape-memory-alloy actuator. *J. Artif. Organs* **2018**, *21*, 238–246. [CrossRef]
32. Soni, A.H.; Harrisberger, L. Roberts' Cognates of Space Four-Bar Mechanisms With Two General Constraints. *J. Eng. Ind.* **1969**, *91*, 123–127. [CrossRef]
33. Soni, A.H. Coupler cognate mechanisms of certain parallelogram forms of watt's six-link mechanism. *J. Mech.* **1970**, *5*, 203–215. [CrossRef]
34. Roberts, S. On Three-bar Motion in Plane Space. *Proc. Lond. Math. Soc.* **1875**, *s1-7*, 14–23. [CrossRef]

mathematics

MDPI

Article

AE-XGBoost: A Novel Approach for Machine Tool Machining Size Prediction Combining XGBoost, AE and SHAP

Mu Gu [1,2], Shuimiao Kang [3,4], Zishuo Xu [3,4,*], Lin Lin [1] and Zhihui Zhang [2]

1 College of Mechatronics Engineering, Harbin Institute of Technology, Harbin 150006, China; gumu@casic.com.cn (M.G.); waiwaiyl@163.com (L.L.)
2 Beijing Aerospace Intelligent Manufacturing Technology Development Co., Ltd., Beijing 100028, China; zhangzhihui@casic.com.cn
3 College of Aeronautical Engineering, Civil Aviation University of China, Tianjin 300300, China; 2022095018@cauc.edu.cn
4 Aviation Special Ground Equipment Research Base, Civil Aviation University of China, Tianjin 300300, China
* Correspondence: 2022011018@cauc.edu.cn

Abstract

To achieve intelligent manufacturing and improve the machining quality of machine tools, this paper proposes an interpretable machining size prediction model combining eXtreme Gradient Boosting (XGBoost), autoencoder (AE), and Shapley additive explanation (SHAP) analysis. In this study, XGBoost was used to establish an evaluation system for the actual machining size of computer numerical control (CNC) machine tools. The XGBoost model was combined with SHAP approximation to effectively capture local and global features in the data using autoencoders and transform the preprocessed data into more representative feature vectors. Grey correlation analysis (GRA) and principal component analysis (PCA) were used to reduce the dimensions of the original data features, and the synthetic minority overstimulation technique of the Gaussian noise regression (SMOGN) method was used to deal with the problem of data imbalance. Taking the actual size of the machine tool as the response parameter, based on the size parameters in the milling process of the CNC machine tool, the effectiveness of the model is verified. The experimental results show that the proposed AE-XGBoost model is superior to the traditional XGBoost method, and the prediction accuracy of the model is 7.11% higher than that of the traditional method. The subsequent SHAP analysis reveals the importance and interrelationship of features and provides a reliable decision support system for machine tool processing personnel, helping to improve processing quality and achieve intelligent manufacturing.

Keywords: machine tool processing; dimension prediction; XGBoost; autoencoder; SHAP

MSC: 68T07; 65D17

1. Introduction

Predicting the quality of the machine tool is the basis and the prerequisite for intelligent machine tool manufacturing and closed-loop control of the machine tool. Therefore, many scholars have carried out in-depth research on the factors affecting machining quality, and analyzed the impact of tools' geometric parameters, cutting parameters, cutting fluid type, CNC component performance degradation, chatter, dynamic and static characteristics of a tool-works-jig machine tool system, thermal deformation and thermal error and other factors affecting machining quality. Based on directional importance sampling, the Monte Carlo simulation, Zhang et al. [1] proposed a reliability evaluation method for machining accuracy that considered both geometric and vibration errors. Sato et al. [2] developed a nonlinear friction model that takes into account the relationship between friction and vibration and proposed a method to evaluate the impact of tool–chip contact on vibration characteristics; then they evaluated the effects of nonlinear friction and process damping through simulation analysis. Sun et al. [3] used laser texture to make pits on tool surfaces and conducted cutting experiments; the results show that the surface roughness of textured tools is lower than that of non-textured tools, and there is a critical value for the pit diameter on textured tools that will affect the surface roughness of the machined workpiece. Zhang et al. [4] developed an integrated model of the ball screw and cutting process and, based on the proposed model and experimental verification, investigated the effect of harmonics on the surface quality of the final machined part. Liu et al. [5] proposed a robust modeling method based on separated unbiased grey relation analysis, aiming to reduce the collinearity of temperature-sensitive points and select the temperature point with the greatest influence weight, thereby reducing the model accuracy decline caused by fluctuations in temperature-sensitive points. Huang et al. [6] established an integrated model for predicting milling machining accuracy by combining mechanical structure, control system, and cutting force, which significantly improved the reliability of CNC machine tool design by accurately simulating actual machining conditions; at the same time, the correct use of cutting fluid, coupled with the application of external lubrication and cooling methods, is also conducive to improving processing quality, thereby improving the performance of the machine tool [7–9].

With the development of technology, neural networks and machine vision technology are applied to predict the machining quality of machine tools. Considering the differences between human-induced faults in a laboratory setting and those encountered in real-world scenarios, Tan et al. [10] introduce a deeply coupled joint distributed adaptive network that enhances the detection of machine tool performance and provides a basis for predictive modeling of machining quality. Liu et al. [11] proposed a tool wear identification method based on analyzing textures generated during machining based on variable-magnifying lenses. Chen et al. [12] proposed a large-scale surface roughness detection method based on machine vision. Shi et al. [13] used wavelet transform to decompose the spindle power signal of the machine tool into feature scale, which was used as an input variable of the support vector machine to predict tool wear and evaluate workpiece machining quality. Song et al. [14] used the deep convolutional neural network model to extract features from the spindle current noise signal and used them as the classification index for four types of milling cutter wear state, thus realizing the monitoring of milling cutter state and workpiece processing quality. Tang et al. [15] developed an online monitoring system for disk milling cutter wear and machining quality prediction by combining current monitoring with the BP neural network and using the GA-BP algorithm to improve the prediction model.

XGBoost [16] is an improved gradient lift tree algorithm that has been widely used in many fields and its effectiveness in solving complex predictive modeling problems has been verified. Qu et al. [17] developed a robust feature recognition model for urban road traffic accidents, which has advantages in identifying key accident features and provides valuable insights for improving traffic safety and developing intelligent transportation systems. Lin et al. [18] established a prediction model of the transverse tensile strength of the self-thrust riveted joint based on the self-thrust riveted dataset of experimental tests and finite element simulation and trained the regression model with the XGBoost algorithm. Dai et al. [19] introduced an enhanced short-term power load forecasting method, which combined the BiLSTM model with an attention mechanism with XGBoost, and with a weighted grey relation projection algorithm for data pre-processing. The accuracy and reliability of the proposed method are verified by predicting the power load in the Singapore and Norway markets. Cao et al. [20] propose an improved XGBoost model that combines a window mechanism and random grid search to enhance short-term regional power load self-prediction and shows better predictive performance and generalization ability on four datasets compared to five alternative models. Han et al. [21] introduce an edge-computing-enabled framework that uses the optimized SMOTE-XGBoost model for unbalanced data quality monitoring in an industrial IoT environment and improves classification accuracy and efficiency during product assembly. Wan et al. [22] used the XGBoost machine learning algorithm to establish a highly accurate mass flow prediction model for refrigerants in electronic expansion valves, which significantly improved the prediction performance, optimized the efficiency of refrigeration systems, and provided effective control strategies. Based on the adaptive self-learning adjustment method, Zhang et al. [23] proposed an improved XGBoost algorithm, which was optimized by the improved bat algorithm to solve the problems of strong coupling and low precision in the existing strip thickness control mathematical model. Chen et al. [24] proposed an optimized XGBoost model based on an improved sparrow search algorithm to predict milling-cutter wear under variable operating conditions. The model integrated a recursive feature elimination algorithm for feature selection and showed high recognition accuracy and prediction performance. Lan [25] uses AE to extract features and reduce dimensions of high-dimensional network traffic data, remove redundant information, and combine with the powerful learning ability of XGBoost to classify and predict the reduced data, which improves detection accuracy. Shan [26] uses AE to reduce noise and extract features from the monitoring data of electric gate valves. XGBoost analyzes features and diagnoses faults, which reflects that AE can deal with data noise and XGBoost can mine potential relationships in data.

In the prediction of tool wear, fault detection, and product quality in machining operations, the main categories usually represent the normal or defect-free machining state. While a few categories indicate the presence of anomalies or defects, these anomalies or defects typically occur much less frequently than canonical states, resulting in an unbalanced data distribution in the collected dataset. For the problem of data imbalance, Chawla et al. [27] put forward the synthetic minority over-sampling technique (SMOTE) to solve the problem of class imbalance in the dataset. They used the SMOTE to improve classifier performance for a few categories in various datasets and compared it with other methods such as under-sampling and changing misclassification loss functions in existing algorithms such as Ripper and naïve Bayes. Khan et al. [28] conducted extensive research on the combination, implementation, and evaluation of ensemble learning methods and data enhancement techniques for solving class imbalance problems, and gained insight into their effectiveness and applicability in various fields.

For the problem of data imbalance in regression tasks, Torgo et al. [29] proposed an improved SMOTE method to synthesize samples to balance the distribution of target variables. Branco et al. [30] introduced a new preprocessing method called SMOGN, which combined under-sampling and two over-sampling techniques to solve the unbalanced regression problem, and evaluated the effectiveness of the proposed method through extensive experimental evaluation of various regression datasets and learning algorithms. Avelino et al. [31] conducted a comprehensive investigation and empirical analysis of resampling strategies for unbalanced regression. They proposed a new taxonomy and validated the effectiveness of various techniques across multiple datasets and learning algorithms while highlighting the impact of dataset characteristics on model performance.

To improve the performance of models in regression tasks affected by unbalanced data, some researchers also explored the introduction of neural networks to solve these problems. Nguyen et al. [32] introduced a new approach to integrate a differentiable fuzzy logic system into a generative adversarial network to enhance its regression capabilities. They emphasized that fuzzy logic is effective in improving the stability and performance of generative adversarial networks in regression tasks.

By studying the current mainstream hybrid machine learning (ML) prediction models, Simona et al. [33] used autoencoders in clinical data for various purposes such as dimensionality reduction, denoising, feature extraction, and anomaly detection. XGBoost was trained based on features extracted from AE features. The combination of the two improves the prediction performance and generalization ability and improves the prediction ability of data in clinical data. In terms of soft sensing modeling, the parallel LSTM autoencoder proposed by Ge Zhiqiang [34] extracts dynamic features through the parallel training of data and models. After the original features are merged, XGBoost trains the model based on this to achieve efficient and accurate soft sensing modeling, which improves the prediction performance and robustness. In the field of machine tool processing, Zhao Hongshan et al. [35] used AE and XGBoost for generator fault diagnosis of wind turbines, which not only improved the prediction accuracy but also reduced the computational complexity due to the dimension reduction in AE and improved the overall performance. In practice, the model performance can be optimized by adjusting the structure of AE and XGBoost hyperparameters, such as the convolutional layer of AE and the number of nodes [36], or the learning rate of XGBoost and the maximum depth of the tree to balance the training speed and prediction accuracy.

Summarizing the previous research results of hybrid machine learning, it is found that the data imbalance is not considered enough in the machine tool machining size prediction: there are problems of data redundancy and high complexity, and there is a lack of effective methods to combine feature extraction and model prediction. Therefore, our proposed AE-XGBoost model fills this gap and inherits the autoencoder for feature extraction. XGBoost is used for prediction, SMOGN is used to process the imbalance data, and finally, SHAP is used for interpretation to help engineers intuitively understand the model behavior, so as to better optimize the processing parameters and model size. Various previous hybrid MLs are shown in Table 1 below.

Table 1. Summary of multiple hybrid ML models.

Hybrid ML Model	Model Composition	Key of Implementation	Application Scenarios	Advantages and Disadvantages of Performance
XGBoost-LightGBM ensemble model	XGBoost + LightGBM	XGBoost and LightGBM models were initialized using open-source machine learning frameworks, and the respective hyperparameters were adjusted to fuse the predicted values through weighted averages or voting mechanisms.	Industrial process monitoring and forecasting based on large-scale datasets.	Advantages: can handle large-scale data; disadvantages: hyperparameter tuning is more complex and more sensitive to data noise.
Random forest-Adaboost ensemble model	Random forest + AdaBoost	Random forest and AdaBoost models were built in Python with the help of the Scikit-learn library to integrate the prediction output.	Prediction of machining size for small machine tools with high machining accuracy	Advantages: good robustness, can handle high-dimensional data; disadvantages: longer training time on large datasets and poor model interpretation.

Table 1. *Cont.*

Hybrid ML Model	Model Composition	Key of Implementation	Application Scenarios	Advantages and Disadvantages of Performance
CNN-LSTM Mixed model	CNN + LSTM	A deep learning framework was used to construct the CNN part, connect the LSTM layer, and train the model with loss functions such as mean square error.	A machine tool process characterized by a space-time sequence	Advantages: it can effectively capture spatiotemporal characteristics, and has strong modeling ability for complex time series data. Disadvantages: model training requires a large amount of data and computational resources, takes a long time to train, and is prone to overfitting.
Stacking fusion model	Base model + meta-learner	The training and validation sets were divided, and multiple base models were trained. A new dataset was constructed using the prediction results of the validation set to train the meta-learner, and the model parameters of each stage were adjusted.	A variety of machine tool processing scenarios, especially when the processing data sources are diverse and complex features	Advantages: it can integrate the advantages of multiple models to improve prediction performance and generalization ability. Disadvantages: high model complexity, cumbersome training process, and high computational cost.
Blending fusion model	Fusing different models trained on different subsets	Different models were trained with different subsets. The fusion weight was determined according to the performance of the validation set, and the fusion predictive value was weighted.	Machine tool processing scenarios that require rapid construction of prediction models	Advantages: the training speed is relatively fast and the model fusion method is simple. Disadvantages: it is sensitive to data subset division and may lose part of the information.
AE-XGBoost Model	AE + XGBoost	The autoencoder architecture was built by PyTorch or TensorFlow, and the coding features were obtained after pre-training, which were sent to the XGBoost model in Scikit-learn for training and prediction.	Machine tool processing data have high dimension, redundancy, and unobvious features, such as size prediction in complex machine tool processing with multi-process and multi-parameter.	Advantages: autoencoder can effectively perform feature extraction and dimensionality reduction, and remove redundant information and noise, while XGBoost can make efficient and accurate prediction based on the extracted features. The combination of the two can improve the performance and generalization ability of the model, and the requirement for data preprocessing is relatively low. Its uniqueness lies in the combination of unsupervised feature learning (autoencoder) and supervised prediction (XGBoost), which gives full play to the advantages of both, and has better adaptability and accuracy when processing complex machine tool processing data.

The following chapters are as follows. Section 2 is the methodology of this paper, introducing the overall description of the model, the three preprocessing methods, the construction of the AE-XGBoost model, and the visualization and interpretation model of the model results—SHAP analysis model in sequence. In Section 3, the experimental verification is carried out, and the data source, software and hardware configuration, Results and Analysis of Data Screening Processing, Results and Analysis of Prediction of AE-XGBoost and XGBoost, Results and Analysis of feature interpretation based on SHAP analysis, Results, and Analysis of Dimensions Interpretation based on SHAP Analysis are presented in turn; the results are then discussed. Section 4 summarizes the findings and suggests future research directions.

2. AE-XGBoost Model Construction

2.1. Global Model Description

The AE-XGBoost model developed in this paper is short for autoencoder-XGBoost. The advantages of AE and XGBoost are utilized to better process and analyze the machine tool machining dimensional prediction problems. An autoencoder automatically learns important features in the input data and compresses high-dimensional data into a low-dimensional representation. The encoder maps the input data to a low-dimensional latent space, and the decoder reconstructs the original data from the latent space. XGBoost is an efficient gradient-boosting algorithm that performs well in classification and regression tasks. It builds strong learners by integrating multiple weak learners (usually decision trees) that are capable of handling complex nonlinear relationships. Combining AE with the XGBoost model can use AE to learn the intrinsic structure of the data to extract features, better characterize the XGBoost input data size, improve the prediction ability of the error data by using the structural characteristics of the AE error robustness, and also reduce the model's dependence on specific data distributions by combining the two to achieve better generalization ability.

In addition, the input data for machine tool prediction usually exists in multivariate data, which increases the workload of data collection and the complexity of problem analysis to a certain extent. Therefore, it is necessary to use the principal component analysis, PCA, method to downsize the data to achieve a reduction in indicators to be analyzed while minimizing the loss of information contained in the original indicators; at the same time, it is necessary to combine with the correlation analysis method because if each indicator is analyzed separately, it is easy to blindly downsize the data and lose a large amount of useful information; therefore, combining with the GRA to study the relationship between data dimensions and the resultant prediction to understand the relative strength of the impact of certain residual size factors on the machining size. The imbalance of machine tool size data is also a common problem, so it is necessary to process the data. The core idea of the SMOGN algorithm selected in this paper is to synthesize new minority samples to balance the dataset. For each size data in the minority class, SMOGN will add a certain amount of Gaussian noise to its feature space to add new size data. The initial data are preprocessed by a combination of PCA, GRA, and SMOGN to provide more effective data input for subsequent prediction models.

SHAP [37] values are calculated based on Shapley values in cooperative game theory to fairly distribute the contribution of model predictions among the individual features and are used in this model to quantify the contribution of dimensional features to dimensional prediction results and to verify safe ranges for important dimensions. The overall model, as shown in Figure 1, demonstrates how the data flow from input, preprocessing, and between the AE, XGBoost, and SHAP analysis modules, as well as the internal structure and connectivity of each module.

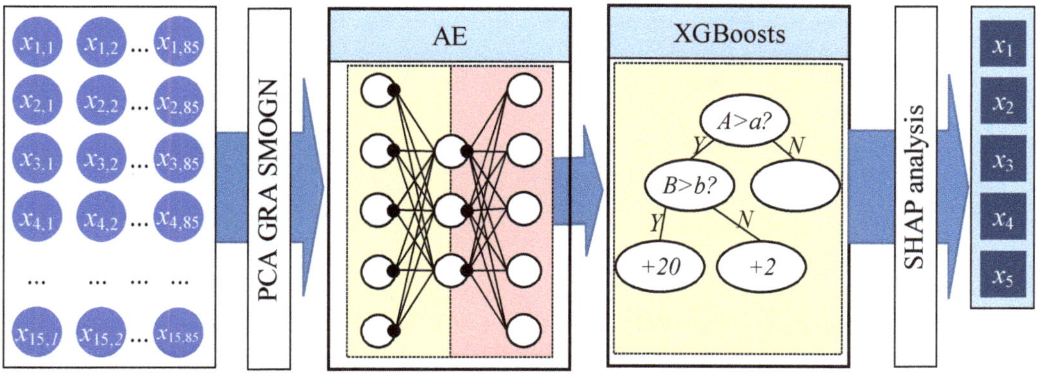

Figure 1. Overall model flowchart.

As can be seen in Figure 1, the data related to machine tool processing is used as input to the overall model, including numerical data such as positioning accuracy, repetitive positioning accuracy, clamping rigidity, etc. The size of the input data is 15 $\times$ 85, which can be used as a part of the subsequent processing; and then, through the data pre-processing, the data are subjected to PCA dimensionality reduction, GRA correlation analysis, and SMOGN imbalance processing in order; then the data are passed into the self-encoder for feature extraction.

Self-encoder contains an encoder, bottleneck, and decoder; the encoder reduces the input size and compresses the input data into coded form; the bottleneck represents a potential space, which contains all the hidden variables, that is, the smallest features that exist in the space obtained, this is the smallest size of the input data, the minimum number of neurons; the decoder is the inverse of the encoder, which is the role of the realization of data reconstruction, so that the coded representation of the bottleneck layer is as close as possible to the original input data, and verifies the model compression effect.

Subsequently, the potential spatial data of the self-encoder are used as the input features of the XGBoost model, and the combination of the original numerical data and the advanced features extracted by deep learning is passed into the XGBoost prediction module; XGBoost constructs multiple decision trees based on the principle of gradient boosting, and each decision tree learns the patterns in the data by splitting the input features to predict the machining dimensions of the machine tool, and the prediction results of the multiple decision trees are weighted by the weighting of the input features. The prediction results of multiple decision trees are integrated by weighted summation to obtain the final prediction value.

The trained XGBoost model is used to create a SHAP interpreter, which calculates the contribution of each input feature to the model prediction (i.e., SHAP value), which can be used to interpret the model's prediction, and shows how each feature affects the prediction result and the interactions between the features through the visualization of the feature importance graph and SHAP dependency graph. The model results contain the XGBoost model predictions.

The model results contain the predicted values of the XGBoost model output machine tool dimensions, which can be used for quality control, process optimization, and other applications in real-world production, as well as the interpreted results provided by the

SHAP analysis, which help to understand the model's prediction process by showing which features are critical factors for further optimization of the model and the machining process.

The information flow is as follows: the raw data first enters the PCA block, where principal components are calculated. These components are then passed to the grey correlation analysis (GRA) block. The GRA block outputs a ranked list of features based on their correlation significance, which is then used as input to the autoencoder. The SMOGN method is applied to the original dataset before PCA to address data imbalance issues, ensuring that the subsequent processing steps work on a more representative sample.

2.2. Data Preprocessing Method

Data preprocessing includes three methods, at first, PCA is used for the dimensionality reduction in data, then relational analysis is conducted based on the GRA, and finally, SMOGN is used for unbalanced processing of data. The following describes how to use each method in detail.

A. Data dimensionality reduction based on PCA

PCA is a method for dimensionality reduction in high dimensional feature data, which makes the machine tool processing dimension dataset easier to use and reduces the computation amount of the algorithm. The raw data features are of high dimensionality and vary considerably in the dimension of the influence of different factors during machining on various machine tools, such as positioning accuracy, repeatability, clamping rigidity, machining material, initial heat treatment status of the material, tool structure, tool material, number of cutting edges, cutting edge length, and the amount of free-state oscillation. According to the PCA method, we first set the dataset $X_{n\times m} = [x_1, x_2 \cdots, x_m]$, representing 15 features, $m = 15$, where each X is an n-dimensional column vector. Decentralization first, and then the average value of each feature is subtracted as follows:

$$X = X - \frac{1}{m}\sum_{i=1}^{m} x_i \tag{1}$$

Then, the covariance matrix $C = \frac{1}{m}XX^T$, and eigenvalue decomposition of the covariance matrix are calculated to obtain the eigenmatrix, arranged in columns from the largest to the smallest eigenvalues, and the first k columns are taken to form the matrix $P_{n\times k}$, where k is the target dimension, P is equivalent to a coordinate system, and each column in P is a coordinate axis. The data after dimensionality reduction can be obtained by projecting the original data into the P coordinate system. $Y_{k\times m} = P^T_{n\times k}X_{n\times m}$ can reduce the dimension of 15-dimensional data to a new space of 5 feature vectors.

B. Data relational processing based on GRA

GRA is a method used to analyze the degree of correlation between factors in a system, and in machine tool dimensional analysis, it is possible to quantify the degree of influence of influencing factors on machining dimensions. GRA can help determine which factors are most closely related to machining dimensions, and it can also be used to screen out key factors efficiently, reducing the complexity of data analysis and making the analysis of machine tool dimensions more efficient and accurate. According to the PCA method, dimensionless processing is carried out on the machine tool dimensions dataset, as shown in the equation below:

$$x_i(k) = \frac{x_i'(k)}{\frac{1}{m}\sum_{k=1}^{m} x_i'(k)} \tag{2}$$

Then calculate the grey relation coefficient of each factor, as shown in the formula below:

$$\zeta_i(k) = \frac{\min_i \min_k |x_0(k) - x_i(k)| + \rho \bullet \max_i \max_k |x_0(k) - x_i(k)|}{|x_0(k) - x_i(k)| + \rho \bullet \max_i \max_k |x_0(k) - x_i(k)|} \tag{3}$$

where $x_0(k)$ is the reference column, $k = 1, \cdots, m$. ρ is the resolution coefficient, ρ represents the differentiation coefficient used to control the degree of differentiation, its value is set to 0.5, the smaller the ρ, the greater the difference between the relation coefficients, the stronger the differentiation ability.

Then calculate the grey-weighted relation degree, and the mean value of this column is the final score, as shown in the formula below:

$$r_i = \frac{1}{m} \sum_{k=1}^{m} \zeta_i(k) \tag{4}$$

C. Data imbalance processing based on SMOGN

The SMOGN algorithm will also be used to deal with the imbalance of the dataset before constructing the XGBoost model, including interpolating the minority class samples to generate synthetic samples to increase the number of minority class samples. Also, this method reduces the number of large samples in the process of generating new samples. The specific steps of the over-sampling algorithm are as follows: first, the distance between the seed sample and its farthest and nearest neighbor is calculated, and half of this distance is selected as the safety margin. Next, a safe zone for the seed sample is established according to this margin. Samples are classified as "safe" or "unsafe" based on whether the distance between the seed and its neighbors exceeds the safety margin. If the selected neighbor is within the "safe" margin, it is suitable to use the synthetic minority over-sampling technique (SmoteR) policy. Conversely, if the selected neighbor exceeds the "safe" margin, it is considered too far from the interpolation. That means in this case, it is best to introduce Gaussian noise to the seed sample to generate a new sample.

Figure 2 shows a composite example of a seed sample and its 5 closest neighbors. "Tgt" represents the samples showing high relation; the high relation category is represented by the blue dotted line with dots at both ends; the low relation category is represented by the red dotted line with asterisks at both ends; the "case" represents the parameters and dimension results corresponding to a certain processing operation, set as the seed sample; and the horizontal and vertical coordinates represent two different processing parameters. The dark gray "Safe" indicates the area where the data points whose processing dimensions are within the safety margin are distributed, while the light gray "unsafe" indicates the area where the data points whose processing dimensions are within the unsafe margin are located. Different interpolation methods are adopted in the two zones. "Five-nearest neighbors" represent the 5 other data points closest to the seed sample in the data control. The effect is that if the dataset has far more qualified data points than unqualified data points, a few classes of samples can be processed based on the division of the "safe" and "unsafe" zones and the nearest neighbor information. A few class samples are selected in the "unsafe" area, and then new minority class samples are generated by using the information of its nearest neighbors through the over-sampling technology in the SMOGN algorithm to balance the dataset and improve the model's ability to identify abnormal processing dimensions.

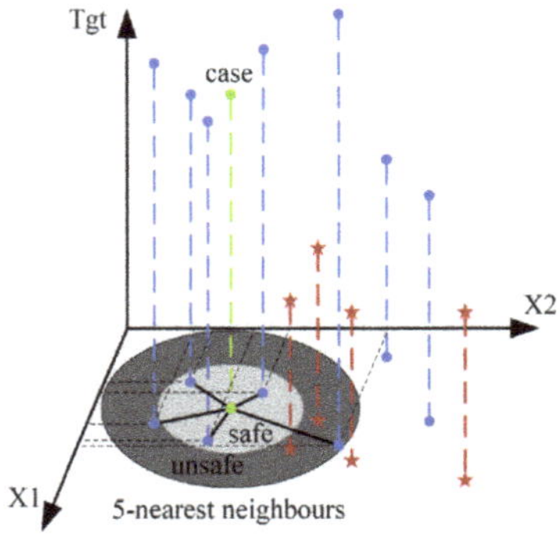

Figure 2. SMOGN sampling.

2.3. AE-XGBoost Model

A: AE Structural Foundations

In a machine tool dimension prediction model based on XGBoost, convolutional neural network (CNN), and SHAP analysis, CNN can be used to automatically extract features from machine tool machining data. CNN is a deep learning model that is good at processing data with grid structure, which can automatically learn features in the data through structures such as the convolution layer and pooling layer. The parameter data in the machining process of the machine tool can be used as the input of the CNN. The structure of the CNN usually includes a convolution layer, pooling layer, and fully connected layer, as shown in Figure 3.

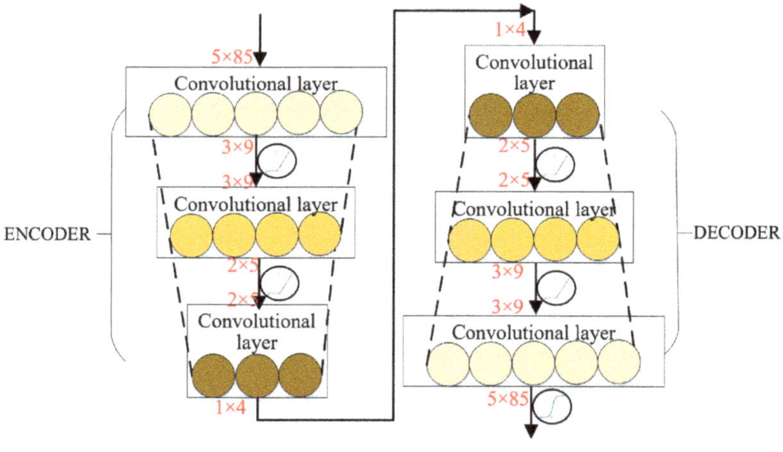

Figure 3. Convolutional neural network diagram.

Convolution layer: involves feature extraction using multiple convolution checks on input data. Convolution nuclei in the convolution layer slide over the machining parameter data to extract different features using local joins and weight sharing; for example, a convolution kernel may detect some interaction pattern between cutting speed and feed rate, which may be related to changes in machining dimensions.

In the training phase, CNN learns the feature representation in the data and then uses the feature output learned by CNN as input for the XGBoost model.

B: AE-XGBoost Model

XGBoost is an integrated learning algorithm, the basic components are decision trees, which are "weak learners" for classification and regression tasks. Based on the principle of gradient enhancement, each successive tree is constructed to predict the residuals of the previous tree, and there is a sequence between the decision trees that make up XGBoost: the latter will take into account the prediction results of the previous tree, i.e., the deviation of the previous tree. Based on the principle of gradient enhancement, each successive tree is constructed to predict the residuals of the previous tree, and there is a sequence between these decision trees: the generation of the latter decision tree will take into account the prediction results of the previous tree, i.e., the bias of the previous tree will be taken into account so that the training samples of the previous tree that made mistakes in the subsequent tree will be paid more attention to, and then based on the adjusted distribution of the samples to train the next decision tree, and the positive and negative results will be gradually optimized by integrating multiple decision trees. The prediction results are gradually optimized, and the regularization term effectively prevents overfitting and improves the model's generalization ability. The feature vectors extracted by AE are used as inputs to the XGBoost model to construct an XGBoost-based regression model to predict the machining dimensions of the machine tool. The combination of these individual tree predictions together produces a collective decision for the final prediction. Let us assume that the tree model trained during the t iteration is denoted by $f_t(x_i)$, then the prediction of the sample i after the t iteration, $\hat{y}_i^{(t)}$ can be expressed mathematically by (5), as follows:

$$\hat{y}_i^{(t)} = \sum_{j=1}^{t} f_j(x_i) = \hat{y}_i^{(t-1)} + f_t(x_i) \tag{5}$$

where x_i is the ith data point in the input dataset. Based on the actual value and predicted value, the loss function is obtained as follows (6):

$$L = \sum_{i=1}^{n} l(y_i, \hat{y}_i) \tag{6}$$

where the $\sum_{i=1}^{n} l(y_i, \hat{y}_i)$ quantifies the difference between the predicted value and the actual value. XGBoost adds regularization terms to the original loss function of the gradient lifting decision tree to improve its performance and prevent overfitting. The improved loss function is expressed in the following Formula (7):

$$obj = \sum_{i}^{n} l(y_i, \hat{y}_i) + \sum_{j=1}^{J} \Omega(f_j) \tag{7}$$

$$\Omega(f_t) = \gamma T + \frac{1}{2}\lambda \sum_{k=1}^{T} w_k^2 \tag{8}$$

In Formula (8), the $\Omega(f_t)$ is a regularization term, T is the number of leaf nodes, w represents the fraction assigned to leaf nodes, γ is used to control the number of leaf nodes and thus affects the complexity of the tree structure, λ ensures that the fraction of leaf nodes does not become too large, helping to maintain balance and prevent overfitting.

By substituting Equation (1) into Equation (3) and performing a second-order Taylor expansion of the loss function, it can be derived that the objective function of the t-th tree, as shown in Formula (9) as follows:

$$obj^{(t)} = \sum_{i=1}^{n} [l(y_i, \hat{y}_i^{(t-1)}) + g_i f_t(x_i) + \frac{1}{2} h_i f_t^2(x_i)] + \Omega(f_t) \tag{9}$$

where the equation has $g_i = \partial_{\hat{y}_i^{(t-1)}} l(y_i, \hat{y}^{(t-1)})$, $h_i = \partial^2_{\hat{y}^{(t-1)}} l(y_i, \hat{y}^{(t-1)})$. For a given tree, we can calculate the best value of the objective function by finding the best weight, thus determining the best leaf node, as shown in Formula (10).

$$w_k^* = -\frac{\sum\limits_{i \in I_k} g_i}{\sum\limits_{i \in I_k} h_i + \lambda} \tag{10}$$

By calculating the gain before and after the segmentation, we can evaluate the quality of the model, as shown in Formula (11).

$$gain = \frac{1}{2}\left[\frac{\left(\sum\limits_{i \in I_k} g_i\right)^2}{\sum\limits_{i \in I_k} h_i + \lambda} + \frac{\left(\sum\limits_{i \in I_R} g_i\right)^2}{\sum\limits_{i \in I_R} h_i + \lambda} - \frac{\left(\sum\limits_{i \in I} g_i\right)^2}{\sum\limits_{i \in I} h_i + \lambda}\right] - \gamma \tag{11}$$

XGBoost parameters determine the performance of the model. We chose max_depth, n_estimators, learning_rate, colsample_bytree, objective, reg_alpha, and reg_lambda for adjustment. max_depth is used to enhance the complexity of the model, and to capture the relationship in the data in a more detailed way; learning_rate adjusts the weight of the residual fitted by each weak learner, and the fitting effect can be improved by adjusting the number of weak learners; n_estimators represents the number of constructed trees, which is used to improve the accuracy of the model. colsample_bytree represents the proportion of features considered during the splitting process of each tree, helping to manage the complexity of the model. reg_alpha and reg_lambda control L1 and L2 regularization, respectively, to reduce the complexity of the model and prevent overfitting. The objective is used to define the objective function to be optimized by the model, with the parameters set as shown in Table 2.

Table 2. The values of AE-XGBoost parameters.

Parameters	Optimal Values
max_depth	6
n_estimators	400
learning_rate	0.05
colsample_bytree	0.8
objective	reg: squared error
reg_alpha	0.05
reg_lambda	0.1

We define the range of the above parameters. By using grid search cross-validation (GridSearchCV), we systematically traverse the parameter space for a comprehensive combinational search, which evaluates the validity of each parameter combination through cross-validation, ensuring a reliable assessment of its predictive performance. Ultimately, we chose the combination with the highest score to determine the parameters used in the XGBoost model.

C: Model Evaluation Indicators

After completing the AE-XGBoost model dimensional prediction, the dimensional accuracy predicted by the proposed model is compared with the actual dimensional accuracy of the machining process. We selected three commonly used metrics to evaluate the model's performance: mean absolute error (X_{MAE}), mean square error (X_{MSE}), and coefficient of determination (X_{R^2}) scores. X_{MAE} measures the degree of average absolute deviation between the predicted value and the true value, as shown in Formula (12) as follows:

$$X_{MAE} = \frac{1}{n}\sum_{t=1}^{n}|y_t - \hat{y}_t| \tag{12}$$

X_{MSE} focuses on the square of the difference between the predicted value and the true value, so it gives a higher penalty for large errors, as shown in Formula (13) as follows:

$$X_{MSE} = \frac{1}{n}\sum_{t=1}^{n}(y_t - \hat{y}_t)^2 \tag{13}$$

The X_{R^2} score is an indicator used to assess the goodness of fit of a regression model, it represents the proportion of the total variation in the dependent variable that can be explained by the regression model, as shown in Formula (14), as follows:

$$X_{R^2} = 1 - \frac{\sum_{t=1}^{n}\left(\widehat{y}_t - y_t\right)^2}{\sum_{t=1}^{n}(\overline{y} - y_t)^2} \tag{14}$$

where n is the number of training data, y_t is the measured machine tool machining dimensions, $\widehat{y}_t$ is the predicted machine tool machining values, and $\overline{y}$ is the average of the measured machine tool machining dimensions.

2.4. SHAP Analytical Explanatory Model

The output of the AE-XGBoost model is used as the input of SHAP analysis, which provides the interpretability of the model prediction. The core idea is to calculate the marginal contribution of the features to the model output, and then interpret the "black-box model" at both global and local levels, and the method is inspired by the Shapley-value-inspired additivity interpretation model. The value-inspired additive explanatory model, the process of the model prediction task is schematically shown in Figure 4.

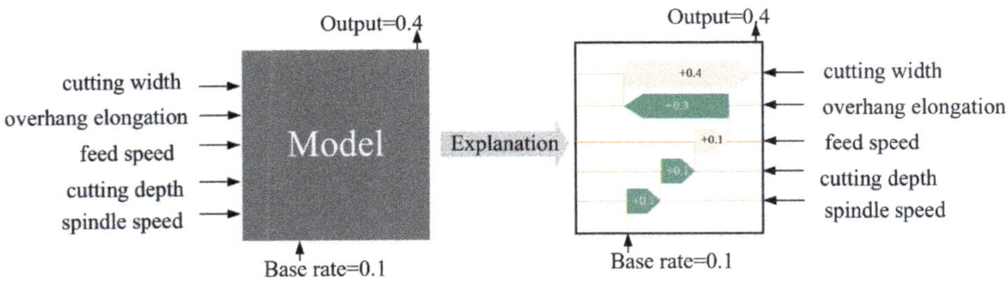

Figure 4. SHAP visual interpretation of machine learning models.

As seen in Figure 4, first of all, input some known conditions to the model (cutting width, overhang elongation, feed speed, cutting depth, spindle speed), then train the model based on the inputs, Finally, the trained model can output prediction results for this condition (output = 0.4). However, it is impossible to know how the calculation inside the model is performed, and the SHAP model can let us know how these known conditions affect the final prediction results.

For a model with n features, the Shapley value ϕ_i of feature i is calculated by considering all possible subsets of features $S \subseteq F$, where F is the set of all features. The specific calculation formula is shown in Formula (15).

$$\phi_i = \pm \sum_{S \subseteq F \setminus \{i\}} \frac{|S|!(|F| - |S| - 1)!}{|F|!} \left[f_{S\cup\{i\}}(x_{S\cup\{i\}}) - f_S(x_S) \right] \tag{15}$$

where $f_S(x_S)$ is the predicted value of the model on the feature subset S, and $|S|$ represents the number of features in the subset S. By iterating over all subsets S that do not contain a feature i, the formula calculates the change (i.e., marginal contribution) of the model's predicted value after adding a feature i to subset S, and carries out weighted summation according to the combination of subsets to obtain the Shapley value of feature i.

The dimensions of SHAP values directly reflect the importance of features to the model's prediction results. A SHAP value with a larger absolute value indicates that the feature has a larger impact on the prediction results, while a SHAP value near zero indicates that the feature has a smaller impact. For the prediction of a single sample of machining dimensions, when the machining dimensions of a workpiece are predicted, the SHAP value of the cutting speed is negative, which means that increasing the cutting speed will make the predicted machining dimensions smaller under other conditions. The SHAP value of the tool material is positive, indicating that the use of a high-quality tool material will increase the processing dimensions. Therefore, based on the SHAP value, it is possible to explain how each feature affects the final prediction of the model. By analyzing the SHAP value of the feature and its positivity and negativity, we can find out whether the feature changes the prediction result in a positive or negative direction.

3. Results and Discussion

3.1. Data Preparation

To analyze the factors that affect the dimensional accuracy in CNC milling, this paper starts from the actual CNC milling process. A total quantity of 850 dimensional machining data points were collected, and each data point recorded the corresponding 15 machining size factors, providing a rich data source for model training and validation. These factors include positioning accuracy, repeated positioning accuracy, clamping rigidity, machining material, initial heat treatment state of the material, tool structure, tool material, blade number, overhang elongation, blade length, free state pendulum momentum, spindle speed, feed speed, cutting width and cutting depth, as shown in Table 3.

Table 3. Influence factors and data source.

Type	Influencing Factor	Data Source
Machine tool	Positioning accuracy	Machine tool
	Repeated positioning accuracy	Machine tool
Jig and fixture	Clamping rigidity	Machining process routine
Processing material	Machining material	Machining process routine
	Initial heat treatment state of the material	Machining process routine
Cutting tool	Tool structure	Tool maintenance center
	Tool material	Tool maintenance center
	Blade number	Tool maintenance center
	Overhang elongation	Tool maintenance center
	Blade length	Tool maintenance center
Cutting tool set	Free-state pendulum momentum	Operational record
Cutting parameters	Spindle speed	Machine tool/CNC program
	Feed speed	Machine tool/CNC program
	Cutting width	Machine tool/CNC program
	Cutting depth	Machine tool/CNC program

Table 3 shows 15 different factors affecting dimensional accuracy, divided into six categories according to type, each factor has a specific source.

For the two factors under the "Machine tool category", "Positioning accuracy" and "Repeated positioning accuracy", the source of the data is the "Machine tool" itself, and these data reflect the performance of the machine tool in terms of positioning, which has a fundamental influence on the accuracy of the machined dimension.

One factor in the "Jig and fixture" category, "Clamping rigidity", is derived from the "Machining process routine", and these parameters affect the fixation of the workpiece in actual machining, which in turn affects the machined dimensions.

Two influencing factors under the category of "Processing material", "Machining material" and "Repeated positioning accuracy", data also from the "Machining process routine", and these information are recorded in the process regulations and used to guide the machining process because different materials and heat treatment states will lead to different deformation behaviors of the material in the cutting process, which affects the machining dimensions.

The five influencing factors under the category of the "Cutting tool", "Tool structure", "Tool material", "Blade number", "Overhang elongation", and "Blade length" are provided with data from the "Tool maintenance center". These parameters are critical to the performance of the tool in the cutting process and they work together to influence the machined dimensions.

One influencing factor under the "Cutting tool set" category is the "Free-state pendulum momentum" data recorded by the operator. These data reflect the mounting accuracy and stability of the toolset, which have a direct impact on machining accuracy.

Four influencing factors under the category of "Cutting parameters" are "Spindle speed", "Feed speed", "Cutting width", and "Cutting depth", for which data are available from the "machine tool/CNC program", and for which changes in these parameters directly lead to changes in the machined dimensions. A total of 850 records are included in the comprehensive dataset. Eighty percent of the collected data is used for training and the remaining data is used for testing.

The model is equipped with a 12th-generation Intel(R) Core (TM)i7-12700H processor manufactured by Intel, George Town, Malaysia. The basic processor frequency is 2.70 GHz. The GPU is NVIDIA GeForce RTX3060 manufactured by Gigabyte, New Taipei City, Taiwan, China. The operating system is Windows 11. The programming language used for model training is Python, version 3.10.14. The deep learning framework used is PyTorch, version 2.2.1, and accelerated with cu121.

3.2. Results and Analysis of Data Screening Processing

A. Results and Analysis of Data Screening Processing based on PCA

The dataset contains 15 kinds of data affecting the machining dimensions of machine tools, and whether or not to use the effect of the effect and how much the effect varies, so data screening based on principal component analysis (PCA) and gray correlation analysis (GRA) effectively reduces the dimensionality of the data, filters the key variables, and reveals the relationship between the variables, which provides strong support for the machining of machine tool machining dimension processing.

In the process of various machine tools, some influencing factors remain unchanged, such as positioning accuracy, repeated positioning accuracy, clamping rigidity, machining material, initial heat treatment state of the material, tool structure, tool material, blade number, blade length, and free-state pendulum. Therefore, these constant features were excluded to prevent the generation of misleading results by the model.

PCA projects the original standardized data into the principal component space through eigenvectors to obtain the principal component score of each sample. The contribution rate of the principal components reflects the proportion of the amount of information they contain about the original data. The composite score is a weighted sum of the samples' scores on each principal component according to the principal component contribution ratio, such that the composite score provides a comprehensive measure of the "importance" of the samples in the principal component space, which is used for tasks such as sample ranking. The formula is shown below.

$$\text{score}_j = \sum_{j=1}^{num} df_{ij} \times \frac{rate_j}{100} \tag{16}$$

where i represents the sample, j represents the principal component, score_j is the composite score of the jth principal component, num is the number of principal components, df_{ij} is the score of the ith sample on the jth principal component, and $rate_j$ is the contribution rate of the jth principal component. Because the principal components with a high contribution rate contain more original information, they are more important in the comprehensive evaluation, and their corresponding scores have greater weights. The top five comprehensive evaluation values are actual mass, tool overhang extension, cutting feed rate, cutting spindle speed, cutting width, and depth of cut, and the comprehensive scores are 15.42762416, 5.497486898, −4.643924089, −5.222349954, −5.396497335, respectively.

B. Results and Analysis of Data Screening Processing based on GRA

For the five major factors selected, the GRA algorithm was used to explore the relation between the factors, as shown in the GRA heat map results in Figure 5.

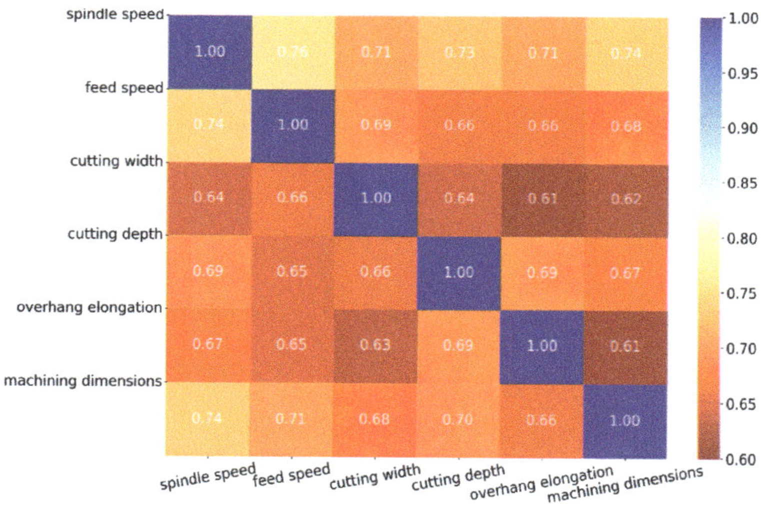

Figure 5. GRA heat map.

As can be seen in Figure 5, the bluer the color, the higher the relation between factors, and the redder the color, the lower the relation between factors. The relation between various factors is shown in Table 4 below.

Table 4. Relation between factors.

	Spindle Speed	Feed Speed	Cutting Width	Cutting Depth	Overhang Elongation
Spindle speed	1	0.74	0.64	0.69	0.67
Feed speed	0.76	1	0.66	0.65	0.65
Cutting width	0.71	0.69	1	1	0.63
Cutting depth	0.73	0.66	0.64	0.66	1
Overhang elongation	0.71	0.66	0.61	0.69	0.69

According to the calculation results of GRA, there are five main influencing factors in the first row and the first column, and the remaining five main influencing factors have a great influence on the GRA value of the machine tool processing dimensions distributed in the range of [0.65, 0.76]. Therefore, overhang elongation, spindle speed, feed speed, cutting width, and cutting depth were selected as the characteristics to predict the machining dimensions.

C. Results and Analysis of Data Screening Processing based on SMOGN

In the unbalanced regression problem, the imbalance in the number of samples may cause the model to perform poorly in predicting samples from fewer categories. To solve this problem, the SMOGN algorithm is used to synthesize the samples to balance the dataset, and the results before and after processing are shown in Figure 6 below, for the size feature of true mass.

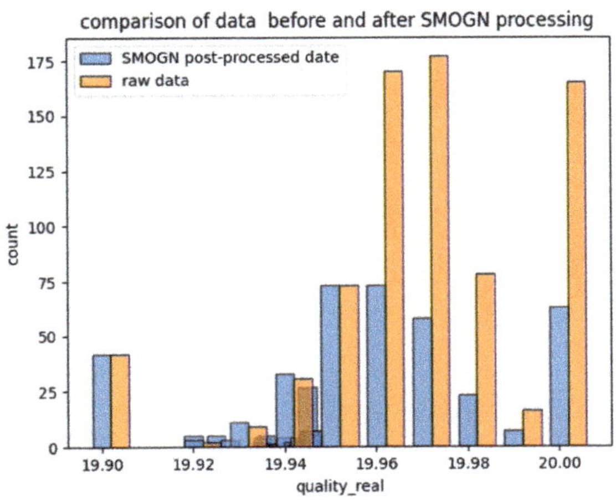

Figure 6. Comparison of quality_real distribution in raw data and SMOGN processed data.

The upper histogram in Figure 6 shows that the x-axis represents the value of real quality in the dataset, ranging from 19.90 to 20.00 and the y-axis represents the number of samples corresponding to each quality_real value, with a scale from 0 to 175.

The blue bars represent the pre-processed data and the orange bars represent the SMOGN post-processed data. The blue bars indicate that the number of samples in the original data is higher for the quality_real values of 19.96, and 19.97, which is around 175, while the number of samples for other quality_real values is relatively low. The orange bars show the distribution of the data after SMOGN processing, and it should be noted that the processed data are weakened on distributions with more quality_real samples, e.g., lowering the number of samples around 19.96, 19.97, 19.98, and 20.00, and re-synthesizing to a certain number of samples on distributions with fewer samples, e.g., raising the number of samples around 19.92, 19.93, and 19.94 near to which the sample size was raised.

By comparing the blue and orange bars, it can be seen that the SMOGN processing has an impact on the data distribution, which makes the processed data more spread out and even in the distribution of quality_real values. SMOGN achieves balanced data and avoids the situation where the number of samples is too much or too little for certain values in the original data, which can improve the generalization ability and stability of the model.

3.3. Results and Analysis of Prediction of AE-XGBoost and XGBoost

After training the XGBoost model, we evaluated the performance of the model with test data. The predicted machined dimensions were compared with the measured mass dimensions and the XGBoost model was compared with the AE-XGBoost model based on three evaluation metrics. The results are shown in Figure 7.

As shown in Figure 7a, the horizontal axis index, ranging from 0 to 80, represents the index of the data points, and the vertical axis values ranging from 19.90 to 20.00 represent the size of the data points; the blue folds in the figure represent the true values, with values ranging from 19.90 to 20.00, and the orange discounts in the figure represent the predicted values from the AE-XGBoost model, with a value range between 19.90 and 19.98; the green discount in the figure represents the value predicted only by the XGBoost model, and the value range is between 19.90 and 20.00. It can be seen in the figure that the predicted value of the AE-XGBoost model is closer to the real value, the value is relatively stable, and it may be closer to the real value around 40, 50, 60, and 70.

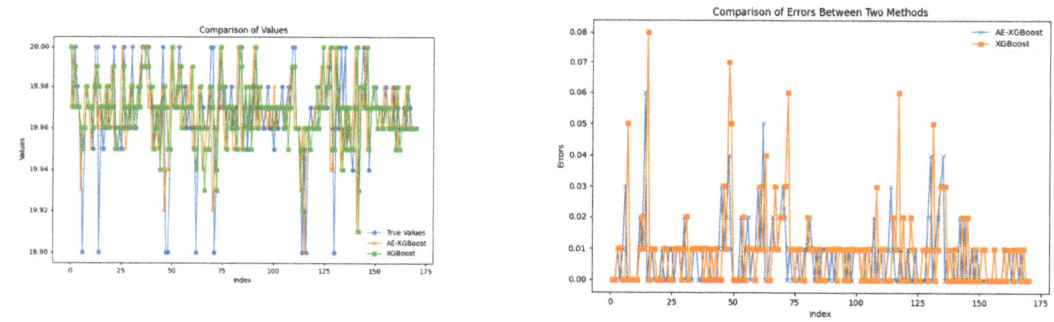

(a) Comparison of the predict values and the true values (b) Comparison of prediction errors between AE-XGBoost and XGBoost

Figure 7. Comparison between real values and predicted values of two methods.

According to Figure 7b, the horizontal coordinate is an index, which ranges from 0 to 80, and the vertical coordinate errors, which range from 0 to 0.008, indicate the magnitude of the error value, the blue dash line represents the error predicted by the AE-XGBoost model, and the orange dash line represents the error predicted by the XGBoost model, and it can be seen that the error value of the two methods is between 0 and 0.1, and the overall level shows that the prediction error of AE-XGBoost is significantly lower than the prediction error of XGBoost model, and at certain indexes, e.g., the positions of 20, 50, and 70, the error of the predicted values of AE-XGBoost model is significantly lower than the prediction error of XGBoost model.

To further quantify the differences in the model before and after the improvement, the mean absolute error, mean square error, and coefficient of determination were calculated for both cases, and the results are shown in Table 5.

Table 5. Evaluation metrics of two methods.

Model	MAE/e-3	MSE/e-4	RMSE/e-2	R^2
AE-XGBoost	7.778	1.655	1.286	0.681
XGBoost	9.415	2.696	1.642	0.480

The table shows that the MAE, MSE, RMSE, and R^2 of AE-XGBoost are 7.778×10^{-3}, 1.655×10^{-4}, 1.286×10^{-2}, and 0.681, respectively, while the evaluation metrics of XGBoost are 9.415×10^{-3}, 2.696×10^{-4}, 1.642×10^{-2}, and 0.480, respectively. Compared with the XGBoost model, the AE-XGBoost model improves on these three metrics by 17.39%, 38.61%, 21.69%, and 41.88%. It can be clearly seen that the improved AE-XGBoost algorithm has effectively improved the handling of the redundancy and imbalance problems in the initial data.

3.4. Results and Analysis of Feature Interpretation Based on SHAP Analysis

After screening the main influencing factors in the original dataset, SHAP analysis is used to interpret the model. The SHAP value of each feature is calculated, and the important features are listed in descending order of importance. The results are as follows:

The horizontal axis in the bar chart of Figure 8a indicates the magnitude of the average effect ranging from 0 to 0.008, the higher the value, the higher the average effect on the model output magnitude, the vertical axis lists five factors and it can be seen that the overhang elongation and the cutting width are of the highest importance, followed by the feed rate, the depth of cut and the spindle speed.

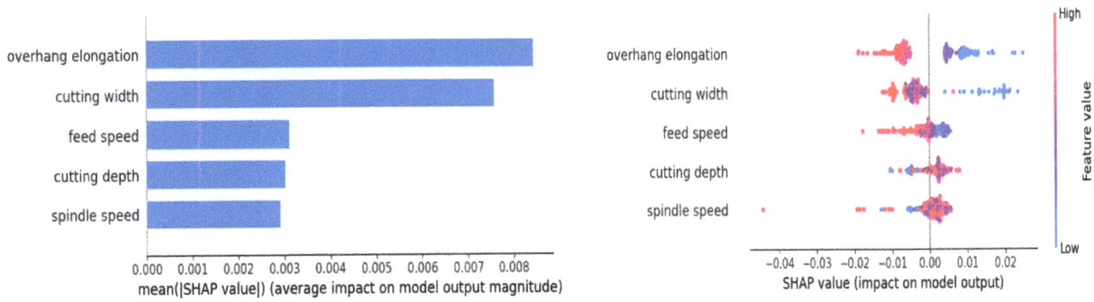

(**a**) Plot of the average influence of the mean absolute value of SHAP values of each feature on model size (**b**) Plot of the influence of SHAP value distribution of each feature on model output

Figure 8. Mean (| SHAP value |) and SHAP summary plot.

The horizontal axis in Figure 8b represents the SHAP values ranging from −0.02 to 0.02, and the vertical axis lists five different features: overhang elongation, cutting width, feed speed, cutting depth, spindle speed. The color of the scatter points change from blue to red, with blue representing a lower value of the feature and red representing a higher value of the feature, which shows the effect of different features at different values on the model output.

Obviously, larger eigenvalues of overhang length and cutting width correspond to smaller SHAP values, which indicates that these two eigenvalues are negatively correlated with the machining dimensions.

3.5. Results and Analysis of Dimensions Interpretation Based on SHAP Analysis

Among the results of SHAP interpretation, the two factors of overhanging elongation and cutting width are of the highest importance. The following is a further study on the influence of these two factors on the machining dimensions. The SHAP partial dependence graph and the SHAP dependency graph are used to analyze these two features in more detail, and the results are shown in Figure 9.

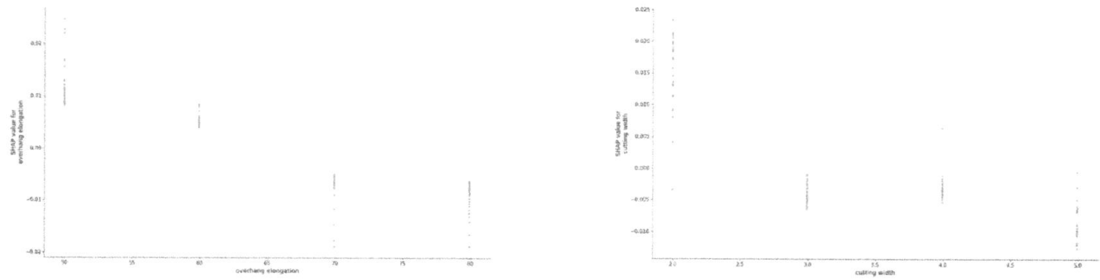

(**a**) SHAP value for overhang elongation (**b**) SHAP value for cutting width

Figure 9. SHAP partial dependence plots of two parameters.

According to the SHAP partial dependence in Figure 9a, we observe that when the overhang elongation is 50 or 60, it has a positive impact on the target value, and a smaller value has a greater positive impact. In contrast, when the value is 70 or 80, the overhang elongation has a negative effect on the target value, and the effect remains almost constant as the value increases. According to Figure 9b, we observe that when the cutting width is 2.0, there is a positive effect on the target value. However, when the value is 3.0, 4.0, or 5.0, the cutting width usually has a negative effect on the target value. In addition, as the number increases, the effect on the target value remains almost constant. However, whether the internal coupling of the two factors affects the value of the factor requires further analysis of the SHAP dependence diagram of the suspension length and cutting width. The SHAP dependence results of the two factors are shown in Figure 10.

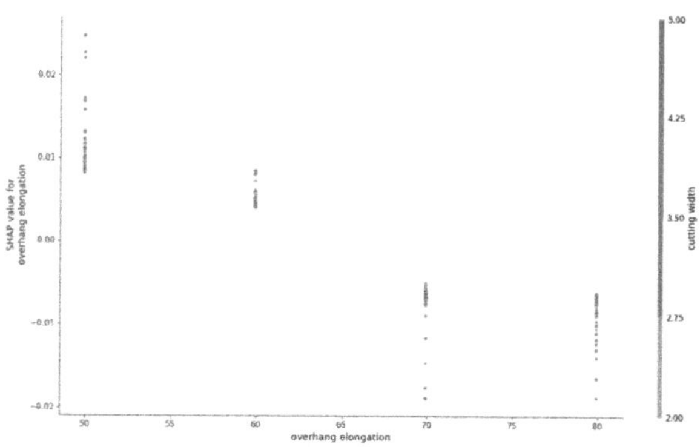

Figure 10. SHAP dependence plots of two parameters.

According to Figure 10, the variation in the influence of suspension elongation on the target value under the same value is attributed to the influence of other characteristics. However, when the overhang elongation is 50 or 60, the increase in the cutting width does not affect its positive effect on the target value. Similarly, when the overhang elongation is 70 or 80, the reduction in the cutting width does not have a negative effect on the target value. This indicates that the coupling relationship between the two features is weak and the parameters can be adjusted independently. The calculation results show that the other three parameters have similar effects on suspension elongation.

3.6. Discussion

We proposed an AE-XGBoost model for predicting machine tool machining dimensions, integrating XGBoost, autoencoder (AE), and SHAP analysis. The experimental results demonstrated the superiority of the AE-XGBoost model over the traditional XGBoost method, with a 7.11% improvement in prediction accuracy. However, a more in-depth discussion of these findings is warranted.

Model Performance and Feature Importance: The improved performance of the AE-XGBoost model can be attributed to its unique architecture. The AE effectively extracts local and global features from the data, reducing noise and redundancy. This pre-processed data is then fed into the XGBoost model, which is known for its ability to handle complex non-linear relationships. The combination allows for a more accurate prediction of machining dimensions. For example, the principal component analysis (PCA) and grey correlation analysis (GRA) pre-processing steps reduce the dimensionality of the data while retaining important information, making the data more suitable for the XGBoost model.

Regarding feature importance, SHAP analysis revealed that overhang elongation and cutting width have the most significant effects on machining dimensions. The negative correlation between the larger values of overhang elongation and cutting width and the machining dimensions, as indicated by the SHAP values, can be explained by the physical processes in machining. A longer overhang elongation may lead to increased tool deflection during machining, causing the actual machining dimensions to deviate from the desired values. Similarly, a wider cutting width may result in greater cutting forces, which can also affect the final dimensions of the machined part. The feed speed, cutting depth, and spindle speed also play important roles, but to a lesser extent.

Comparison with Existing Studies: Compared with previous research in the field of machine tool machining size prediction, our model addresses several limitations. Many existing studies do not adequately consider data imbalance, which can lead to inaccurate predictions. By using the SMOGN method, we were able to balance the dataset and improve the model's generalization ability. Additionally, the integration of SHAP analysis in our model provides interpretability, which is often lacking in other models. This allows engineers to understand how different features contribute to the prediction results, facilitating the optimization of machining parameters.

Limitations and Future Research: Despite the promising results, our study has some limitations. The dataset used in this study may not cover all possible machining scenarios, which could limit the model's generalization to other types of machine tools or machining processes. Future research could focus on expanding the dataset to include more diverse machining conditions. Additionally, although the AE-XGBoost model shows good performance, there is still room for improvement. Exploring more advanced feature extraction techniques or optimization algorithms for XGBoost could further enhance the model's accuracy.

In conclusion, this study provides valuable insights into machine tool machining size prediction. The AE-XGBoost model shows great potential, and the SHAP analysis offers a useful way to interpret the model's predictions. Future research should aim to overcome the limitations of this study and further improve the performance and generalization of the model.

4. Conclusions and Future Work

4.1. Conclusions

In this study, we proposed an interpretable machining size prediction model that combines XGBoost, autoencoder (AE), and SHAP analysis to address the challenges in machine tool machining size prediction. Our approach aimed to achieve intelligent manufacturing and enhance the machining quality of machine tools.

We began by constructing a comprehensive dataset that incorporated actual machining process parameters, machine parameters, and final machining dimensions. Given the data imbalance commonly encountered in practical engineering scenarios, we employed grey correlation analysis (GRA) and principal component analysis (PCA) to preliminarily screen the features. This not only reduced data redundancy but also retained the most relevant information. Subsequently, the synthetic minority over-sampling technique of gaussian noise regression (SMOGN) was utilized to balance the dataset, ensuring that the model could handle different data distributions effectively.

Before training the XGBoost model, we leveraged the autoencoder network to extract data features. The AE was able to capture both local and global features within the data, transforming the pre-processed data into more representative feature vectors. These features were then fed into the XGBoost model, and its optimal parameters were determined through grid search cross-validation.

The experimental results demonstrated the effectiveness of our proposed AE-XGBoost model. Compared with the traditional XGBoost method, the AE-XGBoost model showed a significant improvement in prediction accuracy. Specifically, it achieved a 7.11% increase in accuracy, with mean absolute error (MAE), mean square error (MSE), and coefficient of determination (R^2) values of 1.071×10^{-2}, 2.741×10^{-2}, and 0.570 respectively. These improvements indicated that the AE-XGBoost model was better at handling the redundancy and imbalance problems in the initial data, enabling more accurate predictions of machining dimensions.

We further employed SHAP analysis to rank the feature importance of machining dimensions. Overhang elongation and cutting width were identified as the most significant factors affecting the target variable. Through SHAP partial dependence diagrams and SHAP dependency graphs, we found that an overhang elongation of 50 or 60 had a positive effect on the target, while values of 70 or 80 had a negative effect. For the cutting width, a value of 2.0 had a positive effect, while 3.0, 4.0, and 5.0 had a negative effect. Moreover, the coupling relationship between overhang elongation and cutting width was found to be weak, suggesting that these parameters could be adjusted independently to optimize machining dimensions.

In summary, our research provides a reliable and interpretable model for machine tool machining size prediction. The AE-XGBoost model offers a practical solution for engineers to better understand and control the machining process, ultimately contributing to an improvement in machining quality and the realization of intelligent manufacturing. However, it should be noted that our model still has some limitations. For example, the performance of the model may be affected by the limited diversity of the dataset. Future research directions are discussed in the following section.

4.2. Future Work

Future work could focus on expanding and diversifying datasets and developing new imbalanced data sampling methods, which could help improve model performance under imbalanced data conditions. In addition, more efficient hyperparameter tuning techniques can be explored to further optimize the performance of the XGBoost model. In terms of practical machining applications, this study provides valuable insights for optimizing machining dimensions and adjusting machine parameters, which is helpful in developing more reasonable and effective machining schemes.

Author Contributions: Conceptualization, M.G., L.L. and Z.Z.; methodology, S.K. and Z.X.; software, S.K., Z.X. and L.L.; validation, S.K. and Z.X.; investigation, M.G., Z.X. and Z.Z.; resources, M.G.; data curation, L.L. and Z.Z.; writing—original draft, S.K. and Z.X.; writing—review and editing, S.K. and L.L.; supervision, M.G. and Z.Z.; project administration, M.G., S.K., L.L. and Z.Z.; funding acquisition, M.G. All authors have read and agreed to the published version of the manuscript.

Funding: This research was funded by "Key Research and Development Program" grant number "2022YFE0197600", "Key Research and Development Program" grant number "2020YFB1710501" and funded by "Central University Project" grant number "KJZ53420230039".

Data Availability Statement: Due to intellectual property constraints, the original datasets cannot be publicly released. However, the code (excluding proprietary components) is available in https://github.com/Muxia605/AE---XGBoost-A-Novel-Approach-for-Machine-Tool-Machining-Size-Prediction-.git (accessed on 25 February 2025). Any researcher interested in our work is welcome to contact us at 2022011018@cauc.edu.cn for further information and potential collaboration regarding the datasets.

Conflicts of Interest: Authors Mu Gu and Zhihui Zhang were employed by the company Beijing Aerospace Intelligent Manufacturing Technology Development Co., Ltd. The remaining authors declare that the research was conducted in the absence of any commercial or financial relationships that could be construed as a potential conflict of interest.

References

1. Zhang, Z.; Yang, Y.; Li, G.; Qi, Y.; Yue, C.; Hu, Y.; Li, Y. Machining accuracy reliability evaluation of CNC machine tools based on the milling stability optimization. *Int. J. Adv. Manuf. Technol.* **2023**, *124*, 4057–4074. [CrossRef]
2. Sato, R.; Noguchi, S.; Hokazono, T.; Nishida, I.; Shirase, K. Time domain coupled simulation of machine tool dynamics and cutting forces considering the influences of nonlinear friction characteristics and process damping. *Precis. Eng.* **2020**, *61*, 103–109. [CrossRef]
3. Sun, J.; Zhou, Y.; Zhao, J. Effect of hybrid texture combining micro-pits and micro-grooves on cutting performance of WC/Co-based tools. *Int. J. Adv. Manuf. Technol.* **2016**, *86*, 3383–3394. [CrossRef]
4. Zhang, W.; Zhang, X.; Zhao, W.H. Research on the multi-physical coupling characteristics of the machine tool and milling process based on the systematically integrated model. *J. Manuf. Process.* **2023**, *105*, 46–69. [CrossRef]
5. Liu, H.; Miao, E.; Zhu, X.; Wei, X. Thermal error robust modeling method for CNC machine tools based on a split unbiased estimation algorithm. *Precis. Eng.* **2018**, *51*, 169–175. [CrossRef]
6. Huang, L.; Huang, H.; Wang, Q.W. An Integrated Model Based Prediction of Machining Accuracy for Milling Machine. *Proc. Inst. Mech. Eng. Part C J. Mech. Eng. Sci.* **2024**, *238*, 6499–6517. [CrossRef]
7. Kaynak, Y.; Gharibi, A.; Yilmaz, U.; Köklü, U.; Aslantaş, K. A comparison of flood cooling, minimum quantity lubrication and high pressure coolant on machining and surface integrity of titanium Ti-5553 alloy. *J. Manuf. Process.* **2018**, *34*, 503–512. [CrossRef]
8. Yan, L.T.; Zhang, Q.J.; Yu, J.Z. Analytical models for oil penetration and experimental study on vibration assisted machining with minimum quantity lubrication. *Int. J. Mech. Sci.* **2018**, *148*, 374–382. [CrossRef]
9. Park, K.; Ewald, B.; Kwon, P. Effect of Nano-Enhanced Lubricant in Minimum Quantity Lubrication Balling Milling. *J. Tribol.* **2011**, *133*, 031803. [CrossRef]
10. Tan, Y.; Guo, L.; Gao, H.; Zhang, L. Deep Coupled Joint Distribution Adaptation Network: A Method for Intelligent Fault Diagnosis Between Artificial and Real Damages. *IEEE Trans. Instrum. Meas.* **2021**, *70*, 3507212. [CrossRef]

11. Liu, Y.; Yu, Y.; Guo, L.; Gao, H.; Tan, Y. Automatically Designing Network-Based Deep Transfer Learning Architectures Based on Genetic Algorithm for In-Situ Tool Condition Monitoring. *IEEE Trans. Ind. Electron.* **2022**, *69*, 9483–9493. [CrossRef]
12. Chen, W.; Li, Y.S.; Huang, C.Z. A study of a rapid method for detecting the machined surface roughness. *Int. J. Adv. Manuf. Technol.* **2021**, *117*, 3115–3127. [CrossRef]
13. Shi, D.F.; Gindy, N.N. Tool Wear Prediction based on Wavelet Transform and Support Vector Machines. *Int. Conf. Inform. Control Autom. Robot.* **2016**, *2*, 479–485.
14. Song, K.; Wang, M.; Liu, L.; Wang, C.; Zan, T.; Yang, B. Intelligent recognition of milling cutter wear state with cutting parameter independence based on deep learning of spindle current clutter signal. *Int. J. Adv. Manuf. Technol.* **2020**, *109*, 929–942. [CrossRef]
15. Tang, J.; Li, W.X.; Zhao, B.; Abraham, A.D. The Application of GA-BP Algorithm in Prediction of Tool Wear State. *IOP Conf. Ser. Mater. Sci. Eng.* **2018**, *398*, 012025. [CrossRef]
16. Chen, T.Q.; Guestrin, C. XGBoost: A Scalable Tree Boosting System. In Proceedings of the 22nd ACM SIGKDD International Conference on Knowledge Discovery and Data Mining 2016, San Francisco, CA, USA, 13–17 August 2016; pp. 785–794.
17. Qu, Y.; Lin, Z.K.; Li, H.L.; Zhang, X. Feature Recognition of Urban Road Traffic Accidents Based on GA-XGBoost in the Context of Big Data. *IEEE Access* **2019**, *7*, 17016–170115. [CrossRef]
18. Lin, J.; Qi, C.; Wan, H.; Min, J.; Chen, J.; Zhang, K.; Zhang, L. Prediction of Cross-Tension Strength of Self-Piercing Riveted Joints Using Finite Element Simulation and XGBoost Algorithm. *Chin. J. Mech. Eng.* **2021**, *34*, 36. [CrossRef]
19. Dai, Y.; Zhou, Q.; Leng, M.; Yang, X.; Wang, Y. Improving the Bi-LSTM model with XGBoost and attention mechanism: A combined approach for short-term power load prediction. *Appl. Soft Comput.* **2022**, *130*, 109632. [CrossRef]
20. Cao, W.; Liu, Y.; Mei, H.; Shang, H.; Yu, Y. Short-term district power load self-prediction based on improved XGBoost model. *Eng. Appl. Artif. Intell.* **2023**, *126*, 106826. [CrossRef]
21. Han, Y.; Wei, Z.; Huang, G.T. An imbalance data quality monitoring based on SMOTE-XGBOOST supported by edge computing. *Sci. Rep.* **2024**, *14*, 1151. [CrossRef]
22. Wan, A.; Gong, Z.; Chen, T.; AL-Bukhaiti, K. Mass flow characteristics prediction of refrigerants through electronic expansion valve based on XGBoost. *Int. J. Refrig.* **2024**, *158*, 345–352. [CrossRef]
23. Zhang, F.; Huang, S.; Wang, L.-J.; Zhang, Y.-J.; Li, Y.-J.; Huang, X.-Z. Online segmented thickness prediction of hot rolling strip based on IBA-XGBoost. *Int. J. Data Sci. Anal.* **2024**, *19*, 141–151. [CrossRef]
24. Chen, S.; Yin, Z.; Zheng, L.; Yuan, J. Study of an ISSA-XGBoost model for milling tool wear prediction under variable working conditions. *Int. J. Adv. Manuf. Technol.* **2024**, *133*, 2761–2774. [CrossRef]
25. Lan, R.T. Research on DDoS Attack Detection Method Based on AE-XGBoost Model. Master's Thesis, Southwestern University of Finance and Economics, Chengdu, China, 2022. [CrossRef]
26. Shan, L.F. Research on Condition Monitoring and Fault Diagnosis of Electric Gate Valves Based on AE and XGBoost. Master's Thesis, Harbin Engineering University, Harbin, China, 2022. [CrossRef]
27. Chawla, N.V.; Bowyer, K.W.; Hall, L.O.; Kegelmeyer, W.P. SMOTE: Synthetic Minority Over-sampling Technique. *J. Artif. Intell. Res.* **2002**, *16*, 321–357. [CrossRef]
28. Khan, A.A.; Chaudhari, O.; Chandra, R. A review of ensemble learning and data augmentation models for class imbalanced problems: Combination, implementation and evaluation. *Expert Syst. Appl.* **2024**, *244*, 122778. [CrossRef]
29. Torgo, L.; Ribeiro, R.P.; Pfahringer, B.; Branco, P. SMOTE for Regression. In *Portuguese Conference on Artificial Intelligence*; Springer: Berlin/Heidelberg, Germany, 2013; pp. 378–389.
30. Branco, P.; Torgo, L.; Ribeiro, R.R. SMOGN: A Pre-processing Approach for Imbalanced Regression. *Proc. Mach. Learn. Res.* **2017**, *74*, 36–50.
31. Avelino, J.G.; Cavalcanti, G.D.; Cruz, R.M. Resampling strategies for imbalanced regression: A survey and empirical analysis. *Artif. Intell. Rev.* **2024**, *57*, 82. [CrossRef]
32. Nguyen, R.; Singh, S.K.; Rai, R. FuzzyGAN: Fuzzy generative adversarial networks for regression tasks. *Neurocomputing* **2023**, *525*, 88–110. [CrossRef]
33. Volovăț, S.R.; Popa, T.O.; Rusu, D.; Ochiuz, L.; Vasincu, D.; Agop, M.; Buzea, C.G.; Volovăț, C.C. Comparative Performance of Autoencoders and Traditional Machine Learning Algorithms in Clinical Data Analysis for Predicting Post-Staged GKRS Tumor Dynamics. *Diagnostics* **2024**, *14*, 2091. [CrossRef] [PubMed]
34. Ge, Z.Q.; Zhang, X.Y.; XGBoost Soft Sensing Modeling Method Based on Parallel LSTM Autoencoder Dynamic Feature Extraction. Zhejiang China CN201910421435.6.CN110210495A. 2021. Available online: https://www.cnipa.gov.cn (accessed on 25 February 2025).
35. Wang, S.; Zhang, W.; Zheng, G.; Li, X.; Zhao, Y. Fault diagnosis of wind turbine generator using deep autocoding network and XGBoost. *Power Syst. Autom.* **2019**, *43*, 81–86.

36. Ma, Y.; Wang, X.; Dang, K.; Zhou, Y.; Yang, W.; Xie, P. Intelligent recommendation system of the injection molding process parameters based on CAE simulation, process window, and machine learning. *Int. J. Adv. Manuf. Technol.* **2023**, *128*, 4703–4716. [CrossRef]
37. Lundberg, S.M.; Lee, S. A Unified Approach to Interpreting Model Predictions. In Proceedings of the 31st International Conference on Neural Information Processing Systems, Long Beach, CA, USA, 4–9 December 2017; pp. 4768–4777.

mathematics

MDPI

Article

Optimal Design Considering AC Copper Loss of Traction Motor Applied HSFF Coil for Improving Electric Bus Fuel Economy

Kyoung-Soo Cha [1,†], Young-Hoon Jung [2,†], Soo-Hwan Park [3,*] and Min-Ro Park [4,*]

1 Advanced Mobility System Group, Korea Institute of Industrial Technology, Daegu 42994, Republic of Korea; kscha@kitech.re.kr
2 Department of Automotive Engineering, Yeungnam University, Gyeongsan 38541, Republic of Korea; yhjung@yu.ac.kr
3 Department of Mechanical, Robotics, and Energy Engineering, Dongguk University, Seoul 04620, Republic of Korea
4 Department of Electrical Engineering, Soonchunhyang University, Asan 31538, Republic of Korea
* Correspondence: parksh@dgu.ac.kr (S.-H.P.); minro@sch.ac.kr (M.-R.P.)
† These authors contributed equally to this work.

Abstract

Improving the fuel economy of electric buses requires traction motors that provide not only high-power density but also high efficiency under diverse driving conditions. While high slot fill factor (HSFF) coils such as the maximum slot occupation (MSO) coil improve motor torque and power density, they inevitably increase AC copper losses due to elevated AC resistance, especially at high speeds. Unlike conventional motor optimization studies that mainly focus on efficiency at specific operating points, this paper proposes a drive-cycle-aware design optimization method that minimizes AC copper loss to enhance real-world fuel economy. By combining 2D finite element analysis (FEA) with vehicle-level simulations under three representative driving cycles (Manhattan, HWFET, HDUDDS), an optimal motor design was derived. The optimized motor achieved improvements in fuel economy by 0.20%, 0.86%, and 0.36%, respectively, compared to the initial design. Experimental validation through prototype fabrication confirmed the effectiveness of the proposed method. These results demonstrate that the proposed design approach can contribute to improving energy efficiency and reducing operational costs in electric bus applications.

Keywords: AC copper loss; electric bus; fuel economy; optimal design; traction motor; vehicle simulation

MSC: 49S05

1. Introduction

Recently, along with the rapid development of electric vehicles, various related studies have been conducted. In [1], an analysis of domain- and zone-based automotive architecture topologies with vehicle-centralized or controller-based mappings was conducted. Reference [2] proposed the practical methodology for security analysis of grid-connected electric vehicle charging stations with wind-generating resources. Reference [3] proposed a decentralized resource allocation mechanism based on deep reinforcement learning. Reference [4] proposes a method to enhance the fuel efficiency (FE) of an electric vehicle by altering the winding connection in a wound field synchronous motor. In addition, recent studies have explored the optimization of thermal management in electric vehicle powertrain systems to further improve energy efficiency and overall vehicle performance [5]. Among various studies, there is also a method to improve mileage, which has been pointed out as a problem in terms of electric vehicle (EV) supply [6]. In terms of components, various studies are being conducted on improving the power density and efficiency of a traction motor to improve EV mileage [7].

Proposals for increasing the power density of the motor have included coil technologies [8–10]. The slot fill factor (SFF) of the winding is directly related to the area of the slot and consequently affects the volume of the motor. Essentially, the utilization of high slot fill factor (HSFF) coils, as discussed in reference [11], contributes to the enhancement of the motor's power density. A representative coil technology developed due to the demand for HSFF coils is hairpin winding. Hairpin windings have a SFF of about 60% and are applied to motors in various automotive industries [11,12]. The maximum slot occupation (MSO) coil developed by The Korea Institute of Industrial Technology (KITECH) is also one of the HSFF coils, like hairpin winding. By cutting copper blocks to match the slot's form, MSO coils can achieve a SFF of up to 80%. Thus, applying MSO coils to the motor can lead to an enhancement in the motor's power density.

However, HSFF coils have a large area of the conductor, resulting in large AC resistance due to skin and proximity effects at high frequencies [13]. The motor encounters difficulties in achieving high efficiency because AC resistance leads to additional losses commonly referred to as AC copper loss within the motor. For this reason, the use of HSFF coils can help to improve the power density, but it is difficult to achieve high efficiency. Therefore, to achieve high efficiency as well as the high-power density of the motor using HSFF coils, AC resistance must be considered when designing the motor.

Several papers have reported methods for reducing AC copper loss. Reference [14] reported a decrease in AC copper loss, achieved through the winding transposition techniques. Reference [13] discussed strategies involving the arrangement of the strands bundle to reduce AC copper loss. Reference [15] reported a winding technique aimed at minimizing the AC copper loss of a hairpin winding. However, these methods are not suitable for application in the motor using MSO coils. For this reason, a method for reducing AC copper loss that is suitable for MSO coils has been recently reported. Reference [16] reported the trend of AC resistance of MSO coils according to the current density and the number of parallel circuits. Reference [17] reported a method of decreasing the AC copper loss of MSO coils through the optimal design of the tooth width. However, no research has been conducted on the optimal design that takes AC copper loss into account to enhance the FE of the EV.

The purpose of this paper is to enhance the electric bus's FE by optimizing the traction motor while considering its AC copper loss. First, the influence of the traction motor design variables on its electrical performance is analyzed. Second, a multi-objective optimization is performed using energy consumption as an objective function. Three driving cycles are selected to represent different operational purposes of the bus.

In this study, an optimal design method to increase FE considering AC copper loss of motor for the electric bus traction using the MSO coil is proposed. First, the specifications and issues of electric bus traction motors using MSO coils will be described. Next, the effect of design variables on electrical performance is checked through 2D finite element analysis (FEA). Tooth width and slot opening width are stator design variables related to the slot leakage flux. The slot leakage flux affects the AC resistance, so the tooth width and slot opening width are important stator design variables. Since AC resistance occurs almost on the coil side, the stack length is also an important design variable. Third, a multi-objective optimization for improving the FE of electric buses is conducted. Three driving cycles have been selected to consider the various purposes of the electric bus. The energy consumption according to the driving cycle is defined as an objective function. Additionally, this study conducts a comparative analysis of the FE of electric buses with respect to both the initial motor and the optimal motor resulting from the multi-purpose optimal design. Finally, an optimal motor is fabricated and subjected to testing procedures to validate this study.

2. Electric Bus and Initial Motor for Traction

A bus terminal is a place where all buses begin or end a designated route. For this reason, the bus is more advantageous than the passenger vehicle in applying the electric powertrain system because the battery-charging device only needs to be installed at the bus terminal. Due to this advantage, research is being conducted to replace the powertrain of the bus with an electric system consisting of a motor and inverter instead of an internal combustion engine.

2.1. Initial Motor for Electric Bus Traction

Figure 1 shows the shape of an initial motor, which is an Interior Permanent Magnet Synchronous Motor (IPMSM) using an MSO coil. The initial motor applying the MSO coil is designed for electric bus traction. Reference [18] introduces the MSO coil as one of several coil types developed to enhance the SFF. The bare SFF of the MSO coil is up to 80% because the copper block is cut according to the form of the slot, unlike other coils. An advantage of HSFF coils is that they help to achieve high-torque density or high-power density of the motor. However, at high-speed operation, the large area of the conductor causes AC resistance. For this reason, the motor encounters difficulties in achieving high efficiency because AC resistance leads to additional losses that are commonly referred to as AC copper loss within the motor.

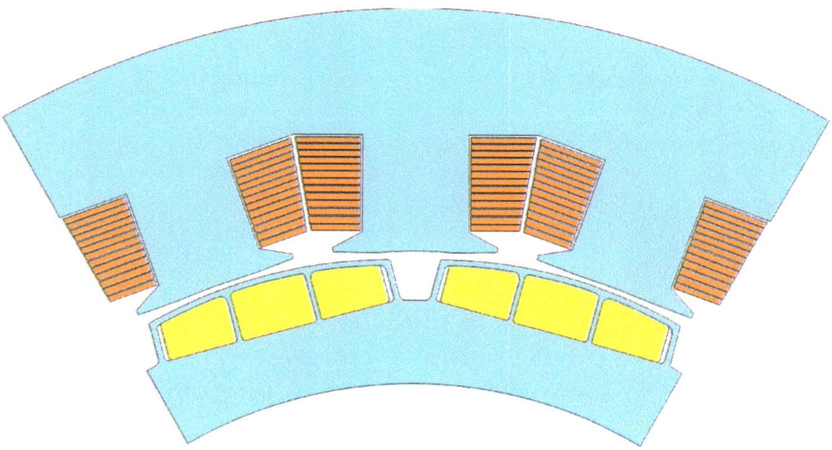

Figure 1. The shape of the initial motor using MSO coil.

Table 1 provides the specifications of the initial motor intended for electric bus traction. For electric bus traction, the motor is required to deliver a maximum torque of 800 Nm, maximum power output of 130 kW, and operate at a maximum speed of 5200 rpm.

Table 1. Specification of initial motor.

Items	Unit	Value
Maximum Torque	Nm	800
Base Speed	rpm	1600
Maximum Speed	rpm	5200
DC Voltage	V_{DC}	360
Maximum Line Current	A_{rms}	500
Stator Outer Diameter	mm	210
Stack Length	mm	83

As per the battery and inverter specifications, the DC-link voltage is 360 V_{DC}, and the maximum line current is 500 A_{rms}.

2.2. *Issue of Initial Motor for Electric Bus Traction*

In general, buses serve three primary purposes: transit, express, and suburban. Each type of bus is tailored to specific operational requirements:

- Transit bus: Designed to operate between short stops within downtown areas.
- Express bus: Intended for long-distance travel between cities, typically covering extensive routes.
- Suburban bus: Geared towards medium-length journeys within metropolitan areas, serving commuters traveling to and from suburban locations.

To summarize the characteristics of the bus, the bus drives at a low or high speed, depending on the purpose. Therefore, it is necessary to design the motor in consideration of all purposes of the bus. As mentioned in Section 2.1, due to the high fill factor of the MSO coil, the initial motor causes additional losses due to AC resistance when operating at a high speed. AC copper loss, which is the additional loss caused by AC resistance, worsens fuel efficiency. The FE is expressed as (1) and obtained by dividing the total driving distance by the total energy consumption. The total energy consumption is obtained as the integral of the input power with respect to time. As shown in (2), the input power is obtained using the output power, the motor efficiency, the inverter efficiency, and the battery efficiency. At this time, the motor efficiency is obtained using the output power and the losses, including the AC copper loss and the iron loss, as indicated in (3). Therefore, an increase in AC resistance results in greater AC copper loss and reduced motor efficiency. The reduced motor efficiency, in turn, increases the input power required for motoring and decreases the input power during the generating operation. Consequently, the FE deteriorates. Conversely, it can be concluded that the reduction in the AC copper loss, which is the design target of this paper, leads to an increase in the FE. Hence, given that buses operate at varying speeds depending on their purpose, from low speed to high speed, it is imperative to design the motor while considering AC copper loss to enhance the FE of electric buses.

$$\mathrm{FE} = \frac{\int V_v(t)dt}{\int P_{in}(t)dt} \tag{1}$$

$$P_{in} = \begin{cases} \frac{P_{out}}{\eta_M \eta_{Inv} \eta_{Bat}}, & T_M \geq 0 \\ P_{out}\eta_M \eta_{Inv} \eta_{Bat}, & T_M < 0 \end{cases} \tag{2}$$

$$\eta_M = \frac{P_{out}}{P_{out} + P_{copper,AC} + P_{iron}} \tag{3}$$

where V_v is the vehicle speed, P_{in} is the input power, P_{out} is the output power, η_M is the motor efficiency, η_{Inv} is the inverter efficiency, and η_{Bat} is the battery efficiency. $P_{copper,AC}$ represents the AC copper loss, P_{iron} is the iron loss, and T_M is motor torque.

3. Stator Design Variables Affecting Efficiency of Motor Using High Fill Factor Coil

This section describes the design variables that affect the efficiency of motors using HSFF coils. First, the reason for analyzing the AC resistance of the motor through 2D FEA due to the limitation of the AC resistance coefficient formula is explained. Next, the influence of tooth width and slot opening width, which are design variables that affect the AC copper loss of a motor using HSFF coils through 2D FEA, is investigated. Finally, the tendency of the torque, copper loss, and line-to-line induced voltage with the change in the design variable were examined to confirm.

3.1. Limitation of Analytical Method for Predicting AC Resistance

Under DC current conditions, the current density in the conductor is uniform. However, under AC current conditions, the voltage induced by the magnetic flux passing through the conductor causes an imbalance in the current density distribution in the conductor [19]. As illustrated in Figure 2a, the current density in the conductor is not uniform for the area of one conductor and is concentrated in a specific area like the red square in Figure 2a. In particular, this phenomenon is remarkable in conductors close to the air gap. The imbalance of the current density, which occurs within one conductor, increases the copper loss because the concentrated areas in the current density have a greater effect on the copper loss than the unconcentrated areas. In addition, the larger the cross-section area of the conductor, the larger the concentrated areas in the current density are, and the more severe imbalance of the current density is. As referenced in [15], larger conductor areas correspond to increased AC copper loss. In addition, as shown in Figure 2a, the current density distribution of the conductor far from the air gap is constant in the horizontal direction and changes in the vertical direction. However, the current density distribution of the conductor close to the air gap is not similar to the current density distribution of the conductor far from the air gap. This is because the leakage magnetic flux flows through the arc-shaped path due to the tooth tip shape, as presented in Figure 2b. These results imply that not only the slot width but also the tooth tip shape affects the AC copper loss.

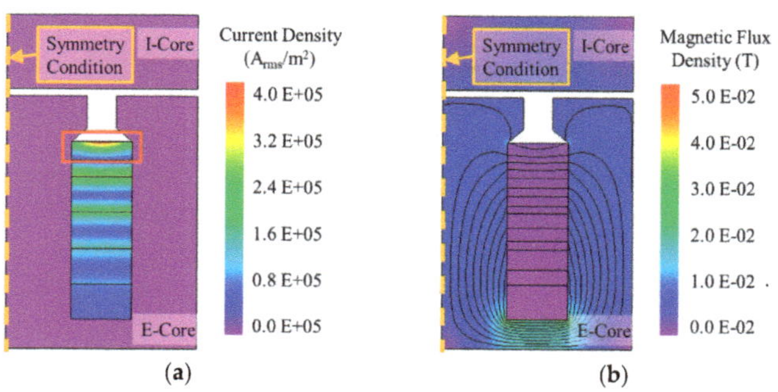

Figure 2. Time-harmonic analysis results of the E- and I-shaped cores: (**a**) current density; (**b**) magnetic flux density and magnetic flux line.

The AC resistance coefficient is a value obtained by dividing the AC resistance by the DC resistance and is a representative coefficient representing the effect of the AC resistance [19]. From [17], it was confirmed that the AC resistance coefficient calculated through the time-harmonic analysis and formula is almost similar. However, the formula for predicting the AC resistance coefficient has the following disadvantages:

- It ignores the influence of field flux.

- Slot leakage magnetic flux generated by the field cannot be reflected.
- It ignores the nonlinearity of the iron core.
- It is impossible to reflect the magnetic flux of leakage in the slot that changes due to the nonlinearity of the stator core.
- Assume that the slot leakage magnetic flux flows horizontally with the air gap.
- It is not possible to accurately reflect the path of the leakage magnetic flux flowing through the arc-shaped path due to the tooth tip.

Due to the above assumptions of the formula for predicting AC resistance, it is difficult to calculate the accurate characteristics of the AC copper loss of the motor through the formula. For this reason, it is necessary to analyze the tendency of AC copper loss through 2D FEA.

3.2. Determination of Design Variables Considering Electric Performance

In this section, the design variables that affect torque and copper loss are defined for the optimization process described in Section 4.3. The design variables are determined by analyzing the trend of motor performance, as the tooth width and slot opening width are varied. This analysis utilizes the results of the 2D FEA, conducted at both the base speed and maximum speed of the initial motor, exploring the impact of the changes in these dimensions on motor performance. When the stator design parameters change, the area of the slot remains constant. Reducing the tooth width while preserving the area of the slot results in the widening of both the yoke width and the slot width. Consequently, the form of the coil adjusts accordingly in response to alterations in the slot form, reflecting the unique characteristics of the MSO coil. In addition, when motor performance according to the change in one design variable is examined, the other variable is kept constant to independently examine the influence of each design variable.

The motor performance to be checked in common at base speed and maximum speed is torque and copper loss. Moreover, at the maximum speed, the peak value of line-to-line induced voltage was additionally checked. At high speeds, since the harmonic component of the induced voltage is remarkable, the line-to-line induced voltage may exceed the DC-link voltage. Due to this phenomenon, sinusoidal current cannot be input in the motor and additional torque ripple may occur due to the current containing harmonics component. This is the reason the line-to-line voltage at the maximum speed is checked.

Figure 3 illustrates the motor performance with varying tooth widths under the condition that the slot opening width is maintained at 15 mm. As shown in Figure 3, when checking motor performance through 2D FEA, the magnitude and phase angle of the current are (500 A_{rms}, 10°) and (350 A_{rms}, 65°) at the base and maximum speed, respectively. Figure 3a presents the torque and copper loss at the base speed, and Figure 3b shows the torque, copper loss, and peak values of line-to-line induced voltage at the maximum speed. Figure 3 depicts several key parameters as follows: the torque is represented by the black line, the copper loss by the red dotted line, the peak value of line-to-line induced voltage by the blue dashed line, and the maximum torque required by the electric bus system, accounting for manufacturing tolerances, is illustrated by the green line with rectangular symbols. To consider potential deviations in the motor performance due to manufacturing tolerances, the target torque was established at 105% of the maximum torque. As the tooth width increases, the torque tends to increase up to a certain dimension, after which it starts to decrease. However, the copper loss decreases and then increases. At the base speed, there is little variation in copper loss between the tooth widths ranging from 30 to 40 mm, all of which fulfill the maximum torque requirement of the electric bus system. Conversely, at maximum speed, there is a noticeable trend of continuous increase in copper loss as the tooth width increases within the range of 30 to 40 mm. Here, the difference between the maximum and minimum copper losses is approximately 61%. In addition, the peak value of line-to-line induced voltage at maximum speed increases and then decreases as the tooth width increases and is largest at 38 mm of the tooth width. Also, 38 mm of the tooth width is the point generating the largest torque at the base speed.

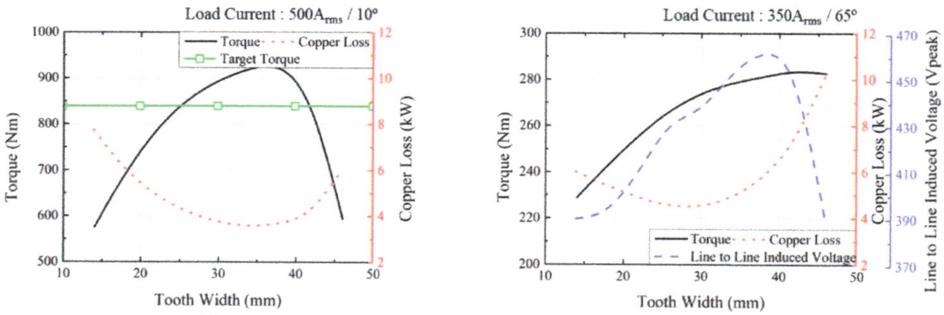

(a) (b)

Figure 3. Electric performance according to tooth width: (**a**) base speed and (**b**) maximum speed.

Figure 4 depicts the motor performance according to the slot opening width. At this time, the tooth width is fixed to 30 mm. As demonstrated in Figure 4, the current condition is the same as when examining the motor performance according to the tooth width. Figure 4a shows the tendency of torque and copper loss at the base speed, and Figure 4b illustrates the torque, copper loss, and peak values of line-to-line induced voltage at maximum speed. In Figure 4, the black line is the torque, the red dotted line is the copper loss, the blue dashed line is the peak value of line-to-line induced voltage, and the green line with a rectangular symbol is the target torque considering manufacturing tolerances. Figure 4a shows that it is not more dramatic than the tendency of torque or copper loss according to the change in tooth width. However, as can be seen from Figure 4b, the slot opening width greatly affects the copper loss or peak value of line-to-line induced voltage at maximum speed. The copper loss and the peak value of the line-to-line induced voltage are the smallest at 11 mm of slot opening width.

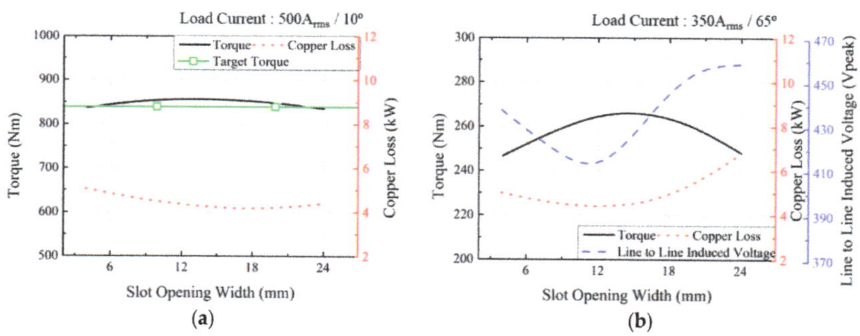

(a) (b)

Figure 4. Electric performance according to slot opening width: (**a**) base speed and (**b**) maximum speed.

Through the above analysis, the tooth width and slot opening width affect the torque, the copper loss, and the peak value of the line-to-line induced voltage. Although not included in the above analysis, the stack length is also one factor that influences the torque, the copper loss, and the peak value of the line-to-line induced voltage. The stack length proportionally affects the torque, AC resistance, and line-to-line induced voltage under the same current condition. As the stack length increases, the effective magnetic flux, conductor length, and flux linkage also increase proportionally, resulting in a linear increase in torque, AC resistance, and induced voltage. Therefore, the stack length is also added as a design variable, and according to the design variables, such as the tooth width, the slot opening width, and the stack length, the optimal design to improve the FE of the electric bus is performed.

4. Multi-Objective Optimization Design for Improving Fuel Economy

This section presents the motor multi-objective optimization design method and its results for enhancing the FE of the electric bus. First, a vehicle simulation model is introduced to evaluate the FE based on the motor's electrical performance. Next, the optimization design process applied to the motor is described in detail. Finally, the performance of the optimized motor is compared with that of the initial motor.

The overall procedure of the proposed multi-objective optimization is illustrated in Figure 5. The detailed steps are summarized as follows:

1. Define the vehicle model and motor design variables.
2. Formulate the optimization problem (objectives and constraints).
3. Design of the experiments using the optimal Latin hypercube design (OLHD).
4. Conduct 2D FEA and vehicle simulation to obtain results.
5. Build a Kriging surrogate model.
6. Validate the surrogate model.
7. Perform optimization using a surrogate model.
8. Obtain an optimal motor design.

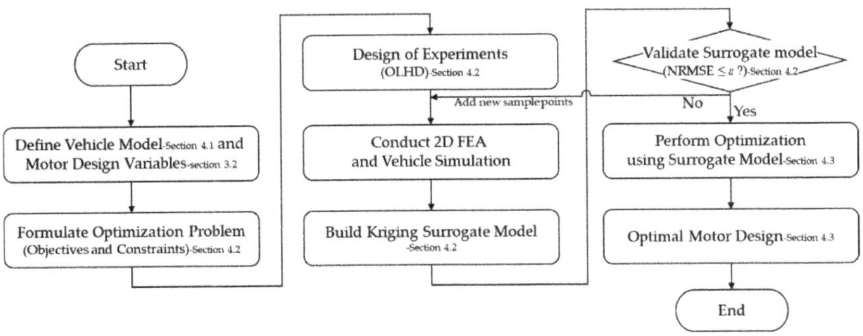

Figure 5. Flowchart of the proposed multi-objective optimization process for the motor design.

4.1. Vehicle Simulation for Calculating Fuel Economy of Electric Bus

Vehicle simulation is a method used to calculate the fuel economy (FE) of a vehicle under specific driving conditions. It enables the evaluation of how various component designs and control strategies impact the overall vehicle's performance without the need for full-scale experiments. In this study, the vehicle simulation model is developed using the ADVISOR platform, a widely validated simulation tool created by the National Renewable Energy Laboratory (NREL) [20]. To ensure accurate simulation results, the model reflects the specifications of the target vehicle and its major components, including the motor, inverter, gear, and battery, as well as the intended driving cycles. All major parameters, such as vehicle mass, frontal area, wheel radius, gear ratio, inverter efficiency, and battery characteristics, are set according to the actual specifications of the target electric bus. The motor efficiency map is generated from 2D finite element analysis (FEA) results and experimentally validated data to accurately represent the motor's electrical performance under various operating conditions. Figure 6 shows a schematic diagram of the vehicle simulation process used to calculate the fuel economy by considering the drive cycle and system characteristics. Through this modeling approach, the established vehicle simulation model reliably reflects the real-world performance characteristics of the electric bus system. This ensures that the subsequent fuel economy evaluation and optimization results are based on a realistic and credible framework.

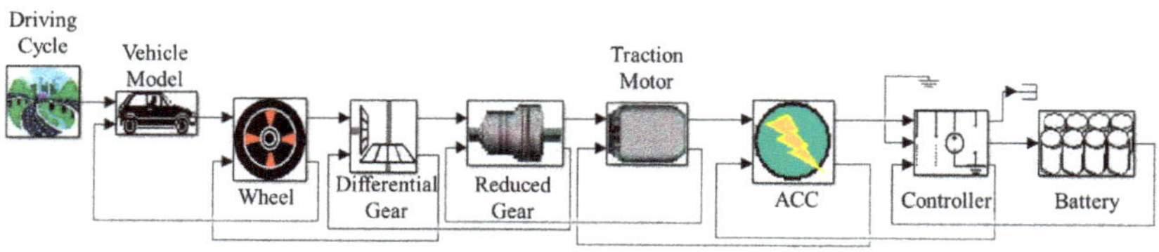

Figure 6. Schematic diagram of the vehicle simulation process.

4.1.1. Longitudinal Vehicle Dynamics

Figure 7 depicts the dynamic force diagram of a vehicle. As shown in Figure 7, there is a rolling resistance, air resistance, and gradient resistance as the resistance forces applied to the vehicle. According to vehicle longitudinal dynamics, the torque demand at the wheel can be calculated as:

$$\begin{aligned} T_w &= (F_R + F_G + F_D)r \\ &= \left(mgf_R\cos\theta + \tfrac{1}{2}A_F C_d \rho_{air} v^2 + mg\sin\theta\right)r \end{aligned} \tag{4}$$

where T_w is the torque demand at the wheel, F_R is the rolling resistive force, F_G is the grading resistive force, F_D is the aerodynamic drag force, m is the vehicle mass, g is the gravity acceleration, f_R is the rolling resistance coefficient, θ is the slope of the road, A_F is the frontal area, C_d is the aerodynamics drag coefficient, v is the vehicle speed, and r is the wheel radius.

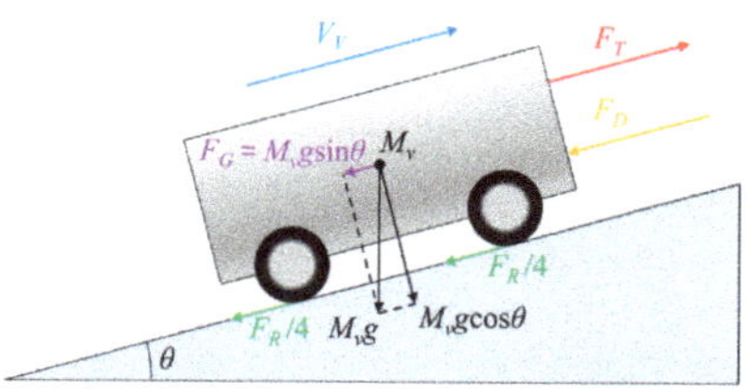

Figure 7. Dynamic force diagram of the vehicle.

In addition, the vehicle's powertrain provides torque demand at the wheel, and the energy balance is as follows:

$$T_w = \eta_T i_g T_M \tag{5}$$

where η_T is the efficiency of the gear, and i_g is the gear ratio.

4.1.2. Motor Model

The motor model needs a motor efficiency map according to the rotation speed and torque to perform vehicle simulation. The efficiency of the motor is predicted over three steps [21]. First, the d- and q-axes based electrical parameters, are calculated through 2D FEA according to the magnitude and phase of the current. Next, the magnitude and phase angle of the current according to the torque and rotational speed are determined through maximum torque per ampere control. Also, the torque equation is used to determine the current condition, which is expressed below.

$$T_M = pp\left[\psi_f i_{oq} + (L_d - L_q) i_{od} i_{oq}\right] \tag{6}$$

where pp is the number of pole-pairs, ψ_f is the rms value of the flux linkage by field, i_{oq} and i_{od} are the magnetizing q-axis and d-axis current, and L_d and L_q are the d, q-axis inductance, respectively. Here, the d- and q-axes equivalent circuit of the motor illustrated in Figure 8 is used to consider the voltage limit [22]. Finally, the motor efficiency is calculated through the copper loss and iron loss calculated by 2D FEA according to the magnitude and phase of the current.

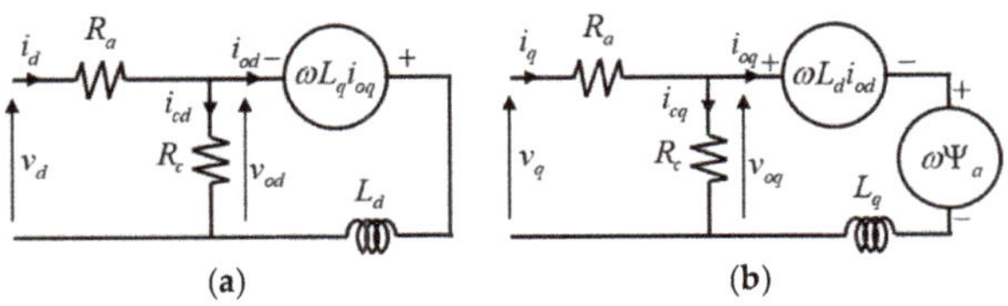

Figure 8. The d- and q-axes equivalent circuit of the motor: (**a**) d-axis; (**b**) q-axis.

4.1.3. Battery Model

The battery model is modeled as a 2nd RC equivalent circuit, as shown in Figure 9. Figure 10 presents the battery model parameters measured through experiments [23–25]. The state-space model of the battery is as follows:

$$\frac{d\mathrm{SOC}(t)}{dt} = \frac{i(t)}{C_{bat}} \tag{7}$$

$$\frac{dv_1(t)}{dt} = -\frac{v_1(t)}{R_1C_1} + \frac{i(t)}{C_1} \tag{8}$$

$$\frac{dv_2(t)}{dt} = -\frac{v_2(t)}{R_2C_2} + \frac{i(t)}{C_2} \tag{9}$$

$$v_t(t) = v_{oc}(\mathrm{SOC}) + v_1(t) + v_2(t) + R_0 i(t) \tag{10}$$

where SOC represents the state of charge, i denotes the current, C_{bat} refers to the nominal capacity of the battery, and R and C indicate the resistance and capacitance, respectively. Further, v_1 and v_2 correspond to the voltages across the first and second capacitors, respectively. R_0 is the ohmic resistance, and v_t represents the terminal voltage. R_1 and C_1 are related to the first RC pair, while R_2 and C_2 are linked to the second RC pair.

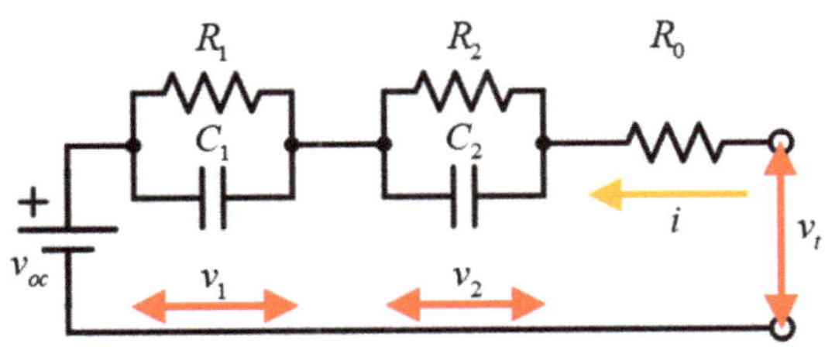

Figure 9. Battery equivalent circuit.

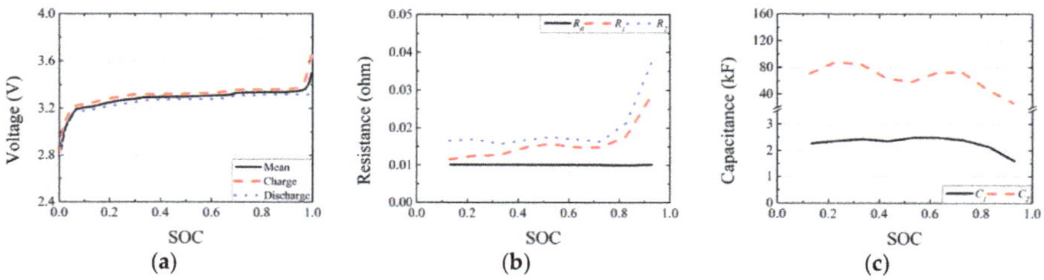

Figure 10. Battery model parameters according to SOC: (**a**) open circuit voltage; (**b**) resistance; (**c**) capacitance.

4.1.4. Vehicle Model and Vehicle Simulation Conditions

The target vehicle for this study is an electric bus. Table 2 outlines the specifications of the electric bus, and Table 3 delineates the vehicle simulation conditions. The gear and inverter are both expected to operate with an efficiency of 95%.

Table 2. Specification of electric bus traction.

Items		Unit	Value
Curb Weight		kg	12,500
Frontal Area		m^2	6.72
Overall Width		m	2.50
Overall Height		m	3.21
Overall Length		m	10.58
Wheelbase		m	5.95
Wheel Radius		m	0.48
Inverter	Efficiency	%	95
Gear	Ratio	-	9.5
	Efficiency	%	95
Battery	Overall Nominal Voltage	V_{DC}	360
	Overall Nominal Capacity	kWh	256

Table 3. Drive condition.

Items	Unit	Value
Air Density	kg/m^3	1.28
Gravitational Acceleration	m/s^2	9.81
Aerodynamic Drag Coefficient	-	0.7
Rolling Resistance Coefficient	-	0.007
Number of Passengers	-	40
Weight per Passenger	kg	65

As explained in Section 2.2, the bus is used for three purposes: transit bus, express bus, and suburban bus. In this study, three driving cycles were selected to conduct the multi-objective optimization design of the motor to improve FE, considering all three purposes of the bus. Figure 11 depicts the target driving cycle. The Manhattan cycle was chosen considering that the electric bus was used as a transit bus because it was developed for the FE test of the transit bus, and HWFET was developed for the highway driving test, so it was selected to consider the case where the electric bus was used as an express bus. The suburban bus has the characteristics of a transit bus and an express bus at the same time. Because HDUDDS reflects the driving characteristics of both the Manhattan cycle and HWFET, it is chosen as a driving pattern of the suburban bus. Thus, based on the depicted driving cycle in Figure 11, a multi-objective optimization design of the motor is conducted with the aim of enhancing the FE of the electric bus.

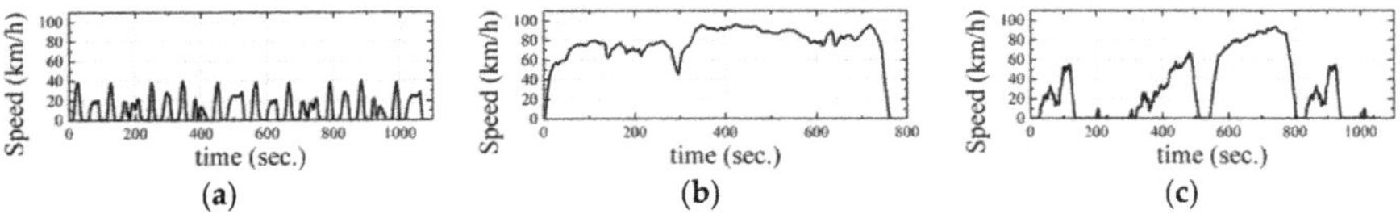

Figure 11. Target driving cycle: (**a**) Manhattan; (**b**) HWFET; (**c**) HDUDDS.

4.2. Multi-Objective Optimization Formulation

As discussed in Section 3, the consideration of AC resistance is crucial when designing motors applying HSFF coil. The form of the stator, as previously mentioned, directly impacts AC resistance. Iron loss, as well as AC resistance is determined by the shape of the stator. In other words, it is necessary to design an appropriate stator shape to increase the efficiency of the motor. However, the motor design that improves efficiency without considering the driving point of the motor is meaningless in terms of vehicle FE. Therefore, the motor design that improves efficiency considering the driving cycle should be made to improve the FE of the electric bus.

Utilizing in-house codes, the multi-objective optimization was conducted employing the Kriging surrogate model. This optimization aimed to confirm the optimal design point across multiple driving conditions [26,27]. The energy consumption according to the driving cycle is defined as an objective function, and a multi-objective optimization model in which all objective functions are combined is defined using the desirability function to minimize energy consumption [28]. The defined objective functions and multi-objective optimization model are as follows:

$$\text{Objectives}: \begin{cases} \min f_1(x) = E_{\text{Manhattan}} \\ \min f_2(x) = E_{\text{HWFET}} \\ \min f_3(x) = E_{\text{HDUDDS}} \end{cases} \tag{11}$$

$$\min: f_o(x) = -{d_1}^{w_1} \cdot {d_2}^{w_2} \cdot {d_3}^{w_3} (w_1 = w_2 = w_3) \tag{12}$$

where f_i denotes the objective function, x is the design parameter, $E_{Manhattan}$, E_{HWFET}, and E_{HDUDDS} are the energy consumption according to the driving cycle, f_o is the multi-objective optimization function, d_i is the individual desirability function, and w_i is the weighting factor, respectively. In this paper, a genetic algorithm was employed to find the optimal design that maximizes the overall desirability. The individual desirability function, d_i, is expressed as follows:

$$d_{\text{i}} = \frac{f_{\text{i}} - f_{\text{im ax}}}{f_{\text{imin}} - f_{\text{imax}}} \tag{13}$$

where f_i is the arbitrary value, and f_{imax} and f_{imin} are the maximum and minimum values of the objective function, respectively [29]. At this time, f_{imax} and f_{imin} are the maximum and minimum among the values obtained from all sample points of each objective function.

In addition to the optimization objectives, constraints have been established, taking into consideration the requirements of the vehicle. Initially, to account for potential reductions in torque due to mechanical loss or manufacturing tolerances, the target torque was set at 105% of the required torque for the vehicle system. Next, the ratio of the peak value of line-to-line induced voltage and the DC link voltage were added to the constraints at high speeds so that the inverter could flow a sinusoidal current to the motor. The constraints can be expressed as follows:

$$\begin{cases} g_1(x) = 800 \times 1.05 - T_{base} \leq 0 \\ g_2(x) = 238.9 \times 1.05 - T_{max} \leq 0 \\ g_3(x) = V_{LL}(n_{\max})/V_{DC} - 1 \leq 0 \end{cases} \tag{14}$$

where g_i is the constraint, T_{base} is the maximum torque required by the vehicle system at the base speed, T_{max} is the maximum torque required by the vehicle system at the maximum speed, V_{LL} is line-to-line induced voltage, $n_{\max}$ denotes the maximum speed of the motor, and V_{DC} is the DC link voltage.

Sample points for multi-objective optimization are sampled using the optimal Latin hypercube design (OLHD) [30]. The initial sample points are sampled as follows:

$$n_s = \frac{(n_d + 1)(n_d + 2)}{2} \tag{15}$$

where n_s is the number of the initial sample points, and n_d is the number of the design variable.

The number of the initial sample points is selected as the boundary values of the input parameters to encompass a feasible region as widely as possible, but the initial sample points are the minimum number to compose the surrogate model. In general, since the more sample points (the higher the accuracy of the Kriging surrogate model) to determine the appropriate number of sample points, a cross-validation method is implemented to evaluate the model's accuracy. Here, calculating the normalized root mean square error (NRMSE) is used as an evaluation index to evaluate model accuracy [6]. Based on this method, the number of sample points was determined to be 40, which is 4 times the number of the initial sample points obtained through (15).

4.3. Multi-Objective Optimization Result and Discussion

Figure 12 presents the contours of the multi-objective optimization function with respect to variations in two design variables, while the other design variable is kept constant. The direction in which the desirability function increases is indicated by an orange-colored arrow. Also, areas that satisfy the constraints are shaded. The shaded area with a dotted red border indicates the area that satisfies all the constraints. As a result, through multi-objective optimization, the tooth width, slot opening width, and stack length were determined to be 31.7 mm, 9.6 mm, and 83 mm, respectively. The optimal design point is indicated by a white circle with a black border in Figure 12.

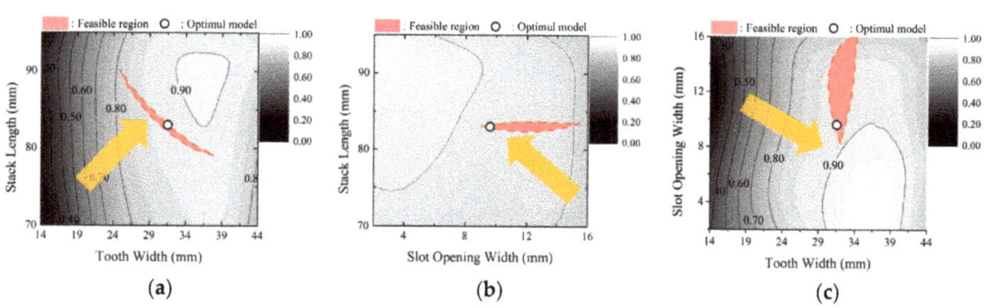

Figure 12. Contour plot of the multi-objective optimization function: (**a**) tooth width–stack length (@ slot opening width: 9 mm); (**b**) slot opening width–stack length (@ tooth width: 29 mm); (**c**) tooth width–slot opening (@ stack length: 85 mm).

Figure 13 shows the initial and optimal motors, and Table 4 lists the dimensions of each design variable according to the motor. The tooth width, slot opening width, and stacking length of the initial motor are 26 mm, 16 mm, and 90 mm, respectively, and those of the optimal motor are 31.7 mm, 9.6 mm, and 83 mm, respectively. As a result, compared to the initial motor, the optimal motor has a wider tooth width, a narrower slot opening width, and a reduced stack length.

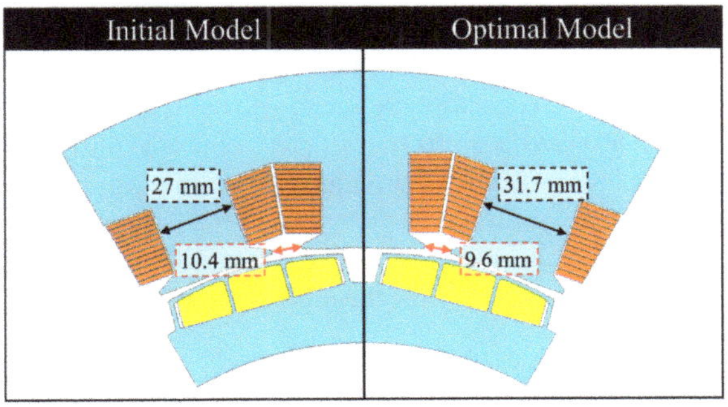

Figure 13. The shape of the initial and optimal motors.

Table 4. Dimension of each design variable according to the motor.

Design Variable	Unit	Initial Motor	Optimal Motor
Tooth width	mm	27	31.7
Slot opening width	mm	10.4	9.6
Stack length	mm	87	83

Figure 14 depicts the FE performance of the electric bus when equipped with different motors. In Manhattan, the optimized motor led to a 0.20% increase in FE, improving from 1.592 km/kWh to 1.596 km/kWh. Similar enhancements were noted in the HWFET and HDUDDS cycles. Specifically, the HWFET exhibited an increase of 0.86%, with FE rising from 1.196 km/kWh to 1.207 km/kWh. Likewise, the HDUDDS showed a 0.36% improvement, with FE increasing from 1.229 km/kWh to 1.233 km/kWh. Overall, these results indicate that the FE has improved across all driving cycles.

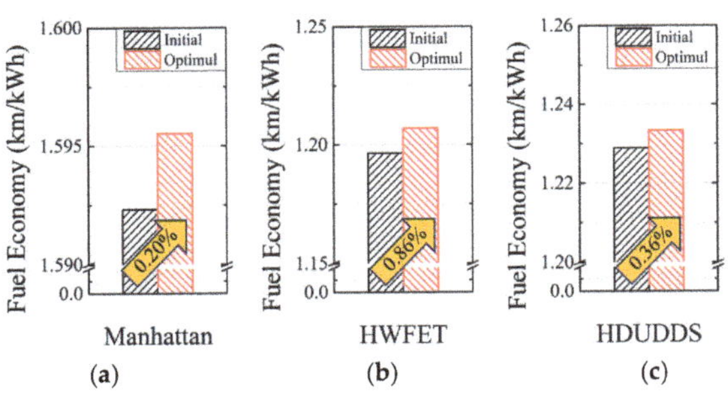

Figure 14. Fuel economy according to motors: (**a**) Mahattan; (**b**) HWFET; (**c**) HDUDDS.

Considering the real-world operations of electric buses, which typically cover 200–300 km per day for about 300 days annually, the accumulated driving distance exceeds 60,000 to 90,000 km [31,32]. Even a 0.5% improvement in FE translates into annual energy savings of approximately 150–200 kWh per vehicle. This contributes to significant operational cost reductions and helps lower the environmental impact by reducing electricity consumption and the associated carbon emissions. In this optimization, design variables related to stator geometry—such as the tooth width, slot opening width, and stack length—were strategically selected and adjusted. By carefully modifying only essential parameters without major structural changes, the optimized motor achieved meaningful improvements in FE while maintaining manufacturability and cost efficiency. Given the already high baseline efficiencies of electric buses, such incremental improvements are considered valuable advancements in electric vehicle technology.

The analysis of FE improvement for each driving cycle begins with an examination of the distribution of operating points (OP) corresponding to each cycle. Figure 15 illustrates the motor operating proportion map across different driving cycles. This map aids in effectively analyzing the motor's OPs. The heatmap visually displays the frequency of motor operation, with the darker colors indicating a higher frequency. Additionally, the bar graph illustrates the operating proportion concerning the motor's speed or torque.

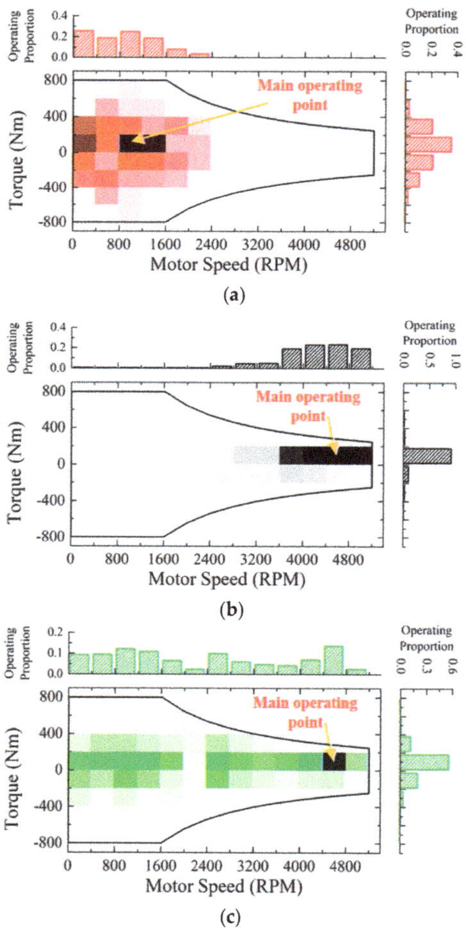

Figure 15. Motor operating proportion map according to the driving cycles: (**a**) Manhattan; (**b**) HWFET; (**c**) HDUDDS.

In the Manhattan cycle, as depicted in Figure 15a, the motor's OPs are primarily concentrated in the low-speed region, with higher torque being utilized more frequently compared to other driving cycles. The main OP is at 1000 rpm and 100 Nm. Likewise, during the HWFET cycle, the OPs are focused on a particular speed. In contrast to the Manhattan cycle, the motor mostly functions in the high-speed range. In the HWFET cycle, the main OP is at 4600 rpm and 100 Nm. In contrast, the HDUDDS cycle shows OPs distributed more evenly across the speed range, but the main OP remains the same as in the HWFET cycle at 4600 rpm and 100 Nm.

Figure 16 displays the efficiency map and the efficiency difference between the initial motor and the optimal motor, generated based on the electrical parameters obtained through 2D FEA. The efficiency of the optimal motor improved across all speed ranges compared to the initial motor, although a slight decrease was observed in the low-speed, high-torque regions. The maximum improvement in efficiency reached up to 3.62%p.

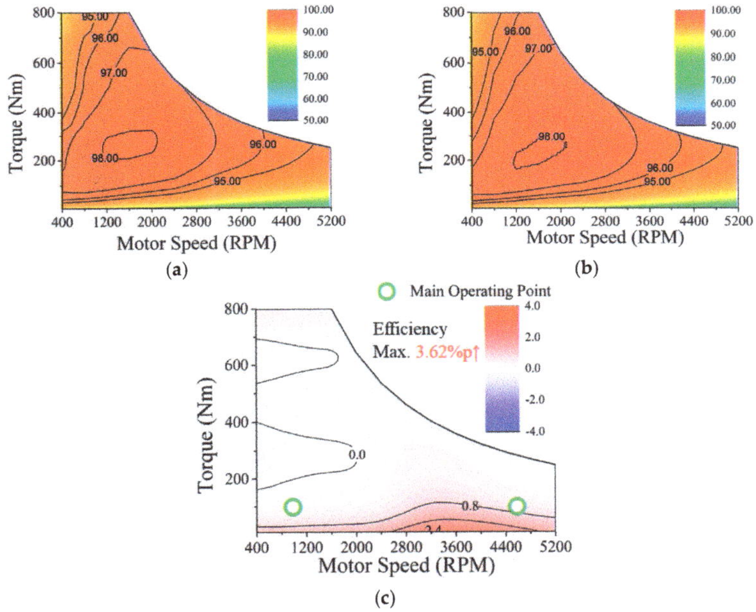

Figure 16. Efficiency map: (**a**) initial motor; (**b**) optimal motor; (**c**) difference between initial and optimal motors.

As shown in Figure 15, the OPs during typical driving cycles for the electric bus are predominantly concentrated in the low-torque region. Based on this observation, the optimization strategy specifically focused on enhancing efficiency in the low-torque operating range to maximize real-world fuel economy (FE).

Therefore, the improvements observed in the low-torque regions of the efficiency map (Figure 16) are consistent with the intended optimization objectives and contribute meaningfully to the FE enhancement across all driving cycles.

In particular, the HWFET cycle exhibited a more significant improvement in FE, as the vehicle mainly operated in the high-speed, low-torque region where the efficiency of the optimal motor was further enhanced. Conversely, in the Manhattan and HDUDDS cycles, the FE improvement was less noticeable because the vehicle also operated in the low-speed, high-torque area, where the efficiency of the optimal motor was relatively reduced.

5. Experimental Verification

The validity of the proposed design method was confirmed via experiments with the fabricated optimal motor. Figure 17 shows the experiment configuration and the fabricated optimal motor. As presented in Figure 17, the pieces of equipment such as inverters, power analyzers, and dynamometers were used in the experiment. The motor was controlled with the current condition obtained through 2D FEA. To calculate the efficiency, the power analyzer recorded the input power, while the output power was determined based on data obtained from speed and torque sensors on the dynamometer. However, due to the limitations of the dynamometer, measurements were limited to only 50% of the power and torque.

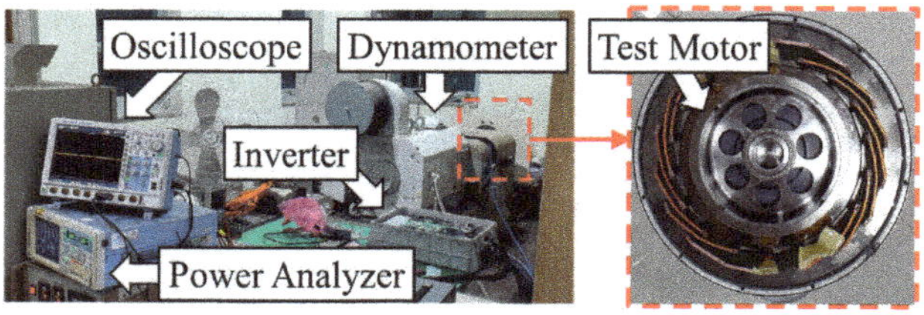

Figure 17. Configuration of the experimental setup and fabricated optimal motor.

The no-load phase BEMF was measured at 1000 rpm. Figure 18 illustrates the waveforms of the phase BEMF of the FEA and experiment. As shown in Figure 18, the FEA and experimental results are almost the same. The peak values of the no-load phase BEMF of the FEA and experiment are 83.3 Vpeak and 83.2 Vpeak, respectively, and the error between the two results is 0.1%. Based on the no-load experimental result, it can be seen that the test motor is well-fabricated.

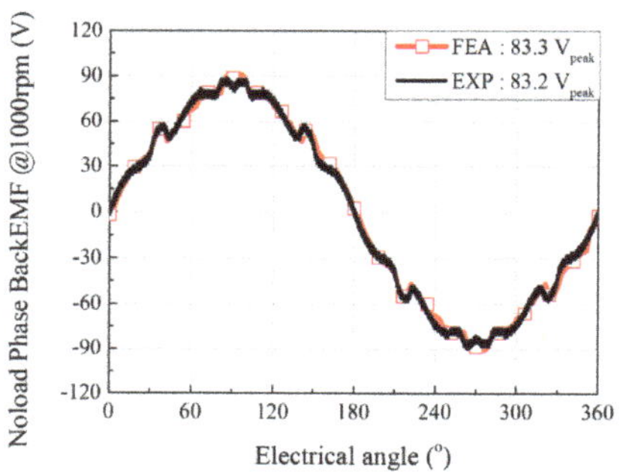

Figure 18. Waveforms of the no-load phase BEMF of the FEA and experiment.

Figure 19a shows the efficiency map measured through the experiment, and Figure 19b depicts the error between the measured efficiency map and the efficiency map calculated using the 2D FEA presented in Figure 16b. Each operating point was measured over 5 s with 10 Hz sampling, and the efficiency results were averaged from 50 samples, ensuring repeatability and reliability of the experimental data shown in Figure 19. Since the main operating points are located near 100 Nm, the experiment was conducted up to 400 Nm. The maximum error and average error between measured efficiency and calculated efficiency through 2D FEA are 2.54%p and 0.73%p, respectively. In other words, the difference between the measured efficiency and the efficiency calculated through 2D FEA is very small. Thus, the experimental results confirm the validity of the proposed design method. Furthermore, the motor experiment results indirectly demonstrate that this method contributes to enhancing the FE of EVs.

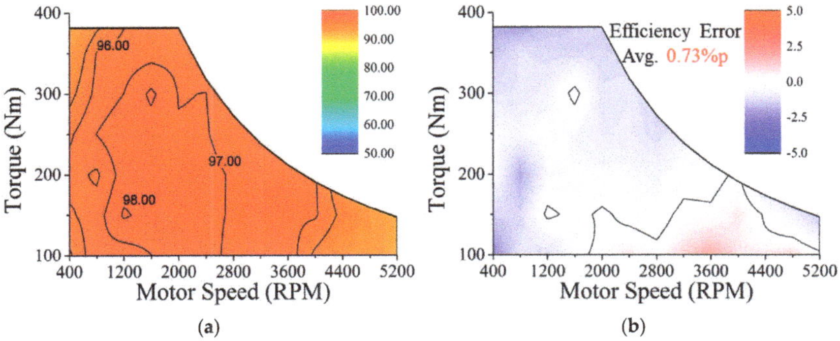

Figure 19. Efficiency map: (**a**) experimental result; (**b**) error between calculated and measured values.

6. Conclusions

This paper proposes a motor design method that accounts for AC resistance in motors' HSFF coils to enhance the FE of EVs. Among the HSFF coils, MSO coils are effective in improving motor torque density. However, HSFF coils inherently have a disadvantage: the large conductor area results in high AC resistance, which, in turn, decreases motor efficiency. To address this issue, a motor design method considering AC resistance has been proposed. Moreover, since designing for efficiency improvement without considering OPs is not meaningful for EV traction motors, the proposed method also considers multiple driving cycles reflecting different vehicle operation purposes.

Through the multi-objective optimization process aimed at enhancing FE, improvements were achieved across all considered driving cycles. Specifically, the FE increased by 0.20%, 0.86%, and 0.36% in the Manhattan, HWFET, and HDUDDS cycles, respectively. To analyze the factors contributing to the FE improvement, OP analysis and efficiency map analysis were conducted. First, the OP analysis revealed that motor operation predominantly occurs in low-torque regions across all cycles. Second, the motor efficiency map demonstrated overall efficiency enhancements in the optimized motor, although a slight decrease was observed in the low-speed, high-torque regions. As a result, the FE of the electric bus was improved through the proposed multi-objective optimization approach. Notably, the HWFET cycle exhibited the most significant FE improvement, primarily because it operates in a high-speed, low-torque region where the optimized motor showed enhanced efficiency. Conversely, the Manhattan and HDUDDS cycles showed less pronounced FE improvements due to a greater proportion of operation in low-speed, high-torque regions, where the motor efficiency gains were relatively smaller. To validate the effectiveness of the proposed motor design method, an optimal motor was fabricated and tested. The experimentally measured efficiency closely matched the efficiency predicted by 2D FEA, thus verifying the reliability of the simulation results.

Although this study primarily focused on simulations under specific vehicle configurations and representative driving cycles, the proposed approach provides a strong foundation for further advancements. Future research will aim to significantly expand the optimization framework by incorporating real-world driving data, accounting for detailed thermal and aging effects, and applying the methodology across a wider range of electric vehicle platforms and operating environments. In addition, the adoption of advanced optimization techniques and the integration of more complex multi-physics models are expected to further enhance the applicability and robustness of the proposed design approach.

In conclusion, this proposed method proves highly effective in improving the FE of electric buses equipped with MSO coils and opens promising pathways for future research and development in motor design optimization for electric mobility.

Author Contributions: Conceptualization, K.-S.C. and Y.-H.J.; methodology, S.-H.P.; software, S.-H.P.; validation, K.-S.C.; resources, K.-S.C.; data curation, Y.-H.J.; writing—original draft preparation, Y.-H.J. and K.-S.C.; writing—review and editing, S.-H.P. and M.-R.P.; visualization, Y.-H.J.; supervision, S.-H.P.; project administration, M.-R.P.; funding acquisition M.-R.P. All authors have read and agreed to the published version of the manuscript.

Funding: This work was supported by the Soonchunhyang University Research Fund.

Data Availability Statement: Data are contained within the article.

Conflicts of Interest: The authors declare no conflicts of interest.

References

1. Frigerio, A.; Vermeulen, B.; Goossens, K.G.W. Automotive Architecture Topologies: Analysis for Safety-Critical Autonomous Vehicle Applications. *IEEE Access* **2021**, *9*, 62837–62846. [CrossRef]
2. Kim, G.; Hur, J. Methodology for Security Analysis of Grid-Connected Electric Vehicle Charging Station With Wind Generating Resources. *IEEE Access* **2021**, *9*, 63905–63914. [CrossRef]
3. Ye, H.; Li, G.Y.; Juang, B.-H.F. Deep Reinforcement Learning Based Resource Allocation for V2V Communications. *IEEE Trans. Veh. Technol.* **2019**, *68*, 3163–3173. [CrossRef]
4. Cha, K.S.; Kim, D.M.; Jung, Y.H.; Lim, M.S. Wound field synchronous motor with hybrid circuit for neighborhood electric vehicle traction improving fuel economy. *Appl. Energy* **2020**, *263*, 114618. [CrossRef]
5. Feng, R.; Hua, Z.; Yu, J.; Zhao, Z. A comparative investigation on the energy flow of pure battery electric vehicle under different driving conditions. *Appl. Therm. Eng.* **2025**, *269*, 126035.
6. Kwon, K.; Seo, M.; Min, S. Efficient multi-objective optimization of gear ratios and motor torque distribution for electric vehicles with two-motor and two-speed powertrain system. *Appl. Energy* **2020**, *259*, 114190. [CrossRef]
7. Fang, L.; Jung, J.-W.; Hong, J.-P.; Lee, J.-H. Study on High-Efficiency Performance in Interior Permanent-Magnet Synchronous Motor With Double-Layer PM Design. *IEEE Trans. Magn.* **2008**, *44*, 4393–4396. [CrossRef]
8. Widmer, J.D.; Spargo, C.M.; Atkinson, G.J.; Mecrow, B.C. Solar Plane Propulsion Motors with Precompressed Aluminum Stator Windings. *IEEE Trans. Energy Convers.* **2014**, *29*, 681–688. [CrossRef]
9. Jung, D.S.; Kim, T.H.; Lee, U.H.; Lee, H.D. Optimum Design of the Electric Vehicle Traction Motor Using the Hairpin Winding. In Proceedings of the 2012 IEEE 75th Vehicular Technology Conference (VTC Spring), Yokohama, Japan, 6–9 May 2012; pp. 5–8.
10. Zhao, Y.; Li, D.; Pei, T.; Qu, R. Overview of the rectangular wire windings AC electrical machine. *CES Trans. Electr. Mach. Syst.* **2019**, *3*, 160–169. [CrossRef]
11. Park, H.-J.; Lim, M.-S. Design of High Power Density and High Efficiency Wound-Field Synchronous Motor for Electric Vehicle Traction. *IEEE Access* **2019**, *7*, 46677–46685. [CrossRef]
12. Momen, F.; Rahman, K.; Son, Y.C. Electrical Propulsion System Design of Chevrolet Bolt Battery Electric Vehicle. *IEEE Trans. Ind. Appl.* **2019**, *55*, 376–384. [CrossRef]
13. Bardalai, A.; Gerada, D.; Golovanov, D.; Xu, Z.; Zhang, X.; Li, J.; Zhang, H.; Gerada, C. Reduction of Winding AC Losses by Accurate Conductor Placement in High Frequency Electrical Machines. *IEEE Trans. Ind. Appl.* **2020**, *56*, 183–193. [CrossRef]
14. Paradkar, M.; Böcker, J.; Cker, J.B. Analysis of eddy current losses in the stator windings of IPM machines in electric and hybrid electric vehicle applications. In Proceedings of the 8th IET International Conference on Power Electronics, Machines and Drives (PEMD 2016), Glasgow, UK, 19–21 April 2016; pp. 1–5.
15. Bianchi, N.; Berardi, G. Analytical Approach to Design Hairpin Windings in High Performance Electric Vehicle Motors. In Proceedings of the 2018 IEEE Energy Conversion Congress and Exposition (ECCE), Portland, OR, USA, 23–27 September 2018; pp. 4398–4405.
16. Chin, J.-W.; Cha, K.-S.; Park, M.-R.; Park, S.-H.; Lee, E.-C.; Lim, M.-S. High Efficiency PMSM with High Slot Fill Factor Coil for Heavy-Duty EV Traction Considering AC Resistance. *IEEE Trans. Energy Convers.* **2020**, *36*, 883–894. [CrossRef]

17. Cha, K.-S.; Chin, J.-W.; Park, S.-H.; Jung, Y.-H.; Lee, E.-C.; Lim, M.-S. Design Method for Reducing AC Resistance of Traction Motor using High Fill Factor Coil to Improve Fuel Economy of eBus. *IEEE/ASME Trans. Mechatron.* **2021**, *26*, 1260–1270. [CrossRef]
18. Lee, E.C.; Soon, O.K.; Lee, H.Y.; Lee, S.W. Method for Manufacturing MSO Coil and Device for Manufacturing Same. U.S. Patent US20200099279A1, 2 August 2020.
19. Pyrhonen, J.; Jokinen, T.; Hrabovcova, V. *Design of Rotating Electrical Machines*, 2nd ed.; John Wiley & Sons: Hoboken, NJ, USA, 2013.
20. Markel, T.; Brooker, A.; Hendricks, T.; Johnson, V.; Kelly, K.; Kramer, B.; O'keefe, M.; Sprik, S.; Wipke, K. ADVISOR: A systems analysis tool for advanced vehicle modeling. *J. Power Sources* **2002**, *110*, 255–266. [CrossRef]
21. Lim, M.S.; Chai, S.H.; Yang, J.S.; Hong, J.P. Design and Verification of 150-krpm PMSM Based on Experiment Results of Prototype. *IEEE Trans. Ind. Electron.* **2015**, *62*, 7827–7836. [CrossRef]
22. Jung, Y.-H.; Park, M.-R.; Kim, K.-O.; Chin, J.-W.; Hong, J.-P.; Lim, M.-S. Design of High-speed Multi-layer IPMSM Using Ferrite PM for EV traction Considering Mechanical and Electrical Characteristics. *IEEE Trans. Ind. Appl.* **2021**, *57*, 327–339. [CrossRef]
23. Perez, H.E.; Siegel, J.B.; Lin, X.; Stefanopoulou, A.G.; Ding, Y.; Castanier, M.P. Parameterization and Validation of an Integrated Electro-Thermal Cylindrical LFP Battery Model. In Proceedings of the ASME 2012 5th Annual Dynamic Systems and Control Conference Joint with the JSME 2012 11th Motion and Vibration Conference, Fort Lauderdale, FL, USA, 17–19 October 2012; pp. 41–50.
24. Perez, H.E. Model Based Optimal Control, Estimation, and Validation of Lithium-Ion Batteries. Ph.D. Thesis, Civil and Environmental Engineeering, University of California, Berkeley, CA, USA, 2016.
25. Klein, M.; Tong, S.; Park, J. In-plane nonuniform temperature effects on the performance of a large-format lithium-ion pouch cell. *Appl. Energy* **2016**, *165*, 639–647. [CrossRef]
26. Diao, K.; Sun, X.; Lei, G.; Bramerdorfer, G.; Guo, Y.; Zhu, J. System-level Robust Design Optimization of a Switched Reluctance Motor Drive System Considering Multiple Driving Cycles. *IEEE Trans. Energy Convers.* **2020**, *36*, 348–357. [CrossRef]
27. Sun, X.; Shi, Z.; Lei, G.; Guo, Y.; Zhu, J. Multi-Objective Design Optimization of an IPMSM Based on Multilevel Strategy. *IEEE Trans. Ind. Electron.* **2021**, *68*, 139–148. [CrossRef]
28. Altinoz, O.T.; Yilmaz, A.E.; Ciuprina, G. A multiobjective optimization approach via systematical modification of the desirability function shapes. In Proceedings of the 2013 8th International Symposium on Advanced Topics in Electrical Engineering (ATEE), Bucharest, Romania, 23–25 May 2013; pp. 1–6. [CrossRef]
29. Costa, N.R.; Lourenço, J.; Pereira, Z.L. Desirability function approach: A review and performance evaluation in adverse conditions. *Chemom. Intell. Lab. Systems* **2011**, *107*, 234–244. [CrossRef]
30. Kim, H.; Kim, S.; Kim, T.; Lee, T.H.; Ryu, N.; Kwon, K.; Min, S. Efficient design optimization of complex system through an integrated interface using symbolic computation. *Adv. Eng. Softw.* **2021**, *126*, 34–45. [CrossRef]
31. Gilleran, M.; Kotz, A.; Eudy, L.; Kelly, K. *National Park Service Bus Electrification Study: 2020 Report*; NREL/TP-5400-78012; National Renewable Energy Laboratory: Golden, CO, USA, 2021. Available online: https://www.nrel.gov/docs/fy21osti/78012.pdf (accessed on 26 April 2025).
32. Prohaska, R.; Kelly, K.; Eudy, L.; Jeffers, M. *Financial Analysis of Battery Electric Transit Buses*; NREL/TP-5400-74832; National Renewable Energy Laboratory: Golden, CO, USA, 2019. Available online: https://www.nrel.gov/docs/fy20osti/74832.pdf (accessed on 26 April 2025).

MDPI AG
Grosspeteranlage 5
4052 Basel
Switzerland
Tel.: +41 61 683 77 34

Mathematics Editorial Office
E-mail: mathematics@mdpi.com
www.mdpi.com/journal/mathematics

www.ingramcontent.com/pod-product-compliance
Lightning Source LLC
Chambersburg PA
CBHW061600210926
51850CB00009B/2168
* 9 7 8 3 7 2 5 8 6 5 0 4 8 *